Jehovah's Witnesses

'Who are those people who knock on your door and want to tell you all about God? How can they go on believing – for generations – that the world is about to end? Why do they prefer to die rather than to kill others, to salute a flag, or to accept a blood transfusion? Andrew Holden addresses, with sensitivity and insight, the many paradoxes to be found in the Watch Tower Society. He helps us to understand not only how different the Jehovah's Witnesses are from the rest of us, but also how they can be seen as ordinary people who have found a rational response to the modern world.'

Eileen Barker, *London School of Economics*

'A serious, perceptive and well-informed account of the Jehovah's Witnesses.'
Bryan Wilson FBA, *Emeritus Fellow of All Souls, Oxford*

'Adds greatly to our understanding of the movement itself, and should . . . take its place as an important account of the nature of the Jehovah's Witnesses in the twentieth century.'
Ian Reader, *Professor of Religious Studies, Lancaster University, England*

Why has a world-renouncing millenarian movement such as the Jehovah's Witnesses, which demands the utmost loyalty from its members, found increasing popularity in a modern age that hedonistically celebrates individual freedoms?

Jehovah's Witnesses: Portrait of a contemporary religious movement is the first major ethnographic study of this enigmatic religious society. Through rigorously investigated case histories based on the real-life experiences of converts, believers and defectors, it describes how the Watch Tower Bible and Tract Society seeks to achieve conformity in devotees and to construct meaningful religious identities in a world whose excesses it vehemently reviles.

Examining the Jehovah's Witnesses' dramatic expansion over the past 130 years, Andrew Holden reveals the dependency of this quasi-totalitarian movement on the very physical and cultural resources which have brought about the privatisation of religion, the erosion of community and the separation of 'fact' from supernatural faith. Asking vital questions about the ambivalent relationship of spiritual meaning to modern secular materialism, *Jehovah's Witnesses* reconsiders the Witnesses' ascetic faith both as an inverted form of pseudo-corporate 'branding' and as an anti-modern quest for certainty in a hostile world of relativism and risk.

Andrew Holden has taught sociology at various levels of further and higher education. He has been conducting fieldwork on millenarian belief systems for over a decade.

Jehovah's Witnesses

Portrait of a contemporary religious movement

Andrew Holden

London and New York

First published 2002
by Routledge
11 New Fetter Lane, London EC4P 4EE

Simultaneously published in the USA and Canada
by Routledge
29 West 35th Street, New York, NY 10001

Routledge is an imprint of the Taylor & Francis Group

Typeset in Sabon by Steven Gardiner Ltd, Cambridge
Printed and bound in Great Britain by
The Cromwell Press, Trowbridge, Wiltshire

British Library Cataloguing in Publication Data
A catalogue record for this book is available from the British Library

Library of Congress Cataloging in Publication Data
Holden, Andrew, 1964–
Jehovah's Witnesses: portrait of a contemporary religious movement
/ Andrew Holden.
    p.   cm.
Includes bibliographical references and index.
ISBN 0–415–26609–2 – ISBN 0–415–26610–6 (pbk.)
1. Jehovah's Witnesses. I. Title.
BX8526.H65 2002
289.9'2 – dc21   2001045726

ISBN 0–415–26609–2 (hbk)
ISBN 0–415–26610–6 (pbk)

To Mum, Dad and Anne
You truly are the wind beneath my wings

Contents

Preface

To the die-hard sceptic, holding millenarian beliefs at the beginning of the twenty-first century is like remaining on board a sinking ship. Opinion polls in recent years have shown a significant decline in religious participation in the West; so much so, that few would dispute that this point of the geographical compass is, in a very real sense, disenchanted. As the 1960s started to swing, so began the relentless attack on superstitious dogma, sexual morality and traditional authority – an attack most unlike anything that had preceded it. Time has passed, and the children of the 1960s have now grown up; only to have produced children of their own who are themselves, by and large, indifferent to matters religious – certainly to millenarianism. While the same polls reveal that people continue to hold some loose concept of a supernatural deity, if religious conviction is to be ascertained by frequency of attendance at a place of worship or the regular (or even irregular) engagement in sacred rituals, secularisation has undoubtedly taken root. We live in an adversarial culture in which it is fashionable to reject what those responsible for our moral and spiritual welfare preach. Even the people whose wisdom we would once have cherished (teachers, religious leaders and the like) appeal to us to interrogate their counsel for fear that they might somehow be charged with denying us our rights. So far as my own profession is concerned, this story is all too familiar. As a teacher of the social sciences, I am subject-bound to encourage my students to question all that they read and to treat much of what I tell them with caution (at least, that is, if I want them to do well in their examinations). Whatever the difficulties, this is something with which my colleagues and I have had to learn to live. For all this, I remain an optimist. For one thing, I have little desire to suppress either my own or my students' quest for knowledge, and, for another, I would not welcome a return to the widespread fear of authority that historians have spent so much time documenting. In the great scheme of things, I am happy with life in the twenty-first century; far happier, it would seem, than the devotees of some of the religious movements I have been studying for the last ten years.

For those who belong to ascetic millenarian communities, the freedom offered by secular culture is nothing to celebrate. This is a culture in which debauchery is rife and where people have lost all sense of moral duty. It is a culture riddled with deceit, uncertainty, anxiety, sleaze, drug abuse, alcoholism, sexually transmitted diseases and a whole host of other evils caused by the inherent flaws in the human condition. It is only when people come to their senses and turn back to God, claim the millenarians (or, better still, when God exacts vengeance on those too crippled by their own depravity to see the error of their ways), that the world will really change. This time, they say, is looming. The world has reached the point not of human liberation but of moral meltdown. Original sin has indeed come home to roost.

People who espouse world-renouncing creeds seldom have trouble-free lives, particularly if they are successful in recruiting others to their cause. The mass media thrive on stories of vulnerable individuals unable to escape from dangerous cult leaders who force their docile followers to obey their every command. Not surprisingly, this kind of sensationalism has distorted public perception of religious conversion. Although there is no doubt that some movements have involved their members in life-threatening activities (including suicide), these incidents are rare. But conversion need not affect life and limb to cause a public stir. When people deviate from convention, conformist onlookers are always at the ready with a fixed repertoire of explanations. Over the years, tabloid newspapers (with the aid of anti-cult activists) have fuelled public contempt for heterodox religion with scare stories of brainwashing and psychological manipulation.

To suggest that individuals have been brainwashed is to strip them of their sanity. It is to infer that their actions are the result of some powerful external force over which they have no control. I am unwilling to accept the brainwashing thesis for several reasons. First, it is a metaphor that reduces the mental state of so-called victims to such an extent that it becomes difficult either to hold them accountable for their actions or to take what they believe seriously. The day we allow this to happen will be a sad day for the social sciences. My second objection concerns empirical measurement. Unless the term can be clearly defined, it is impossible to use any kind of research instrument to test its validity; hence, there is little hope either of exposing those who allegedly employ this process and even less of exonerating them from blame. By far my biggest concern, however, is that the brainwashing metaphor can be used to undermine any political or religious ideology that happens to be unpopular. Stories of brainwashing serve much the same purpose in our culture as accusations of witchcraft in remote African villages. They are an effective means of undermining wayward beliefs and denying a voice to those who hold them. They may even be used to expel religious dissidents from secular communities. It is, perhaps, little wonder that millenarians retreat to the margins of society. Whether we like it or not, most of the available social scientific evidence suggests that, though their behaviour may be anti-social, the majority of those who join millenarian movements are making an informed choice. If this research means anything, people who reject religious orthodoxy are doing little other than expressing their dissatisfaction with tradition. It does not mean that they are of a different species. For what it is worth, I too find millenarian evangelists unconvincing, but it is only by listening to what they have to say that we can achieve a better understanding of their way of life and of how others come to view them with suspicion. For this, we need an appropriate methodology.

And so to the objectives of this book. I write for an academic community, or indeed for anyone with a sociological interest in religious movements. For many years, I have been inspired by the American anthropologist Clifford Geertz, and particularly by his brilliant work on symbolism. There is little I would not give to be able to write as well as he. Next to Geertz's work, my ineptitude stands revealed. Alas for that! In the pages that follow, I offer a glimpse of the modern world through the eyes of a group of religious devotees – the Jehovah's Witnesses. The Witnesses are a well-known community of people whose doctrines defy convention. I write for those who know little or nothing about their beliefs; hence, in Chapter 2, I offer a brief account of the movement's early history and an overview of its teachings. The book is ethnographic and, as such, it is concerned with the Witnesses' version of reality. There are times, however, when I step back from my ethnographic descriptions in an endeavour to bring some theoretical considerations to bear. I use modernity theory to inform my empirical data and to establish the Witnesses' general status in the new millennium. Needless to say, the book is not about comparative religion but about the lives of a group of people who claim to be *in* but not *of* the world. Some students may, therefore, prefer to treat it as a case study. My hope is that those who are relatively new to the sociology of religion enjoy the book sufficiently to pursue some further secondary research and to recognise the value of an ethnographic approach.

Acknowledgements

I would like to express my sincere gratitude to all those people who have helped me in the preparation and writing of this book. My heartfelt thanks go to Professor Eileen Barker at the London School of Economics for her suggestions regarding content and style. I hope she feels the advice she gave me was worthwhile. I owe an enormous debt to Professor Suzette Heald and Dr Sarah Franklin for commenting on my earlier drafts and listening to my incessant talk about the sociology of religion. I am grateful to Professor Larry Ray at the University of Kent for helping me to refine my theoretical framework and for steering me towards literature of which I was only dimly aware. Thanks also to Professor John Urry and Professor Ian Reader, both from the University of Lancaster, for talking to me about the finer details of publishing.

My biggest tribute goes to my parents and to my sister, Anne, for all the love they have shown me over the years. It is to them that I dedicate this work. As with everything else I have done, they have been a dependable source of support throughout the whole period of my research when it must have appeared to them like they were the last thing on my mind. Their forbearance is quite remarkable.

My next acknowledgement is also rather special. It is to my friend Joyce Donnelly, who spent hundreds of hours proofreading my text and helping me with presentation. I used her shamelessly for both these tasks and she asked for nothing in return. I am overwhelmed at Joyce's kindness and at the relentless sacrifices she made, especially when her own workload was every bit as demanding as mine. But then she is like that.

It would be remiss of me not to record my appreciation to the Watch Tower Bible and Tract Society for granting me permission to quote from its tracts. I am particularly grateful to the devotees of the Blackburn congregation for welcoming me into their homes and answering my questions. Elder Joe Bennett deserves a special mention for being so generous with his time and so impervious to my naivety. Without his assistance, I would not have been able to carry out the fieldwork or make contact with other members. I hope he will forgive me for failing to join him in his spiritual mission!

Finally, I would like to thank Routledge for publishing my work and for assigning to me a proficient copy-editor. Any textual errors or inadequacies are, of course, entirely my responsibility.

Andrew Holden

1 The end is nigh

There could be no period more appropriate than the beginning of a new millennium in which to consider the activities of those who hold beliefs about the end of the world. In 1872, a Pittsburgh draper named Charles Taze Russell founded what later became known as the Watch Tower Bible and Tract Society – the official name for the organisation of Jehovah's Witnesses. Russell had a fascination for biblical eschatology – a fascination which would play a huge part in the expansion of what is now a huge international corporation with over six million members. The Witnesses are members of a world-renouncing puritanical movement that claims to monopolise truth, and for this reason they refuse all ecumenical relations with other religious denominations. In a modern age in which people are free to construct their own aesthetic identities, the Witnesses stand out as authoritarian, calculating and aloof, and this makes their organisation distinctive from other social movements. The Witnesses are now active all over the world. Their worldwide membership increased from a mere 44,080 in 1928 to an extraordinary 6,035,564 in 2000, making a total international net growth of more than 5 per cent a year. Although these are the move-ment's own figures, there is no reason to doubt them. For one thing, they are consistent with government estimates as well as those of independent scholars and, for another, the Society publishes losses as well as gains.[1] Indeed, the Witnesses are loath to include anyone other than active evangelists over the age of sixteen in their annual statistics. Even the most conservative estimates indicate that, by the year 2020, there will be 12,475,115 members worldwide (Stark and Iannaccone 1997: 153–4).[2]

The Watch Tower Society has had a chequered evolution. Almost from the moment of its foundation, devotees have lived in anticipation of a new Messianic Kingdom in which all earthly wickedness would be destroyed and paradise be inaugurated. The years of 1874, 1914, 1918, 1925 and 1975 were all earmarked, to a greater or lesser extent, as times for the Second Coming of Christ, yet all brought bitter disappointment. Despite this persistent prophecy failure, the Witnesses have managed to recruit and expand with remarkable success and have now (paradoxically) been on the scene for almost 130 years. This book is about their continued appeal and status at the beginning of the twenty-first century. It is about life inside the Society from the point of conversion and how the Witnesses manage their relations with the outside world. I also consider what causes some of these Witnesses to defect. Those who are expecting answers to questions concerning philosophical or theological truth should read no further. I write as a sociologist, and am thus concerned with the *effects* of supernatural beliefs rather than their validity. My aim is to highlight some of the challenges that the modern world presents to the movement, and to consider the ways in which devotees manage their religious identity in an age of cultural fluidity.

It is astonishing to find that there is a dearth of academic literature on the Witnesses, given the remarkable success of their evangelistic mission. Beckford (1975a, 1975b, 1976), Wilson (1974, 1978, 1990) and Dobbelaere and Wilson (1980) have carried out the most extensive empirical research, although these studies are now quite dated. Moreover, the Witnesses are not given anything other than a brief mention in most of the key textbooks on the sociology of religion. There is, as one might expect, a slightly larger number of published articles on the Watch Tower movement in *Social Compass*, *Sociological Analysis*, *The Journal of Modern African Studies* and *The British Journal of Sociology*, but not nearly as many as those devoted to obscure (and relatively unsuccessful) new religious movements. By far the best known study of the Witnesses is James Beckford's *The Trumpet of Prophecy* (1975a). The first three chapters of Beckford's book are devoted to the historical development of the Watch Tower Society. In them, Beckford makes use of the few earlier sociological studies on the Witnesses as well as the organisation's own published literature. These chapters tell us about the movement's social composition and its postwar expansion in Britain and the USA. Beckford's work contains important quantitative and qualitative data collected from ten congregations representing the geographical divisions of England, Wales and the Scottish Lowlands. Although the book is largely empirical, Beckford offers some theoretical analysis of conversion and affiliation to the organisation that aids our understanding of the Witnesses' worldview.[3] Beckford's discussion of the factors that influence membership and the internal forces that maximise long-term commitment informs some of my analysis in Chapters 3 and 4. Whatever strengths Beckford's work might have, however, the fact remains that it is now more than twenty years old. My aim, therefore, is to produce not only a current monograph on the Witnesses but one that is unlike anything that has been published to date. My hope is that this will help to redress the neglect I have described as well as some of the more general shortfalls in the academic literature on religion identified by sociologist Robert Wuthnow (1997):

> One feature that most clearly distinguishes contemporary scholarship from, say, the 1950s or 1960s is its rejection of . . . 'linear narratives of disembodied trends'. Recent studies not only dispute the claims of

theories that emphasize, for instance, secularization and modernization; they also reject the value of such theories, preferring instead to talk about gender differences, multiple vocabularies, local cultures, contra dictory impulses, negotiation, and the construction of meaning.

(248)

Mindful of Wuthnow's warning that idiosyncratic details of religious organisations can hinder cumulative (theoretical) knowledge, I have used sociological theory to inform my ethnographic description of the Witnesses' system of beliefs. There is, I believe, a current shortage of empirical studies of religious movements that make anything other than brief reference to the wider issues of modernity. What follows is an attempt to chart some of this territory.

Research perspective and method

Before embarking on a discussion of the movement's beliefs, I want to explain how I became interested in the Watch Tower community and to describe the kind of sociology in which I have been engaged for the last ten or so years. There were two main reasons for my initial interest in the Witnesses. First, my childhood memories of their periodic visits to our home and my mother's impatience with their tireless efforts to recruit us aroused my curiosity. Why did these people persist in knocking on our door when my parents had made it patently clear that we were a Catholic family who had no intention of converting to another faith? What did the Witnesses want to say to us? And why *were* my parents so dismissive of their message without even hearing it? After all, people were not usually turned away from our house with such short shrift. Second, a chance encounter with some Witnesses at a local fitness club several years later led to some interesting discussions about creation, evolution, the meaning of life and what happens to us when we die. I discovered that the Witnesses held exclusive and absolutist beliefs – beliefs that seem strange to the outside world. I had to find out what kind of people converted to the Watch Tower organisation and why they did it. Though I found their theology unconvincing, I could see that *they* were convinced. In the early 1990s, I decided to let the Witnesses tell their story and used what they told me to write my doctoral thesis. I now want to share some of what I learned with a wider audience. This monograph contains fieldwork data collected in my home town of Blackburn between 1991 and 1996, but I have added some new material that will also be of interest to the sociologist of religion.

Carrying out an empirical investigation among fervent evangelists like the Witnesses is far from easy. Although in principle anyone is welcome to attend Watch Tower meetings, dealing first hand with devotees themselves requires a certain amount of sensitivity. When I first entered the field, I was thankful for the support of key individuals, including congregational elders, but I was ever wary of doing or saying anything that could appear antagonistic.[4] Though I had read widely on the evolution of the Society and familiarised myself with its doctrines, I was still aware that, as an outsider, I was different from the rest of the congregation, and I had made it clear that I was not a prospective recruit. Since the Witnesses were under no obligation to help me, I became increasingly aware that the quality of my data would depend on the relationships I formed with people who were willing to answer my questions and talk to me about their lives. I cannot tell a lie. I found some of the members difficult to work with, and my status as a sociologist did nothing to allay the suspicion with which they approach outsiders. Nevertheless, I was hungry for information about this movement and it was going to take more than a group of suspicious devotees to stop me from finding out more.

As an ethnographer, I was interested to learn about the Witnesses' version of reality as *they* perceived it, and this meant giving them a voice. Though I am well aware of the methodological problems involved in 'going native', one of the reasons I believe millenarians are poorly understood is that they are seldom given the opportunity to explain their view of the cosmos. Though it was not (and still is not) my intention to rehabilitate the Witnesses from public misrepresentation, I wanted to know why they renounced the world in the way they did and to see how they operated in their own place of worship. The information contained in this book has been culled from participant and non-participant observation, transcripts from unstructured interviews (pseudonyms have been used in order to protect the identity of all interviewees), extracts from the Watch Tower Society's own published literature and extensive analysis of the writings of former members.

Although there are numerous texts and journal articles offering guidance to researchers about the styles and strategies that can be employed in the collection and presentation of ethnographic data, there is still a great deal of mystery surrounding the way in which researchers engage in data analysis. This owes something to the complexity of interpreting the lives of others and presenting qualitative data. No matter how much care ethnographic researchers take in collecting and handling data, their interpretations will always be subjective. Ethnography is no less flawed (or no more for that matter) than any other method in the social sciences, and even the poorest ethnographer knows better than to claim otherwise. We would do well to heed the words of anthropologist Clifford Geertz: 'The culture of a people is an ensemble of texts, themselves ensembles, which the anthropologist strains to read over the shoulders of those to whom they properly belong' (Geertz 1973: 452).

What Geertz is suggesting here is that human societies are analogous to texts that can be read in different ways. The essence of a text (a collective text in the case of culture) is that its meaning is freed from the author's position. According to this view, everyone is entitled to a reading, but there are still issues of interpretation to consider. Texts, for example, can be read and written in ways that detract from the intentions of participants. This book is no exception. I have drawn on the subjective experiences of the Jehovah's Witnesses to help illuminate a social phenomenon, but in so doing I am mindful of my own sociological perspective. My decision to examine the social interactions of the Witnesses in the context of a rapidly changing world that cannot easily accommodate their beliefs indicates that I have chosen to view their relationship with modern forces as something that is characterised by tension. Although few people (including devotees themselves) would argue that this was an unreasonable claim, I could be charged with making the assumption that the values of secular society are, for most non-sectarians, unproblematic. Moreover, my decision to allow the Witnesses to speak through my text involved judgements about which issues were worthy of attention and how best to tell the story.

There are dozens of monographs in which researchers explain how they combined hard data and thick description, but, in the last analysis, the primary role of the ethnographer is to present the experiences of those with whom they are working to an academic community. Geertz distinguishes between the world of the native and the knowledge or interpretations of the researcher, and he refers to these two perspectives as *experience near* and *experience distant* (Geertz 1983). The skill of the ethnographer lies in his or her ability to move to and fro between them. In my own study, the vocabulary of the Witnesses contrasts sharply with that of the academic. Watch Tower concepts such as 'truth', 'love', 'brother' and 'sister' could be regarded as *experience near* concepts and tell us something about the Witnesses' way of thinking. *Experience distant* concepts, on the other hand, belong to the specialist vocabulary of the academic who would replace a concept such as 'truth' with one such as *Weltanschauung*. In his passion for understanding the world of others, Geertz argues that the *local* knowledge of participants should be combined with that of the social scientist:

> so as to produce an interpretation of the way a people lives which is neither imprisoned within their mental horizons, an ethnography of a witchcraft as written by a witch, nor systematically deaf to the distinctive tonalities of their existence, an ethnography of a witchcraft as written by a geometer.
>
> (1973: 57)

It is only by understanding the natives' worldview that ethnographers are able to make sense of an individual act, but these interpretations can only be partial and must be subjected to continual revision. The spatial and temporal gap between author and interpretation is brought together by tradition and by what Geertz calls 'a fusion of horizons', but such a gap can never be fully bridged. Reading the lives of others is, in the final analysis, only a reading; and there is no irrefutably correct interpretation. With this in mind, I have tried to examine Watch Tower culture in terms of how the devotees themselves experience it. Though I neither disdain nor applaud the way the Witnesses choose to live, their lifestyle can be understood only by a methodology that allows them to explain their religious perspective. But epistemological claims are themselves everything but impartial. Sociologist Eileen Barker (1987) sums up some of the difficulties of ethnography in her analogy of the observer as an actor in a live theatrical performance:

> Professional stage actors, like participant observers, have to learn to recognise within themselves the emotions that they share with the rest of humanity, but which will have been developed to different degrees and will have taken different forms in each one of us. They have to learn the form and the strength of such ingredients as compassion, jealousy, idealism, ambition and fear, and they have to understand how these operate in the situations in which the characters they play find themselves. But, at the same time, although they will be drawing on their own emotions, and can have very genuine tears flowing from their eyes, they must still make sure that their choked words can be heard from the back of the gallery, and that they wait for the audience's laughter to subside before taking up a cue. And if the properties-man has forgotten to set the dagger with which the abandoned mistress is about to kill herself, the actress has to be sufficiently distanced to notice this and rapidly work out what the hell to do next.
>
> (142–3)

As I became a more familiar figure at the Kingdom Hall (the official name for the Witnesses' place of worship), I realised that I was both subjectively involved on the inside and dispassionately collecting data from the outside. This was my first real insight into a reflexive ethnography.[5] Like an actor, I felt that I was performing and, at the same time, I was aware that the activities in which I partook were being carefully constructed by those with whom I had little in common. Needless to say, my relationships with individuals in the congregation were all different. To some, I was a polite but sceptical academic with nothing other than a quasi-professional interest in their way of life. To the elders, I was an enthusiastic young man of apparently agnostic disposition who needed help in collecting what was to them rather futile information. To others still, I was a friendly acquaintance (rather than a friend) who, unlike most other outsiders, had a comprehensive knowledge of their mission and with whom they could hold an intelligent conversation.

Throughout my study, I interviewed many Witnesses who told me that their religious conversion had brought them happiness and well-being – a declaration that flies in the face of the generally negative profile which religious movements have been given over the years by the popular press. The mass media thrive on stories of families being torn apart by the loss of their loved ones allegedly enticed by religious maniacs demanding total compliance. Sensationalism of this kind tends to portray *all* heterodox religious devotees as brainwashed extremists, and this makes their zeal difficult to comprehend. While I too find these movements unappealing, I respect the rights of others to join them. Such rights are, I believe, part and parcel of the democracy which few would wish to jeopardise. My ethnography gave me a better understanding of something I had always treated with caution. In the end, I recognised that the confusion and conflict that derive from religious conversion are often the result of people's inability (and sometimes their unwillingness), to understand a different way of life from their own. Throughout the whole period of my research, I met hundreds of Jehovah's Witnesses; some were warm and friendly, others were aloof and cynical. I watched, I listened and I collected some interesting data. I chatted to the Witnesses at meetings and visited them in their own homes. I asked some naive questions and made some embarrassing mistakes. I experienced fascination, humour, sadness and frustration. I felt anger, tension, disappointment and bewilderment. I made friends and I made enemies. But most importantly, I learned what it was like to enter an unfamiliar world and to listen intently to those who inhabited it. It was a journey that forced me to confront my own prejudices and to challenge the prejudices of others. I wouldn't have missed it for the world.

The millenarian option

Since the foundation of their movement around 130 years ago, the Witnesses have maintained that we are living on the precipice of the end of time. Their eschatology is based on the texts of the New Testament and almost all of their literature makes reference to the annihilation of evil at Armageddon; hence, they see their mission as having to proselytise to as many prospective converts as possible. It is no coincidence that their belief in the imminence of a New Kingdom corresponds with the evidence they present in their publications that they are one of the fastest-growing religious movements in the world. The Watch Tower Society teaches that the end will come only when Jehovah's true word has been ministered to the ends of the earth. Millenarian tenets are, by their nature, potentially disruptive since they challenge other systems of belief and patterns of behaviour, religious and secular. Where societies allow people space in which to establish their own lifestyles, millenarian communities can prosper by presenting themselves as exclusive organisations that make clear distinctions between members and non-members. Since many such movements are critical of mainstream religion, their appeal lies in their alternative way of life. Historically, millenarian movements were usually formed by dissidents who rejected the authority of the church and its pontiff and were regarded as a form of religious deviation or protest. Worse still, some of these movements advanced new doctrines which met the wrath of mainstream Christianity; hence, most millenarians have a history of tension with the wider society.

There are two main approaches in the academic literature to the analysis of millenarian beliefs – the first sees millenarianism as a *reaction to*, and the second as a *manifestation of*, secular forces. In the former case, it could be argued that the Watch Tower community appeals to people who are experiencing a renewed interest in the sacred,[6] while, in the latter, it is considered to be one of the final outposts of religion in a secular society.[7] The first argument is fraught with difficulty. Though I agree with some of the basic principles propounded by the secularisation theorists, and echo their contention that there has been a general erosion of the sacred, the expansion of several world-renouncing millenarian groups challenges this assertion. While there can be no doubt that exclusive religious organisations are marginalised in that they isolate themselves to varying degrees from the secularising influences of the wider society, some have managed to maintain strong beliefs and commitment and have expanded at a rate worthy of attention. It is also worth noting that, historically, many movements (though not necessarily millenarian) existed in sectarian form for generations before evolving into huge denominations, as in the case of Methodism and the Quaker movement throughout the 1900s.

Despite their aggressive evangelistic ministry, the Witnesses continue to preach an exclusive message which declares that although a great multitude of righteous people, including those who do not necessarily share their faith, will be granted eternal life on earth, only 144,000 Witnesses will enter heaven. Moreover, their heterodox purity code, which prohibits among other things blood transfusions, Christmas celebrations and unnecessary association with non-members, dictates that they are highly unlikely, despite their worldwide ministry, to recruit anything other than a small number of people from a whole population. Some interesting questions therefore emerge. How, for example, are the Witnesses managing to expand at such an impressive rate when secularisation theorists maintain that religion is losing social significance? How has the Watch Tower community retained its exclusivity and at the same time managed its relations with the outside world? And why do the Witnesses continue to pledge their allegiance to an organisation that appears to demand a high degree of loyalty?

Millenarian movements such as the Watch Tower Society are characterised by explosions of discontent and have emerged inside all religions including Christianity and Islam. Equally, some modern political ideologies (such as the European socialist vistas of the late nineteenth and early twentieth centuries) have been interpreted as millenarian in that they promise radical social and economic change for which there exists no immediate feasible means. These 'new societies' are constructed as egalitarian and just. Prophecies of the transformation of the world by supernatural intervention constitute an important part of the mythology not only of the Witnesses but also of Mormons, Seventh-Day Adventists and Christadelphians. It would be wrong, however, to suggest that apocalyptic visions like those of the post-Armageddon paradise are a new phenomenon. Historian Norman Cohn

(1957) traces the origins of millenarianism to Western Europe between the eleventh and sixteenth centuries. During this period, prophecy was a device used by Jews and Christians alike to console, fortify and assert themselves when confronted by the threat or reality of oppression. The Book of Revelation predicts that, after his Second Coming, Christ will reign for a thousand years in his earthly kingdom before the Last Judgement. The citizens of this Kingdom will be the resurrected Christian martyrs – a prophecy which, says Cohn, later Christians interpreted in a much more liberal sense to include themselves as the suffering faithful. Cohn goes on to describe the historical development of millenarian beliefs and their various characteristics. Millenarianism was necessarily collective in that the visions of the Messianic Kingdom depicted large numbers of faithful people enjoying salvation. This salvation would be realised on this earth rather than some extra terrestrial place such as heaven, and not only was the event imminent, it would also occur suddenly. Transformation of life would be total, in the sense that eternal bliss would replace suffering and imperfection. According to Cohn, the event would also be miraculous since it would be accomplished by, or with the help of, supernatural agencies. Cohn documents a variety of millenarian movements throughout medieval Europe ranging from rigorous ascetics drawn from the dominant classes, to the rootless involuntary poor of town and country whose lot was relentless insecurity. It was this latter group that demonstrated the most violent and anarchic forms of millenarianism, largely in the quest for improving its material conditions. Apocalyptic visions provided peasants and artisans with spiritual ammunition for annihilating the ruling classes, and this sometimes provided the basis for collective action, as in the case of peasant revolts. However, Cohn maintains that millenarianism had its greatest impact in expanding urban areas which were characterised by rapid social change.[8] In much the same way that Weber argued that charismatic leaders would emerge to give a new moral basis to modern societies, Cohn emphasises the tendency of those living on the margins of society to offer deference to leaders who present themselves not simply as holy individuals but as prophets and saviours. This might help to explain why, in late nineteenth-century America, there was a huge proliferation of evangelical movements. Rising entrepreneurs plundered their way to new wealth while the masses fought hard to resist urban poverty. Christian activists of every persuasion preached a social gospel that addressed the unworthiness not only of the individual but of society as a whole (Carter 1980).

It was against this background of collision between owners and workers that Russell founded the Watch Tower organisation. The passing of several turbulent years of social disruption and military catastrophe seemed for Russell to point towards the cataclysm that was to precede the Second Coming of Christ as predicted in the Book of Revelation. His strong disagreements with orthodox Christian explanations of the ills of American society provided the context for his new movement. The escalating international arms race, the spread of famine and the outbreak of war were all events for which Russell's prescription for cure (that is, the annihilation of the wicked at Armageddon) differed from many of his Christian contemporaries; hence, it would appear that the attraction of world-renouncing doctrines in late nineteenth-century America lay in the hope they gave for the end of social injustice. But the Witnesses were by no means the only heterodox religious movement, nor the earliest, to be founded during this period. The Mormons had entered and settled in the valley of the Great Salt Lake in the late 1840s and early 1850s, by which time the Seventh-Day Adventists had begun their missionary outreach, and in the 1870s Mary Baker Eddy founded Christian Science. This suggests that the Witnesses were founded at a time marked not only by great social unrest but also by the birth of a number of other world-renouncing movements. While immigration was of key significance in the expansion of the Mormon church, the renunciation of the world appealed largely to those for whom social and political agitation were signs of the end.

When people convert to the Watch Tower organisation, they defer unquestioningly to the authority of those who are appointed to enforce its doctrines. In this respect, the individual becomes the property of the whole community. This tightly bound movement within which uniform beliefs about the world are shared provides new recruits not only with a ready-made explanation for their life experiences but also with status and prestige. In other words, Watch Tower conversion is about *belonging*. Could it be, therefore, that the Witnesses are offering these particular individuals something that can be achieved only by religious conversion? What does this kind of millenarianism signify at the beginning of the twenty-first century? And what exactly is its relationship with modernity?

Recent sociological literature has addressed the way in which the shift from an urbanised, industrialised society towards a de-urbanised one which is characterised by technology and consumption has encouraged an unprecedented range of alternative beliefs (Bruce 1995, 1996, Heelas 1996). The diminishing number of people who continue to engage in religious behaviour do so in an increasingly individualistic fashion which is arguably more akin to leisure than to moral duty. Bruce claims that this is especially so with the New Age religions which increased in popularity in the late 1980s. Bruce suggests that the present cultural milieu of tolerance has created an almost complete acceptance of alternative versions of reality. He argues that universal authority has given way to self-government and that this has allowed New Age rituals such as paganism, psychosynthesis, Shamanism, Taoism and astrology to flourish. Yet, despite the recent increase in tolerance and decline in traditional authority to which Bruce refers, the Watch Tower Society with its patriarchal, hierarchical structure and disdain for ambiguity is still managing to win recruits in numbers of which any religious organisation offering an alternative to mainstream Christianity would be proud. For this reason, the Witnesses warrant attention. If, in the midst of the religious pluralism described by Bruce, the Watch Tower Society continues to expand at the rate that it has, now is the time to bring it to the centre of the academic arena. After all, movements that manage to increase their annual membership over such a long period take some slowing down. So why, in an age of cultural diversity, do some individuals choose the Watch Tower option and how does the organisation manage to sell itself to prospective recruits?

Millenarian doctrines such as those of the Watch Tower Society are as significant in the twenty-first century as at any other time in history. These doctrines convey a great deal about contemporary culture; or at least people's perceptions of it. No matter how hard cultural theorists try to persuade us that the world is now a safer place than ever before (at least, that is, if the figures for mortality and morbidity mean anything), public fear is a growth industry. The mass media constantly bombard us with stories of abhorrent violence, stranger danger, food contamination, sexually transmitted diseases, environmental disasters and a whole host of other catastrophes which threaten our well-being if not our entire planet. This anxiety about trends in the contemporary world is, I would suggest, one of the reasons for the endurance of doomsday beliefs. Uncertainty about the future stems from our inability to predict the outcome of present actions and events. The suspicion associated with modernity, particularly that resulting from technological development, leaves even the most optimistic individuals (including scientists) with the feeling that they are living in a hi-tech purgatory – a place where risk is impossible to ascertain and where the future cannot be known. For the Witnesses, however, human misery is not a fearful possibility, it is a *fait accompli*. Although the anticipation of an imminent paradise ostensibly gives them hope in a world which they claim is heading for disaster, it is, in fact, a means by which they are able to combat their own uncertainty and to consign their opponents to a future holocaust. In this respect, millenarianism is a form of resistance that serves to strengthen the conviction of a people who see themselves as persecuted. It provides devotees with the assurance that God will exact vengeance on evil. It is an exhortation to stand firm against all adversity.

The Witnesses draw clear boundaries between themselves and non-members, establish strict entry criteria and keep their involvement with the wider society to a minimum. While other religions throughout the world are entering the public sphere in order to make themselves heard, the Watch Tower Society's Governing Body continues to resist denominational status and forbids its members to partake in civil activities. In addition to a strong condemnation of the outside world, the Witnesses' millenarian orientation involves the rejection of all other faiths as errant. Any indications of disloyalty or failure to adhere to the Society's principles can lead to suspension or ostracism which, in terms of their own beliefs, could lead to the risk of the transgressors' exclusion from the utopian Kingdom to come. The 'freedom' offered by the modern world is bad news for the

Witnesses. One does not need to be in their company for very long to realise that secular society is regarded as a place of moral contamination – a place where the righteous are seduced by the devil. Yet, despite tenaciously upholding doctrines that disparage the rest of humanity, members of the movement do not live communally. This raises a number of interesting questions. For example, given that the Witnesses live in the world, why do they continue to renounce it so vehemently? How do they manage to maintain their secular roles in the public sphere? How does the organisation ensure that devotees remain loyal to its cause? What kind of tensions arise from contact between Witnesses and non-Witnesses? And how are these tensions resolved?

As a movement that stands in antithesis to modern society, the Witnesses have, in effect, produced a religion that enables them to resist secular forces. To put it another way, the Witnesses' deference to absolute authority is a solution to all perceived forms of risk. Among the most influential writers to have developed sociological perspectives on the relationship between risk and modernity are Ulrich Beck (1992) and Anthony Giddens (1990, 1991), both of whom are concerned with the cultural changes which they suggest have led to crises of personal identity. Giddens points out that, in late modern societies, individuals find themselves in a constant state of self-questioning as they learn that knowledge has no foundation. This means that we reflect on our behaviour more than ever before, with greater ability to choose new courses of action. Giddens refers to this self-critical, self-questioning aspect of modern life as *reflexivity*. He compares people's constant awareness of many forms of knowledge within and across cultures to that of riding an uncontrollable juggernaut. Giddens argues that not only does reflexivity govern life choices, it is also the tool of modern epistemology (Giddens 1990). Beck develops a similar argument about reflexivity by suggesting that, while scientific progress has brought about health and life risks, the individual has been freed from collective institutions and from tradition. Beck argues that societies have become *destabilised*; characterised by personal insecurity as more and more hazards become apparent. He maintains that, in order for societies to progress, we must all now learn to adapt to the universal principles of progress and the impersonal nature of social institutions. Beck uses the term *modernisation* to describe the transitional period of Western societies that began in the nineteenth century and argues that these societies have undergone enormous changes in the relationship between social structures and agents. Actors have been freed from structural constraints and this marks the dissolution of industrial society and the beginning of a new modernity; thus, *simple* modernity is a feature of late industrialisation while the individualised *reflexive* modernity characterises the society of high risk (Beck 1992: 3). Giddens's work on reflexively organised life planning focuses more on the psychological aspects of insecurity with particular regard to attitudes of trust. An example of this might be the way in which people learn to trust governments and other

organisations to deal as effectively as possible with environmental disaster
and other such risks which have the potential to threaten life. According to
Giddens, basic trust of this nature is a determining element in whether or not
an individual is constantly plagued with anxiety (Giddens 1991).

In the risk societies described by Beck and Giddens, there can be no doubt
that reflexivity undermines the certainty of knowledge. However, Giddens
argues that systems are in place to ensure that possible events or issues
are *bracketed-out* in order that the fear of risk and danger may be kept to a
minimum (1991: 181–3). This might involve strategies such as giving the
fear over to someone else to worry about, placing it in the hands of fate,
diminishing its effects by adopting the belief that all will turn out well,
or trusting some higher authority to deal with it in the way described
above. Both Beck and Giddens provide a crucial context for the study of
millenarians such as the Witnesses whose strategies for dealing with the
world centre on their puritanical beliefs and apocalyptic message. Watch
Tower doctrines provide them with what Giddens calls *ontological security*
(by which he means a sense of continuity and order in events including those
outside the perceptual environment of the individual) and play a crucial
role in the construction of their identity. The Witnesses' pessimistic view
of humanity can thus be seen as symptomatic of their anxiety about the
future.

Throughout this book, I use the concept of risk to examine the various
ways in which the Witnesses manage their interactions with the outside
world; but it is risk as *moral danger* that provides the most appropriate
context for discussion. As far as the Witnesses are concerned, risky behaviour
is that which threatens their salvation, and this has enormous implications
for how they deal with outsiders. Drawing on cultural theory, anthropologist Mary Douglas regards risk as part of *all* reality – not just the
modern world. Like Beck and Giddens, Douglas sets risk in the context of
danger, but her theory is, I believe, more universal than theirs, since she
offers a general analysis which can be applied to all people and for all times.
Although Douglas gives several examples of the uses of risk as a central
concept in policy-making, she also examines its significance among closed
communities in their attempts to achieve cultural homogeneity (Douglas
1992: 38–54). In the case of small millenarian movements, this makes
possible an analysis of sin and taboo; hence, we can begin to examine the
ways in which members of such organisations conceptualise risk as well
as their ways of dealing with it. In other words, while risk is part of the
vocabulary of those who practise science and technology or who work in
local government, it still constitutes plain *danger* for millenarians who want
to protect their boundaries. Douglas argues that the only real difference
between these two concepts is that risk suggests precise calculation:

> Risk, danger, and sin are used around the world to legitimate policy or
> to discredit it, to protect individuals from predatory institutions or to

protect institutions from predatory individuals. Indeed, risk provides secular terms for rewriting scripture: not the sins of the fathers, but the risks unleashed by the fathers are visited on the heads of their children, even to the *nth* generation.

(Douglas 1992: 26)

Douglas's notion of risk as danger allows us to examine the Witnesses' behaviour from their own millenarian perspective. Throughout the 1970s and 1980s, the Witnesses used the environmental threat of nuclear war as a topic of conversation for their door-to-door proselytising in order to win recruits; but this was by no means the only way in which their revulsion for humankind manifested itself. Their constant references to evil revealed much more about their attitude to risk than it did their fear of global catastrophe. Douglas's ideas support my analysis of how the Witnesses use their doctrines to fend off those aspects of secular life which threaten their *Weltanschauung*. Douglas also aids our understanding of why, in an age of cultural fluidity and semiotic pastiche, certain individuals should choose to join and remain in such an authoritarian organisation.

Though there are fundamental differences between the essentially modernist notion of risk propounded by Beck and Giddens and Douglas's idea of risk as a means of averting wrongdoing, all three writers contribute something useful to my overall analysis. However unambiguous the Witnesses' version of sin might be, they must continue to uphold it in a world in which all manner of options are available. If the Watch Tower Society is to continue to be successful in its ministry and recruitment, it must protect its members from secular forces that might well threaten the authority of its leadership. This means assuaging anxieties about high-consequence risks while at the same time allaying any other wicked temptations that the modern world might present.

Each chapter of this book explores a different aspect of the Witnesses' way of life. In Chapter 2, I offer some background information about the history and doctrines of the Watch Tower Society and introduce a number of key themes which I believe make for an original sociological analysis. I discuss the importance of fundamentalist beliefs and practices in the Witnesses' own terms and the strategies prescribed by their Governing Body for dealing with secular society. In Chapters 3 and 4, I use empirical material to examine the current meaning of Watch Tower conversion and the significance of belonging to a closed community. The chapters contain details of how devotees make use of cultural resources to strengthen their appeal, and a description of the weekly activities in which they engage in order to maintain their religious status. This is followed in Chapter 5 by an examination of how those who convert to the Watch Tower Society learn to adopt a millenarian worldview as part of their new identity. The overall purpose of the chapter is to show how the Witnesses' brand of millen-arianism is more dependent on the modern world than we might think or than they might be prepared to admit. Chapter 6 focuses on how the members negotiate their contact with those who do not share their faith. I consider the ways in which they manage their identity in a number of social contexts including the workplace, in the company of friends and, in some cases, within marriage. I argue that negotiating across symbolic boundaries always carries risks, while crossing them is prohibited. I also discuss the strategies deployed by the Witnesses in their negotiations with outsiders. Chapter 7 concerns second and subsequent generation members and how the movement deals with their responses to the Watch Tower regime. The chapter contains interview data that help to inform my analysis of three key issues; namely, socialisation, education and rebellion. In Chapter 8, I examine what causes some Witnesses to abandon the community. The chapter portrays life inside the organisation through the eyes of lapsed members and explains what happens to them when they decide to leave of their own accord. I use published autobiographical accounts of former members to establish whether defection signals a shift in attitude towards modern secular society.

Most of the existing scholarly literature on millenarian religious movements stresses their incompatibility with life outside. Although this assertion may be true, it needs to be demonstrated rather than assumed. Although this book focuses on Jehovah's Witnesses in Britain, it is not essentially about their 'Britishness'. Rather, it is a study of their relationship with the modern world; hence, Britain is important for no reason other than the fact that it is a modern society. While I have given special consideration to local issues and events, the principal tenets of modernity discussed throughout the book can be applied elsewhere. The Witnesses have undoubtedly been successful (more so than in the UK) in non-Western contexts – Japan and Africa being prime examples – but the most relevant secondary material for my analysis (with the exception of some autobiographical literature) has been published by British academics.[9]

In the pages that follow, I will argue that the relationship between the Witnesses and modern society is complex and ambivalent. On the surface, it would appear that Watch Tower theology represents a backlash against secular life, but closer investigation reveals that, in other respects, it is part of the very forces it condemns. Only through an ethnographic study of the Watch Tower community and a general examination of its appeal can a better understanding of the movement's current position in the world be attained. As they patiently await Jehovah's intervention, the Witnesses' relationship with modernity remains something of a paradox. On the one hand, they are rational in the sense that their belief system lacks the mystical content often found in orthodox Christianity (and materialistic in that it is not uncommon to find them employed in well-paid jobs and occupying houses in sought-after areas), but, on the other, they are anti-modern in their resistance to individual freedom and many of the rights of Western citizenship. With the start of a new millennium, the implications for the future of the Watch Tower Society and for the direction of empirical research on its members are enormous. Whatever the epistemological contributions of twenty-first-century academics, such work will undoubtedly be received by a fascinated audience.

2 The Jehovah's Witnesses in the modern world

Before we can begin to establish the Witnesses' status at the beginning of the twenty-first century, we need to know something about their organisation's evolution and doctrines. These details help us to understand the culture in which the Witnesses operate and allow us to consider the various compatibilities and incompatibilities between the Watch Tower Society and the outside world. Moreover, the hierarchical structure of the movement enables devotees to resist those forces that might threaten their status as bona fide members of a system they call 'the truth'. In short, an enquiry into what the Witnesses believe, how they came to believe it and how they are able to reaffirm these beliefs internally aids our understanding of their relationship with modernity.

History, doctrines and internal structure

From origin to present day

The history of the Watch Tower Bible and Tract Society spans 130 years and is rich in controversy. From the moment of its foundation by Charles Taze Russell (1852–1916) to the present day, reactions towards the movement include fascination, compassion, anger and hatred. Although the available literature indicates that their world-renouncing theology and adherence to millenarianism have been the sources of great strain in terms of their liaison with secular bodies (particularly the legal system), the Witnesses have managed to gain converts and expand on an international scale.

Surprisingly, there is very little information about Russell's background. Rogerson's sociological research reveals that Russell was educated in state schools and then by private tutors (Rogerson 1969). Russell inherited Presbyterian beliefs from parents of Scottish–Irish descent, but his mother died when he was only nine years of age. In 1867, at the age of fifteen, he entered into partnership with his father, who ran a chain of men's clothing stores in Allegheny, Pennsylvania. Russell was an astute businessman. Before he was thirty years of age, he had expanded his father's clothing store, which he sold for $250,000 – the equivalent of more than a million dollars today.

He also sold what he called 'miracle wheat' to credulous farmers at $60 a bushel. The fraud was eventually stopped by the federal authorities, who made him refund the money (Ripley 1982: 1–12). During his initial years as a draper, Russell abandoned Presbyterianism in favour of more liberal Congregationalist beliefs, but even these eventually gave way to a firm conviction that an omnipotent, omnipresent and omniscient God was incompatible with conventional doctrines of suffering and hell. This left Russell in a state of perplexity and doubt, as his own reflections confirm:

> Brought up a Presbyterian, indoctrinated from the Catechism, and being naturally of an enquiring mind, I fell a ready prey to the logic of infidelity, as soon as I began to think for myself. But that which at first threatened to be the utter shipwreck of faith in God and the Bible was, under God's providence, over-ruled for good, and merely wrecked my confidence in human creeds and systems of Bible misinterpretations.
> (*The Watchtower* 1916: 170–2 quoted in Rogerson 1969: 5–6)

At this point, Russell became an avowed sceptic and discarded the Bible altogether; but in 1870 he attended a meeting held by some Seventh-Day Adventists in a basement near his store in Allegheny. It would appear that this meeting was a significant influence in the restoration of Russell's faith, for, although he failed to join the Adventists, they did at least persuade him of an alternative creed to Christendom. He gathered together some like-minded friends and acquaintances and they formed a Bible study group in Pittsburgh where they met on a regular basis. Witnesses today believe that this was the point at which Russell returned to the Bible and discovered real truth. Undoubtedly influenced by the Seventh-Day Adventists, Russell espoused doctrines such as the annihilation of the wicked, the denial of hell, the extinction of the soul at death and a new code for salvation. His interest in the Bible became almost obsessive, and, between 1870 and 1879, he wrote several pamphlets and a new periodical called *Zion's Watch Tower and Herald of Christ's Presence*. This new magazine was to play a crucial role in the expansion of the movement, and by 1880 some thirty congregations had sprung up in several American states. By 1884, 'Zion's Watch Tower Tract Society', managed by Russell, was given legal charter (Hoekema 1984). The Society printed tracts, papers, pamphlets, magazines and other materials in various languages and, in 1886, over six million copies of Russell's first publication, *Millennial Dawn* (later called *Studies in the Scriptures*), came to be sold. By now, Russell saw himself as 'the Servant of the Truth'. Not surprisingly, his opponents accused him of conceit. By the late 1880s, Russell had employed thousands of colporteurs (today called *pioneers*) who worked almost full-time preaching the theology and distributing millenarian literature. Russell devoted all his time to the study of the Bible and the administration of his fast-growing organisation. In 1889, a new building was finished in Pittsburgh to house the printing works and to act as the Society's central office. In 1900, the first branch office was established in London.

Russell wrote specific instructions for selling his literature and employed virtually every device of modern advertising to disseminate his biblical message. By the early 1900s, he had travelled to Ireland, Scotland, Russia and Turkey to deliver his sermons. By 1917, there was a total of ninety-three *pilgrims* (today known as *circuit overseers*) travelling from congregation to congregation. Russell had laid the foundation of a movement that would inevitably expand. Most of Russell's written work consisted of elaborate biblical chronology that applied to his own time. His books reveal that he was greatly concerned with dates and events. He related social, political and economic issues to biblical prophecy and was fond of debating the exact meaning of the original Greek and Hebrew words in scripture. In a court in Ontario, Canada, in 1913, he declared under oath to be an expert scripture scholar, but when handed a Greek New Testament he was forced to admit that he did not even know the Greek alphabet. Neither did he know Latin or Hebrew. Few, if any, academic theologians in the universities of the world today acknowledge Russell as a scholar in any sense of the word (Ripley 1982: 1–2). Most Jehovah's Witnesses know little or nothing of Russell's prophecies, but they are all convinced that he correctly predicted the heavenly establishment of the Kingdom of God in 1914. When 1914 finally arrived, it was too late to persuade his followers that he might be wrong. Some left the movement in disappointment, but those who remained were confused about what was going to happen. The Witnesses have since claimed that, in some way, Russell predicted the First World War, but, for Russell himself and his successor Joseph Rutherford, the beginning of a war in Europe was of little significance. Russell was still convinced that heavenly glory was soon to come. In 1916, Russell's health deteriorated rapidly and he died on Tuesday 31 October that year.

In January 1917, Joseph Franklin Rutherford was elected President of what was now known as the Watch Tower Bible and Tract Society. Rutherford called himself 'Judge', although some sources claim that he never held an official appointment as such. At the age of twenty-two, he was admitted to the bar and began to practise law, later serving four years as public prosecutor for Booneville. He had frequently defended Russell in court and had become an ardent supporter of the movement. When he became President, he proceeded to restructure the Society and to encourage devotees to engage in a more active programme of Witnessing. He was dissatisfied with the Board of Directors, over which he adopted total control.[1] This culminated in open rebellion, after which several disaffected leaders were dismissed from their official positions. This led to the formation of small schismatic groups. In July 1917, the seventh volume of the *Studies in the Scriptures* series, *The Finished Mystery*, was published. This book, compiled by Watch Tower editors from the earlier works of Russell, was chiefly a commentary on Ezekiel and Revelation.[2] According to this tract, Catholic and Protestant organisations together represented Babylon, which was soon to pass into oblivion. Possession of these publications was forbidden in Canada, where the movement had been declared illegal. On 8 May 1918, together with other Russellites, Rutherford was arrested under the United States Espionage Act for spreading dissent in the army and navy and sentenced to twenty years' imprisonment. He served only nine months, although, like his predecessor, he was frequently accused of fraudulent practices, even by his own followers. Unlike Russell, Rutherford developed a hatred of his avowed enemy, the clergy.[3] It was during this period that Rutherford began to teach that Christ had returned *invisibly* in 1914, and that Armageddon was imminent.[4] Rutherford claimed that this would be the point at which worldly organisations (including of course, Christendom) would perish. In 1931, he devised the new title 'Witnesses of Jehovah' and publicised the slogan 'Millions now living will never die'. He was not one of the millions! He died in 1942 in the palatial villa he had had built at San Diego as an official residence pending the return of Christ. He had been President of the movement for twenty-five years.

During Rutherford's presidency, the Society had moved from a more or less democratic to a theocratic structure, in which the directors of the various local congregations were no longer elected by local assemblies but were appointed by a Governing Body in Brooklyn. Rutherford was succeeded in 1942 by Nathan Homer Knorr, who had worked as a full-time preacher and co-ordinator of all printing activities within the organisation and General Manager of the publishing plant. In 1934, Knorr had been appointed one of the directors of the New York corporation and in 1940, he became Vice President of the Pennsylvania corporation (Watch Tower Bible and Tract Society of Pennsylvania 1959: 196). Knorr immediately began a face-lifting and public relations programme that has since paid dividends in recruits. Several doctrinal books were published during Knorr's presidency, including *Theocratic Aid to Kingdom Publishers* (1945), *Equipped for Every Good Work* (1946a) and *Qualified to Be Ministers* (1955a). These three books contained information about scripture, door-to-door canvassing and history, but there were other books which were considered authoritative guidelines taking the place of previous publications by Russell and Rutherford, including *The Truth Shall Make You Free* (1943), *Let God Be True* (1946b, revised in 1952) and *Make Sure of All Things* (1953, revised in 1957). The books are summaries of doctrines, and millions of later editions have been printed and sold all over the world. *From Paradise Lost to Paradise Regained* was published in 1958 and is often used along with *Make Sure of All Things* and the more recent *Reasoning from the Scriptures* (1989b) as a handy reference book by the Witnesses in their doorstep ministry.

Another important project carried out under Knorr was the translation of the Bible into modern English. This began in 1950, and in 1961 the entire Bible in *The New World Translation* was published in one volume.

Those members who were responsible for the translating requested that they should remain anonymous. Under Knorr's presidency, door-to-door evangelists no longer carried a portable gramophone and collection of Rutherford's records. Rather, devotees were given a thorough training in speech and non-verbal communication that enabled them to deliver their own sermons. To this day, the Witnesses hold regular meetings, during which training and demonstrations take place to enable them to minister more effectively to the general public. During Knorr's regime as President, there was a huge expansion of the Witnesses' work worldwide. In 1942, evangelism took place in only fifty-four countries, but by 1971 it had spread to 207. The movement grew by 25 per cent during the 1930s and 1940s, with a total of 20,842 active members in Britain by 1950. By 1971, the country in which the Witnesses were most active was West Germany (87,976 members listed), followed by Nigeria with 75,372, and Brazil with 66,460. The British Isles followed with 62,813, then the Philippines with 54,264 and then Zambia with 52,369. Next was Mexico with 51,256 members, then Canada with 48,100. Other countries in which the Witnesses claim to have had more than five thousand active members in 1971 include Argentina, Australia, Belgium, Chile, Colombia, Congo (Kinshara), Denmark, Finland, France, Ghana, Greece, Italy, Jamaica, Japan, Korea, Malawi, New Zealand, Norway, Portugal, Puerto Rico, Rhodesia, South Africa, Spain, Sweden, Switzerland and Venezuela (Watch Tower Bible and Tract Society of Pennsylvania 1971). Millions of copies of the Society's two magazines *The Watchtower* and *Awake!* are sold throughout the world every year, and Witnessing takes place in over two hundred countries. The 1 January 2001 issue of *The Watchtower* recorded 126,297 Witnesses in Britain alone in 2000 and over ninety thousand congregations worldwide (Watch Tower Bible and Tract Society of Pennsylvania 2001).[5] All the countries cited above have seen fairly substantial increases in membership over the last three decades, although in recent years the movement has remained static in Australia, Belgium, Britain, Germany, Scandinavia and Spain. The Witnesses are, however, continuing to expand in Eastern Europe, Latin America and many parts of Africa. Albania, Cambodia and Mongolia all claimed at least a 25 per cent increase in their total membership between 1998 and 1999.

James Beckford tells us that Russell founded his movement amidst a certain amount of dissatisfaction with what was regarded as 'modernism' among Protestant thinkers in late nineteenth-century America. Russell opposed this with what he considered to be fundamental religious truths – truths that he feared were being replaced by individual-oriented Arminianism.[6] Beckford writes:

> Russell chose precisely to oppose modernist philosophy, theology and ecclesiology by restating what he understood to be the unchanging principles of Christianity and by organizing a religious movement with

the explicit goal of propagating those principles . . . His proposed solution to the twin problems of 'infidelity' and 'modernism' was to restore faith in the 'principle (that) seems to be disappearing in respect to religious matters',[7] and his own set of teachings crystallized in the attempt to oppose error with truth and liberalism with 'principle'.

(Beckford 1975a: 3)

Beckford goes on to describe how a movement which became known as The Social Gospel played a significant role in convincing Russell that churches were becoming tainted with secular influences, and that the clergy had begun to neglect their primary duty of ministry for superficial reform. Although there are few sources that link Russell's way of thinking to the social, cultural and political climate of late nineteenth-century America, it would appear that his disillusionment with modern society in general and orthodox Christianity in particular led him to establish a monosemic, scriptural theology which he argued was rational and irrefutable. To this day, the Witnesses regard the international expansion of their movement as evidence of the gospel of the Kingdom having been preached throughout the whole world predicted in Matthew 24, and have countered what they perceive as the immoral conditions of modern liberal society with puritanical doctrines.

Watch Tower teachings

Watch Tower theology is the Society's most crucial resource, and devotees are expected to adhere to all doctrines established by the Governing Body. These doctrines pervade almost every conceivable sphere of life. The theology plays an important part in uniting devotees into a close-knit community and separating them symbolically from the outside world. It should be borne in mind, however, that Watch Tower theology cannot be summarised without doing gross injustice to its complexity. Were it to be presented in its entirety, the thoughts and questions that will be prompted by this book would undoubtedly receive more attention. In the pages that follow, accounts of the Witnesses' beliefs are intended only to illuminate a social phenomenon. It is the task of the theologian, not the sociologist, to engage in debates concerning scriptural interpretation.

Ever since the organisation was founded, there has been no mechanism for contributing to or criticising the canon of official teachings. The establishment of doctrines has been very carefully restricted to, and controlled by, the Society's Governing Body. This means that Jehovah's Witnesses around the world are recipients of an absolutist message rather than free-thinking agents who are actively involved in the formulation of religious ideas. What is significant about this is the effect of such a uniform set of doctrines on the Witnesses' social relations. Doctrines prescribed by an autocratic administration play a crucial role in the construction of a tightly bonded community. Where inconsistencies are noticed by devotees, personal questioning is abrogated in favour of the safe conviction that those responsible for the formulation of Watch Tower doctrines must also be able to deal effectively with any criticisms. Witnesses at grass roots level often argue that, if inconsistencies were real, then the organisation would not have gained the widespread popularity that it has. It is possible that this acquiescence has brought about even greater support than any serious attempt to deal with questions of doctrinal consistency would do. This is why an analysis of the symbolic meaning and presentation of doctrines serves a greater purpose for this book than details of the doctrines themselves.

The Witnesses see themselves as members not just of a religious movement but of one that monopolises the word of God. For this reason, they feel they are called upon to proselytise. Nonconformist ideas that were widespread during the period in which the Society was founded provided the basis for some of its teachings. The one imperative belief, however, is that the Bible, from beginning to end, is the inspired word of God. This means that all Watch Tower teachings are scripturally supported and most, but not all, the Bible is interpreted literally. The exceptions are the recorded visions in the Books of Daniel and Revelation. The rest the Witnesses regard as historically accurate, including the stories in the book of Genesis. The following transcript from an interview with a local elder conveys the importance of this biblical literalism. He is worth quoting at length:

The Bible is the fundamental foundation of doctrine and I would say to someone interested in our faith, 'Are you willing to adjust to it in order to be pleasing to God whom you have faith in?' So we would have a Bible study. For instance, I would say to you, 'Do you believe that God is a single person?', and, depending on how you answered, I would go to references in the Bible that would show you what our beliefs are. Now, when you've heard that clarification it's up to you whether you accept it or not, and then we would go to other angles of fact. I would say, 'When you die, what do you expect will happen to you?', and then I'd say, 'Well, let's see what the Bible has to say about death and why we die, and let's see if there's a different future to the one you envisage'. So, the main fundamentals are, 'Do you believe the Bible is the inspired word of God?' and 'Do you believe in the truth of its doctrines?' and 'What do you think happens when you die?', and then we'd turn to the Bible and give you the biblical answer, and if the Bible is the foundation of doctrine and action and way of life, are you willing to adjust to it in order to be pleasing to God? The Bible can be likened to a rule. The rule is a measurement which is internationally accepted, so the Bible becomes the measure of faith and therefore if you measure your conduct by the Bible's measure, then you're doing what Jesus said, you're in the truth. We're convinced we have the truth because the Bible says it's the truth. Jesus in his speaking said, 'Thy word is truth' – that's from John 17 verse 17. Now when he said that, he was speaking of the Old Testament, because the New Testament hadn't been formulated. So when he said, 'Thy word is truth' or 'Your word is truth' as the modern language would say, we believe that the Bible is an accurate account of facts – historically, scientifically, genealogically and all the other angles of life, and so when Jesus said, 'The first Adam was made flesh', when he talks about 'as it was in the days of Noah' and when he talked about 'the patience of Job', he was making factual references, not allegories. So, when you go therefore to what Jesus referred to as 'the truth', the Old Testament, then you study its narrative, its history, you look at the genealogical lives which are very well recorded in the book of Luke – where Luke said, 'I want to trace things back to the beginning' and he goes back genealogically and ends up with Adam. So therefore, that's why we feel we've got the truth. We try to see things from the biblical viewpoint, which is God's viewpoint.

In contrast with the pick-and-mix philosophy of many of the New Age religions, this elder's comments demonstrate the absolutist nature of the authority to which he defers. Scriptural texts are used by the Witnesses as a constant frame of reference. World catastrophes such as war, famine, murder, environmental pollution, genocide and terrorism provide them with evidence in support of their theology. When ministering on the doorstep, it is not unusual for Watch Tower evangelists to refer to a recent world event and use biblical texts to explain its occurrence. These events are also taken as evidence of signs of the Last Days. It seems that the more the Witnesses hear about social and economic crises when they turn on their television sets, the more their monosemic view of the world is validated.

The Governing Body of the Society teaches its members that God has a personal name – Jehovah (Exodus 9: 16 is used to support this). The Witnesses' God is the God of the Old Testament, and they reject the Trinity doctrine, declaring it unscriptural. Although Jesus is regarded as inferior to Jehovah, it is believed that, together, both Jesus and Jehovah produced perfect spiritual beings that possessed free will. Satan was one such spirit. The Witnesses maintain that, since the deception in the Garden of Eden, Satan has misled the world, and the most important reason for the existence of humankind (as revealed in the Bible) is the vindication of Jehovah over Satan. Instead of destroying Satan, Jehovah decided to test the loyalty of the rest of humankind and to prove to the rest of creation that Satan was a liar. Jehovah has set a time limit of six thousand years for this challenge (the period would have ended in 1975 – the year in which the Society expected Armageddon), after which, the Witnesses will be rewarded for their loyalty to his divine plan.

The Witnesses believe that the Fall (recorded in Genesis) is responsible for death, but they reject the doctrine of the immortal soul. They do not, however, believe that death is the end for everyone (although the Society does teach that this is so for those who fail to pass future millennial tests). They maintain that the reason we die is that our first parents rejected God's law, and human governments have been controlled by Satan ever since. Human misery is the result of Satan's power in a world in which he will soon be destroyed. The Witnesses claim that some kind of existence after death can be expected for most human beings and this will take the form of resurrection. They also believe that, since Pentecost, Jehovah has been preparing a 'Bride of Christ', a 'Little Flock', a body of 144,000 people (a figure mentioned in Revelation 14: 3) to share heavenly life and leadership. Thus, an anointed class of 144,000 Jehovah's Witnesses will win heavenly reward, while the remainder (along with non-Witnesses whom Jehovah deems worthy) will spend eternity in a different paradise here on earth. The righteous who are asleep in death will be raised from their graves (Watch Tower Bible and Tract Society of Pennsylvania 1955b).

Like their founding fathers, Witnesses today continue to renounce the conventional Christian doctrine of hellfire on the basis that it is unscriptural and contrary to Jehovah's loving nature (Watch Tower Bible and Tract Society of Pennsylvania 1989b: 168–75). They claim that hell is nothing more than an insensible state. To support this, they quote Ecclesiastes 9: 10, which describes both Jacob and Job in moments of depression wanting to enter Sheol; and Acts 2: 24–7, 31, and Romans 10: 6, 7, which mention that Jesus himself was in Hades. This, say the Witnesses, would be very difficult to understand if hell were a place of eternal torment. For them, hell is complete annihilation that Jesus will execute upon Satan and his demons at Armageddon, after which there will be no resurrection (Rogerson 1969: 93). Armageddon is the battle in which Christ will purge the earth of Satan's influence – a battle symbolising Jehovah's victory over evil. But Armageddon is not incompatible with the pragmatic nature of building new headquarters for the administration of Watch Tower activities and the continuation of all other features of daily life. Since the Witnesses believe that the just will be saved at Armageddon and that the wicked will be destroyed, the doctrine plays an important role in Watch Tower ministry. The promise of eternal bliss in the post-Armageddon Kingdom informs them that world chaos and life-threatening events are not meaningless but part of a larger system of order.

The Society forbids its members to participate in annual events such as Christmas, Easter, birthdays and national festivals. It teaches that Jehovah does not acknowledge these events since, wherever they are cited in the scriptures, they are always in the context of sin or apostasy. According to the Witnesses, the only two birthday celebrations mentioned in the Bible involve people who were not true believers. These are a pharaoh of Egypt and the Roman ruler Herod Antipas (Genesis 40: 18–22; and Mark 6: 21–8), whose celebrations ended in misery. Though they recognise that the birth of Christ is presented as a joyful occasion by the synoptic writers, devotees refuse to partake in the celebration on the grounds that we do not know the precise date of an event that has, in any case, become tainted with secular images such as lights, trees, tinsel and mistletoe. As far as Easter is concerned, the egg is historically a pagan symbol for the celebration of the return of spring and the rabbit was an emblem of fertility, neither of which is connected with the resurrection of Christ (Watch Tower Bible and Tract Society of Pennsylvania 1989b: 179). Furthermore, the Witnesses associate annual celebrations with immodest behaviour and excessive alcohol consumption – practices that they say are contrary to the counsel of Romans 13: 13, 'As in the daytime let us walk decently, not in revelries and drunken bouts, not in illicit intercourse and loose conduct, not in strife and jealousy.' This explains why, in addition to their eschatological beliefs, devotees adopt a puritanical lifestyle.

Despite their belief that Satan controls the world, the Witnesses do not generally go as far as members of religious organisations such as the Plymouth Brethren in isolating themselves completely from outsiders. None the less, their persistent refusal to engage in political activities such as voting in elections or joining pressure groups shows their disdain for secular society. The Witnesses continue to object to both jury and military service (on the grounds of pacifism and neutrality), and they do not support local or national charities. Although some devotees join social and leisure clubs and progress to post-compulsory education, Watch Tower officials encourage Kingdom interests and frown upon activities that detract from the Society's teachings. The Governing Body officially condemns behaviour that violates these teachings. Devotees are expected not to smoke and to drink alcohol only in moderation. The dualistic nature of Watch Tower theology means that, in principle, Witnesses everywhere are expected to adhere to a strict ascetic code. Sexual purity is high on the agenda of moral regulation. Adultery, fornication, masturbation and homosexuality all flout the organisation's teachings on sexual conduct. Anything other than highly controlled heterosexual activity is regarded as immoral, and sexual intercourse is confined to marriage. Drug abuse, smoking and the excessive consumption of alcohol, although not symbolically polluting, are believed to be physically polluting and offensive to Jehovah. Blood transfusions are both symbolically and physically polluting. These moral boundaries must be understood and accepted by every individual prior to baptism. In its advice to its younger members, the Governing Body has this to say:

> The Bible describes a young man who meets a promiscuous woman. She kisses him and says: 'Do come, . . . let us enjoy each other with love expressions.' Then what happens? 'All of a sudden he is going after her, like a bull that comes even to the slaughter.' (Proverbs 7: 7–22) Obviously, this youth's passions were aroused not simply because his hormones were at work but because of what he saw and heard. Similarly, one young man admits: 'The root of my whole problem with

masturbation boiled down to what I put in my mind. I would watch TV programs that included immorality and in some cases watch programs on cable TV that would show nudity. Such scenes are so shocking that they stay with you. They would surface again in my mind, providing the mental fuel needed to engage in masturbation.'

(Watch Tower Bible and Tract Society of Pennsylvania 1989a: 200)

The tract goes on to explain how marriage is the only legitimate structure in which sexual desires can be satisfied and that masturbation endangers future happiness between a married couple, since the masturbator risks disregarding his or her spouse's needs. Implicit in the Society's rules of sexual purity is the notion that the body is a temple of God and must therefore be freed from moral contamination. Of all these sexual activities, homosexuality is regarded as probably the most vile and unnatural. In a much earlier tract, but one still widely used by devotees, we read:

masturbation can lead into homosexuality. In such instances the person, not satisfied with his lonely sexual activity, seeks a partner for mutual sex play. This happens much more frequently than you may realize. Contrary to what many persons think, homosexuals are not *born* that way, but their homosexual behaviour is learned. And often a person gets started when very young by playing with anothers' sexual parts, and then engaging in homosexual acts.

(Watch Tower Bible and Tract Society of Pennsylvania 1976: 39)

The passage continues with an anecdote about a young man who became 'hooked' on homosexual practices and was able to fight them only by realising that God viewed them as unnatural. As usual, the story ends with a biblical injunction against homosexuality: 'God's Word is very clear on this matter, saying: "Make no mistake: no fornicator or idolater, none who are guilty either of adultery or of homosexual perversion . . . will possess the kingdom of God"' (1 Corinthians 6: 9, 10).

I attended several Kingdom Hall meetings at which homosexuality was referred to as an unnatural perversion. At a *public talk* that was delivered by a highly enthusiastic young man who aspired to become a *pioneer* for the Society,[8] I listened to a forty-five minute sermon about whether homosexuals are 'born that way' or if their sexual behaviour is learned. At this, as at most other Watch Tower sermons, reference was given to the widespread nature of homosexuality, but used only in a way that reinforced the organisation's own teachings – that is, that the world has become unashamedly wicked. There can be little doubt that it would be very difficult for someone with a gay orientation to remain a Witness without experiencing a great deal of injury to his or her personal identity, not least because the Society fails to distinguish between the homosexual condition and homosexual practice.[9]

Of those Watch Tower doctrines that condemn impurity, however, it is the refusal of blood for which the Witnesses are best renowned. This issue has undoubtedly earned the movement the most attention from the outside world (particularly from the courts), and yet, surprisingly, it is not one that often appears on the agenda at Kingdom Hall meetings. Nor is it discussed regularly by elders or even among devotees themselves. Blood prohibition is rarely selected as a key topic for a doorstep sermon, not only because it has given the Witnesses a negative profile (exacerbated over the years by the popular press) but also because it is unlikely to entice new recruits. The Society teaches that blood transfusions are strictly forbidden since blood is a source of life that is sacred to Jehovah. However, the Witnesses insist that most modern surgery can be performed successfully without the use of blood (the Governing Body has no objection to the use of non-blood plasma expanders). Watch Tower publications also warn against the risks of bacterial infection, transfusion reactions and Rhesus sensitisation in their condemnation of the practice. Genesis 9: 4 and Leviticus 17: 11–12 are among the scriptural references used by the Society in support of the doctrine, but it is Acts 15: 28–9 that is most frequently quoted in Watch Tower literature: 'For it has seemed good to the Holy Spirit and to us to lay upon you no greater burden than these necessary things: that you abstain from what has been sacrificed to idols and from blood and from what is strangled and from unchastity.'

Blood transfusions are thus considered physically and morally unclean. As in the case of sexual impurity, receiving blood is tantamount to polluting oneself as well as offending the community. This belief demonstrates the strict purity code that characterises so many Watch Tower teachings. The emergence of AIDS during the 1980s also provided the Witnesses with secular if macabre confirmation of the virtue of the doctrine as well as a powerful justification to abstain from blood on health grounds. It is also worth noting that, prior to its prohibition of blood transfusions in 1945, the Society objected to vaccinations and inoculations, although this never became an official Watch Tower teaching in quite the same way. Sociologist Richard Singelenberg (1990) argues that the patriotic period of the Second World War (ideologically anathematised by the movement) provided a breeding ground for the prohibition to crystallise. The American population was regularly incited to donate blood for its injured soldiers and, in this way, blood transfusions became part of nationalistic manifestation such as armies, national anthems and flags, to which the Witnesses were already vehemently opposed (519–20). The Society's condemnation of blood transfusions constitutes a rule of pollution and purity that is instrumental in creating structural boundaries. In a period marked by state opposition to Watch Tower doctrines (particularly in the USA), devotees needed to maintain their exclusivity in order to re-establish their universal collective identity and to detach themselves from orthodox Christianity. The Witnesses' refusal of blood is functionally analogous with Jewish dietary laws – it confirms that sacrifice is part of the price of membership and reinforces internal cohesion by distinguishing between purity and pollution. Blood is a powerful symbol of allegiance simply because of its lack of meaning for other cultures.

Like most other religious movements, the Watch Tower Society imparts a theology that embraces a large number of highly complex issues and each member usually has at his or her disposal several tracts containing hundreds of biblical references which are used to substantiate beliefs. The doctrines outlined above are those which, in my view, pose the greatest challenge to the Witnesses when they find themselves in the company of non-members and, as such, provide the ethnographer with some important analytical material. I would wish to suggest not that the Witnesses can never circulate in secular environments without experiencing hostility from those who do not share their doctrines, but, rather, that their disillusionment with the world has important implications for how they manage their private beliefs in public. Whatever happens, the Witnesses' loyalty is first and foremost to an organisation that secures their salvation.

Internal organisation and control

As far as the communication of Watch Tower doctrines is concerned, all information is transmitted by central headquarters (that is, the Governing Body) through direct channels to individual members. The result is that Witnesses at all levels are kept aware of the activities of their brethren abroad. The Society's official mission is the key to understanding the relationships that hold devotees together in something that can be called a religious movement. This calls for an examination of the forces of integration and disintegration, the distribution of authority and the internal factors affecting growth and change. Such an exercise involves a description of the activities in which the Witnesses participate. As one might expect, there is a division of labour within the organisation as well as inevitable differences in status and roles.

The Witnesses make use of two corporations – namely, the Watch Tower Bible and Tract Society of Pennsylvania and New York, and the International Bible Students Association. The Pennsylvanian Corporation has voting members who live in all parts of the world. They meet annually and elect or re-elect seven directors of the corporation, who themselves elect officers. The President of the corporation is therefore, elected not by popular vote but by the directors, who choose one of their members for the post. The International Bible Students Association is a London Corporation. It owns property in Britain and is responsible predominantly for British affairs. The President is responsible for the central administration of door-to-door evangelism and travels extensively to check on the progress of the movement worldwide. Doctrinal edicts are the responsibility of a larger body of Jehovah's Witnesses known as the *remnant class* – a spiritual committee comprising the President and other devotees. The Society has an extensive printing factory in New York, consisting of four large inter-connected buildings in which millions of magazines, tracts and other publications are printed every year. This literature appears in nearly every language as well as in Braille. Factory workers are all fully baptised members of the community. There are also Branch Offices in London, which have a printing factory producing several million magazines each month. For administrative convenience, the country under the Branch Office is divided into *districts* that are further divided into *circuits*. At the time of writing, the Society also has three official internet websites.[10]

The Witnesses have no ordained clergy. They refer to all members as *ministers* or *publishers* (or, more personally, *brothers* and *sisters*). This is based on the belief that hierarchies are contrary to biblical teaching. However, closer examination reveals that there *is* a visible hierarchy, and Witnesses in over fifty thousand congregations throughout the world are assigned responsibilities. The chain of posts and the graduation of authority upwards from *Minister* (or *Publisher*) to *Pioneer, Special Pioneer, Circuit Overseer, District Overseer, Branch Official* and *Governing Body* suggest a complicated system of command and promotion. Strange as it may seem to outsiders, all positions are viewed as positions of service with no visible or official exaltation of individuals. At every level of the organisation, those in authority oversee those below them, which means that every Witness is under official surveillance. Nevertheless, it would be wrong to argue that the movement does not contain any informal structures, since kinship relations often facilitate a flow of information outside official channels. Beckford (1975a) argues that kinship links have helped the organisation to expand without threatening the efficient pursuit of goals. Legitimation of official authority is claimed on the grounds that the Society acts as Jehovah's earthly agent and as Christ's instrument for the forthcoming Kingdom.

In sociological terms, the Watch Tower Society is Durkheimian in that there can be no division between God and society. In such a system, the sense of self-discovery or self-exaltation is minimised – often even non-existent, as conveyed in the following passage from a Watch Tower publication:

> There are, of course, many factors involved in being a faithful servant of God. But basic to all of them is reliance on Jehovah and his provisions. How do we show such reliance? One way is by attending congregation meetings. The Scriptures urge us not to neglect them. (Heb. 10: 23–5) Those who have continued to be faithful witnesses of Jehovah, whether in the face of public apathy or of persecution, have exerted themselves to be regular in attending meetings with fellow worshippers. At these meetings our knowledge of the Scriptures is increased, but it is not mere fascination with new things that draws us ... We are drawn close to our Christian brothers in united worship and we personally are strengthened to continue doing God's will. Jehovah's

spirit provides direction through the congregation, and by means of that spirit Jesus is in our midst when we assemble in his name. (Rev. 3: 6; Matt. 18: 20)
(Watch Tower Bible and Tract Society of Pennsylvania 1983b: 170–1)

This passage is rich in detail about the all-powerful congregation over the subordinated self. Although devotees recognise that each human life comes from Jehovah, individual exaltation is given little space. The individual Witness who attends meetings regularly and ministers truth with passion can never pursue personal interests. Many riches await those who are prepared to sacrifice their metaphysical curiosity and personal innovation for the public symbolic system that has stamped its authority on every member of the congregation. In Durkheimian terms, success in the world is incompatible with the given categories of truth in which the internal consciousness of the private person matches that of the collective whole. Witnesses who spend the most number of hours in ministry work and become pioneers or elders are admired and respected for their loyalty and commitment. Individuals derive satisfaction from the knowledge that the community has benefited spiritually from their efforts, while personal success is considered self-indulgent. The following excerpt from an interview with an elder confirms how difficult it is for the Society to allow individual Witnesses to cherish their own achievements:

Involvement in business isn't discouraged except if it's going to overrun and remove your time and energy for spiritual things. You see, Jesus did give an illustration about a man who had grown fat and wealthy and he decided to pull down his barns and build some more barns, 'cos he thought it'd be nice to have some more barns. But Jesus said, 'Beware', and, that very night, the man died. Now many of our younger people do begin to enter into business and that's OK provided it doesn't injure their spiritual activities. Now as far as education is concerned, the organisation through its literature tells our young people, 'Get as much education as you can while you're at school'. Now when it comes to college and university, caution is needed because of the philosophies that can be anti-spiritual and association can be as well.

This elder's comments show how devotees are strongly advised to 'seek first the Kingdom', and there seems to be great pride expressed among active members when their children decide to leave school and become full-time evangelists (or *pioneers*). Financial success can never compensate for one's status as a Witness. The separation of oneself from the community could well mark the beginning of breaking away from it. Unquestioning loyalty of this kind has undoubtedly helped to play down doctrinal inconsistency. The failed prophecies of 1914, 1918, 1925 and, most significantly, 1975 could no longer be taught after these years came and went, and yet the movement has since managed to expand. At the same time, certain doctrines were introduced long after the Society was founded, only to be phased out years later. Examples of these include the ban on vaccinations and the prohibition of organ transplants between 1967 and 1980 (I have also mentioned that blood transfusions were not prohibited until 1945). The movement has been successful in persuading its members that such change comes from the Almighty who never tires of teaching them new things: 'the path of the righteous ones is like the bright light that is getting lighter and lighter until the day is firmly established' (Proverbs 4: 18).

It could well be that many Witnesses have not yet been in the organisation long enough to realise that 'new lights' have a habit of growing dimmer, while old ones are sometimes switched back on! For example, in its guidelines on sexual conduct within marriage in the early 1970s, the Governing Body prohibited certain forms of stimulation, foreplay and intercourse; but in 1978 it advised that it was inappropriate for congregational elders to attempt to control marital intimacy. In 1983, the pendulum swung back when an article in *The Watchtower* of 15 March issued an 'amplification and adjustment in understanding' of the 1978 guidelines, asserting anew the Society's right to examine sexual relations and to impose sanctions, including *disfellowshipping* (the official term for the expulsion of dissident members), on those whose marital behaviour was considered immodest. For Witnesses who have lived through these inconsistencies, leaving the Watch Tower community poses a more painful option than doubting its version of reality. As I will show in Chapter 8, the part that such inconsistencies might play in causing members of other religious organisations to abandon their beliefs is missing in the case of the Witnesses, many of whose loved ones are also members. Loyalty, emotional dependence and a strong sense of community have enabled the movement to survive. Former Witness David Reed (1989a) also suggests that the main reason for the Society's success is that it is able to impart a certain mystique about the authority of the presidency. Until recently, members of the Governing Body remained completely anonymous to Witnesses at grass roots level. Their photographs were never to be seen in Kingdom Halls or in any of the organisation's literature. Witnesses everywhere continue to believe that God is using the Governing Body as his channel of communication, and any correspondence for which it is responsible is endorsed only by the Society's official rubber stamp. The role attributed to the Watch Tower presidency thus carries the same symbolic significance for the Witnesses as the papacy for Roman Catholics.

The structure of the movement and the intense loyalty demanded of each individual at every level demonstrates the characteristics of totalitarianism identified by Friedrich: namely, an elaborate total ideology making chiliastic claims with a promise of a utopian future, a single mass party, a monopoly of the means of communication and central direction and control of activity through bureaucratic co-ordination (Friedrich 1954). Although, historically, totalitarianism has been heavily over-laden with ideology, the Watch Tower Society controls millions of people who are denied freedom of speech, freedom of the press, freedom of assembly and freedom of conscience yet, paradoxically (or so it would seem to the outsider), devotees regard themselves as free, and non-members as oppressed or 'in shackles'. When people join the Watch Tower Society, they must adhere to its teachings, which means subjecting themselves to the theocratic rule of God himself and to judicial committees that claim the right to function as a literal government. In the Witnesses' eyes, these committees supersede secular courts since they act as divine judge and jury over eternal destiny (Reed 1989a). Why, then, do the Witnesses submit to this kind of authority?

Introducing modernity

I explained in Chapter 1 how, despite its international success, the Watch Tower Society has been largely neglected by academic writers. Other than the small amount of literature that addresses Watch Tower conversion and recruitment, most of the remaining sources focus on tension of one form or another between the Witnesses and secular states. With the exception of the historical examples of persecution of Watch Tower evangelists (which was often a result of their own attacks on official authorities), this tension mainly derives from the Witnesses' refusal to participate in activities pertaining to citizenship. Though some of the material raises important issues concerning the relationship between the Watch Tower community and secular society, most of this is written from a macro perspective and fails to examine the strategies which the Witnesses adopt for managing their beliefs in the various contexts of their daily lives. In addition to this, there is a serious shortage of academic literature on defection. Although Botting and Botting (1984) comment on the long-term effects of Watch Tower theology on former members, their discussion centres on those who have been disfellowshipped rather than on voluntary defectors. Most of the available material on defection is autobiographical and therefore lacks sociological analysis. There is, of course, always the potential for further research in every substantive area of social science, but by far my biggest concern about the current sociological literature on the Watch Tower Society is that there is little or no material on the relationship between the Witnesses and modernity. This is not to suggest that research to date is wholly empirical, but, where academics have attempted to theorise the current position of the movement, it is usually in relation to conversion and/or continuation of membership.[11] Search as I may in the sociological, anthropological and historical material, I find no attempt to link the beliefs and activities of the Witnesses to the general characteristics of modern secular society. This is where I believe the concept of modernity is useful.

The literature on modernity is, as anyone who has ever consulted it knows, abstract and dense. The concept has no simple definition and there is very little consensus among sociologists about when modern societies broke with traditional ones.[12] Modernity is complex and multi-layered and involves contrasting and contradictory principles. In the following account, I have outlined a number of issues that provide a backdrop for my analysis. Although the content of this chapter is by no means a blueprint of the modernity thesis, the literature emphasises three main spheres of modern life – the economic, the political and the cultural. Broadly speaking, the economic sphere involves the dominance of industrial capitalism; the political sphere involves the rise of liberal democracy and the consolidation of the nation state; and in the cultural sphere rationality replaces traditional authority (Jones 1993). Other literature focuses on the impact of these structural changes on the construction of modern identities (see, for example, Giddens 1991, Hall and Gieben 1992, Weeks 1992). More dynamical, perhaps, is the claim that the modern age is being replaced with a new social order which is characterised by flexible forms of technology (that is, post-Fordism), globalisation and a cultural ethos containing a radically new set of art forms, lifestyles and values.[13] Bauman, however, sees modernity as:

> a historical period that began in Western Europe with a series of profound social-structural and intellectual transformations of the seventeenth century and achieved its maturity: (1) as a cultural project with the growth of the Enlightenment; (2) as a socially accomplished form of life with the growth of industrial (capitalist and later communist) society.
>
> (Bauman 1991: 4)

There can be little doubt that industrialisation has altered the religious landscape in the West. Some modernity theorists suggest that capitalism has had a corrosive effect on our sense of moral order.[14] The rapid expansion in economic scale bolstered by technological innovations (particularly throughout the twentieth century) gave rise to the enormous loss of confidence in environmental matters and the subsequent emergence of a mood of uncertainty – a mood in which religion has taken on new and sometimes unexpected roles. On the one hand, market demands have required larger economic units in order to expand internationally while, on the other, people have felt inclined to reassert local and national identities in their search for psychological security. These contradictory economic and cultural pressures have brought about some significant changes in religious expression. Sociologist Paul Heelas argues that one of the most important consequences of modernity is the decline in mainstream religion and the emergence of a society in which the individuals are free to negotiate their own identities as consumers. For Heelas, modernity lies at the heart of the New Age movement, which he defines as:

the faith which has been placed in obtaining progress by way of scientific expertise, together with the application of reason to the management of social and individual affairs; the faith which has come to be placed in the promises of consumer culture; the loss of faith in religion, in particular in northern Europe.

(Heelas 1996: 135–6)

Similarly, Chief Rabbi Jonathan Sachs invites us to think about the consequences of the transition from traditional communities, where life chances, beliefs and identities were narrowly circumscribed, to a modern situation in which lifestyles, relationships and careers are open to a multiplicity of options:

> Modernity is the transition from fate to choice. At the same time, it dissolves the commitments and loyalties that once lay behind our choices. Technical reason has made us masters of matching means to ends. But it has left us inarticulate as to why we should choose one end rather than another. The values that once led us to regard one as intrinsically better than another – and which gave weight to words like 'good' and 'bad' – have disintegrated, along with the communities and religious traditions in which we learned them.
>
> (Sachs 1990: 6)

All these writers suggest that rationalisation has led to the increased differentiation of social institutions. Industrial societies with high levels of technology have seen the freeing of communities from religiously sanctioned controls and the emergence of autonomous individuals driven by their own values. The loss of community and the rise of individualism are regarded by modernity theorists as essential features of secularisation – a process which arguably has its roots in the 'modern' discourses of the seventeenth and eighteenth centuries.[15] Since then, modernity has become identified with major changes associated with industrial capitalist societies including the rise of the secular state, the expansion of a capitalist economy, the formation of classes, the emergence of distinctive patriarchal relations between men and women, racial divisions and 'the transition from fate to choice'. Over a long period of time, so we are told, these processes brought about a materialistic social order governed by individualistic, instrumental and rational impulses. These historical trends and changing social patterns resulted in a variety of lifestyles and a huge proliferation of consumer products. Life chances both within and between nation states have since become enormously complex and asymmetrical. Throughout the twentieth century, modernity became a progressively global phenomenon (Hall and Gieben 1992).

Davie (1994) offers a historical analysis of religious expression in her examination of the relationship between the ordering of societies and the cultural forms with which they have become associated. Though she acknowledges that there are disagreements among historians about the origins of modernity, Davie argues that the shift from pre-industrial to production-based societies made heavy demands on organised religion. Migration away from the countryside to what eventually became large industrial conurbations brought about lower levels of religious practice than had previously been the case (particularly among the working classes) across the whole of Western Europe. Davie suggests that this was mainly because of the increasing detachment of many people from their previous churches. In the case of the sizeable minority who, for whatever reason, were able to find employment, Sunday in its traditional form as a day of rest had become like any other – a day of struggle. Davie goes on to explain how, since the eighteenth century, the scrutiny of all knowledge has led to widespread pessimism in both Eastern and Western societies. The undermining of the traditional formulas of the earlier period infected religious and secular life to the extent that creeds of both kinds began to be replaced by continuous self-questioning. As far as Britain is concerned, Davie argues that this has caused the mutation rather than the disappearance of religious life in a society which plays a crucial role in a global economy but which is still rooted in the Judaeo-Christian tradition.[16] Although Davie believes that the sacred will continue to persist, the forms in which it will do so will be fundamentally different from those of previous times. The various manifestations of religion at the beginning of the twenty-first century reflect the age of heterogeneity and self-fulfilment described by postmodernists. In short, individual freedom has led to the adoption of beliefs that are as unconventional as they are diverse.

The weakening of tradition and the rise of individualism have also blurred the boundaries between the public and the private spheres, both in our emotional lives and in our relationships with wider society. Individuals have become increasingly aware of their own ability (and often their own need) to construct new identities in a world which is atomised and fluid.[17] One does not need to have read modernity literature to realise that this is a condition that has caused some considerable concern to current scholars, as expressed in the following passage by Gehlen:

> Any individual transplanted into our times from the vigorously concrete cultures of antiquity, of the Middle Ages, or even of the baroque era, would find most astonishing the conditions of physical proximity, and the lack of structure and form, in which the people of our time are forced to vegetate; and would wonder at the elusiveness and abstractness of our institutions, which are mostly 'immaterial states of affairs'.
>
> (Gehlen 1980: 74)

Gehlen's commentary hints strongly at a culture without shared meanings. Particularly significant (at least for the purpose of this book) is the effect that the 'elusiveness' to which he refers have had on religious beliefs. The abstract nature of social institutions and the absence of an overarching religious ideology has left us increasingly alone in an impersonal (some might say *heartless*) world (Lasch 1980, 1991). With the weakening of mainstream Christianity, monosemic beliefs have become ever more obscure and difficult to uphold, and this has led to significant changes in religious behaviour. The plurality of religious movements indicates that faith is now well and truly a matter of choice, and is no longer part of one's membership of society. Davie (1994) suggests that the majority of people lack discipline in their spiritual orientation in a society in which it is common to believe without belonging. This modern form of religious expression allows the individual to select at will from a variety of goods that can be tailored to meet his or her lifestyle.[18] Faced with so many rival movements – traditional, cultic and postmodern – no single religion can ever be the final arbiter of truth and falsity. In the absence of clear divisions and boundaries, a variety of religious beliefs and practices exist alongside monosemic and revelatory doctrines. The religious eclecticism of the modern world operates on the basis that we can *all* discern reality and that all versions of it are equally valid, as Bruce explains:

> Like the hominid creature drawn on charts of human evolution, who starts on the left-hand side as a small hunched hairy beast and gradually grows and sheds hair until he turns into the sleek human on the right, modernization has seen the individual grow and stand erect. From a stunted and ill-formed beast, subordinate to his Gods as he was subordinate to his political masters, the individual has risen in confidence, claiming first the right to make choices in ever-expanding spheres of behaviour and now insisting, . . . on the right to define reality and then, because the definitions clash, asserting relativism as the practical attitude.
>
> (Bruce 1995: 134)

The relativist's insistence that we are all now released from social constraints and free to decide what counts as knowledge poses a threat to those who extol rational thinking.[19] But the coexistence of individual sovereignty and rationality represents one of the contradictions to which modernity theorists draw our attention. The modernists' belief that it is both possible and desirable to produce valid knowledge has long been recognised as one of the main sources of dispute between modernity and postmodernity theorists.[20] However, modernity writers also contend that self-authoritarian, pluralistic societies are likely to undermine notions of rational knowledge. They call this condition *anti-foundationalism*. Individuals who yearn security in the modern world of contradictions often experience personal and emotional crises (Giddens 1990, 1991, Wagner 1994). The Watch Tower Society has managed to offer its devotees a meaningful identity at a time when free thought has shaken the very foundations on which substantive value systems are built. To the Witnesses, the modern world presents risk – risk of moral contamination, risk of physical harm and, ultimately, risk of eternal damnation. So what is the significance of their monotheistic system with its literal interpretation of scripture and non-negotiable prescription for salvation in a world where polysemic beliefs and absolutist cosmologies occupy the same stage?

Certainty in an uncertain world: the Witnesses' response to ambiguity

In his article on the modern world in the *Guardian* on 3 April 1997, journalist Douglas Rushkoff commented:

> It's a place where nothing is fixed and everything is uncertain. Facts are reduced to conjecture. Linear arguments are deconstructed into discontinuous obscurity. Stories no longer have absolute endings. Authorities have no advantage. Autonomy is the only rule. The holy maxim: empower thyself. So let the celebrations begin. We are liberated from linear thinking and its determinist conclusions. Now we can live in a reality where anything can happen. We don't need heroes, saints, martyrs or messiahs – especially not ones who enforce their messages with a terrifying day of judgment to divide the saved from the damned.

In this passage, Rushkoff offers a concise description of the anti-foundational society. But while the days of catechisms, commandments and absolutes may be regarded as a thing of the past for religions which allow individuals to construct their own identities, the Watch Tower Society claims to offer its adherents the same degree of existential security in the twenty-first century as it did 130 years ago. By renouncing modern notions of individual freedom and liberty, the Witnesses have won recruits year by year and managed to maintain their exclusivity throughout the world. The real problem that modernity poses for the Witnesses is the problem of *choice*.

For sociologist Peter Wagner (1994), modernity is haunted by ambiguity. Wagner argues that although the Enlightenment celebrated freedom and autonomy, modern societies have never allowed liberation in its fullest sense to take place. The state, for example, has always had to safeguard what have been regarded as important objectives of the modern project as well as maintain social order. Far from fulfilling the humanist promise of self-realisation, it has had to restrict practices and discipline individuals to such an extent that total human emancipation has become untenable. At the same time that societies have become marked by difference and plurality, the decline in traditional authority has made the construction of modern identities an ever more precarious and anxious exercise. One of the paradoxes of modernity is that the disembedding of people from their social and cultural contexts at the end of the nineteenth century led to a situation in which the autonomy of one individual meant the exploitation of another. Wagner argues that this is part of the general ambiguity of modern *reasoning* and modern *practice* (1974: 22–4). The capacity to choose new ways of life has weakened tradition to such a degree that we are now living in what Berger calls 'the terror of chaos' (Berger 1977: 109), and it is against these uncertainties of modernity that the Witnesses seem to have launched their appeal. One way of surviving in a pluralistic world is to select one particular fragment of what is on offer and transform it into an all-encompassing worldview. Joining the Watch Tower community enables individuals to eschew those secular institutions that weaken identity. In this sense, the Witnesses have successfully constructed certainty and reduced the risks caused by confusion. But on what cultural resources have they drawn in order to achieve this?

As far as the *certainties* of modernity are concerned, Heelas contends that the enterprise culture of Thatcher and Reagan throughout the 1980s created a climate in which it was impossible (at least in principle) not to think of individuals as more autonomous and better able to take control of their own lives than ever before. This self-empowerment marks a shift away from the influence of traditional, overarching systems towards one's own inner sources of authority and responsibility. But if self-authority is an indicator of certainty, the Watch Tower Society hardly exemplifies it. The Witnesses' continued deference to external authority suggests that they are in no way inclined to gravitate in the same direction as those involved in the New Age. This is not to suggest, however, that the Witnesses' worldview is the complete antithesis to modernity (their movement was, after all, founded as a result of the rejection of orthodox Christianity) for, although world-renouncing tenets undoubtedly curtail life options, modernity theorists do not deny that even some so-called moderns continue to hold absolutist beliefs. In exercising their freedom to choose a post-traditional lifestyle, the Witnesses have solved the problem of finding ontological security in a world of uncertainty. For them, absolutism is the essence of a meaningful identity that eradicates risk and ambiguity with one fell swoop.

The Witnesses' version of truth is the answer to modern doubt. Reactions that advocate the complete transformation of society are part of a phenomenon which sociologists call *fundamentalism*.[21] This is a highly problematic concept (not least because it is used in a pejorative sense to stigmatise beliefs and behaviour that are considered widely unpopular or of which people disapprove), but can, if used accurately, help to illuminate the status of various social movements in the modern world. Some writers regard fundamentalism as a product of late capitalism, and it can take a variety of forms, both religious and non-religious (Davie 1994, 1995, Harris 1994).[22] The available literature suggests that fundamentalist movements arise out of conditions of uncertainty. Generally speaking, it is the passion and simplicity of fundamentalism that gives it its appeal. Fundamentalists are known for their preoccupation with an all-encompassing explanation of the world and their defence of essential truths. According to Davie, they evoke the reaffirmation of these truths 'within a situation that has been profoundly disturbed by the pressures of an expanding global economy and the effects that this has had on social, political or ideological life' (Davie 1995: 2–3).[23] Fundamentalism can thus be seen as a by-product of the modern age. *Religious* fundamentalists see God and the devil as active forces in everyday life and ascribe the most mundane events and decisions to divine authority. Most believe that we are not far from the final judgement where God will intervene, ridding the world of all its ills and rewarding the righteous with everlasting life. The main goal of religious fundamentalism is to protect society from moral decay. This is usually accompanied by a programme of radical reform. Fundamentalists often deliver public sermons to warn nation states – be they communist or secular humanist – of the dangerous forces of atheistic and liberal thinking. Their level of activity ranges from supporting right-wing causes to engaging in direct political action against certain social and moral issues (Davie 1995: 3–4).

The sociological literature on fundamentalism provides an appropriate starting point for an analysis of the Watch Tower movement. The Witnesses' literal interpretation of the Bible can be seen as a retreat to the certainties of fundamentalism by a people who are threatened by the loss of a stable sense of self. Hunter (1991) argues that, in the case of religious fundamentalism, sacred texts play an essential part in sealing beliefs and activities with the approval of divine authority. 'Given the moral and religious ambiguities that seem intrinsic to modern and post-modern thought and aesthetics, the text becomes the source of all religious and moral authority, establishing safe, definable and absolute standards of life and thought' (157–8).

The belief that the inerrant word of God has been correctly translated from original Greek and Hebrew manuscripts has earned Watch Tower theologians a deference not unlike that of papal infallibility. As far as the Witnesses are concerned, religious conviction is not just about attending meetings at their local place of worship, or even believing in the existence of an omniscient being; it is about substantiating beliefs with tangible evidence. Scriptural literalism signifies a *revealed* truth that guards against polysemic beliefs by presenting a one true interpretation of the Bible that holds good for the whole of humanity. Polysemy would seriously undermine the exegeses of Watch Tower interpreters.[24] The certainty that devotees construct from scriptural texts is a proverbial stick with which to beat moral danger. These texts enable them to consult Jehovah on every aspect of their lives.

Although religious fundamentalism is a relatively recent phenomenon, there can be no denying its tension with modernity. Bruce (1990) argues that fundamentalism is never likely to be a major social force because of the ideological dominance of science, technology and humanism, all of which are better able to accommodate cultural diversity. Fundamentalist tenets are in direct conflict with most definitions of liberalism, and liberal thinking is anathema to the Witnesses as they step up their appeal for a puritanical lifestyle based on literal biblical interpretation. Though they are a product of modern conditions, the Witnesses have also successfully resisted some of the very features of the modern world theorised by the above scholars. Only an organisation as highly insulated as the Watch Tower Society would be able to enforce fundamentalist doctrines and a puritanical code of conduct with such a high degree of conformity. The outside world is clearly a world that requires careful management on the part of the Witnesses, who jeopardise their eternal salvation when they cross the organisation's ascetic boundaries. Millenarian beliefs act as a defence against those forces that threaten the fabric of the community. But since the Witnesses represent only a tiny percentage of the world's population, no empirical study of their social relations can constitute either an acknowledgement or a devastating critique of the modernity thesis. What such a study can do, however, is help us to understand how they perceive the world, and what they are able to offer prospective recruits.

3   Finding a home

My argument so far is that the Witnesses construct their identity in a world that is characterised by a plurality of life options, and that their fundamentalist theology is a modern phenomenon which can be seen as a response to certain conditions of modernity – particularly that of uncertainty. In this chapter, I address a number of key questions; namely: To what kind of people do the Witnesses appeal? At what point in an individual's life does conversion become a serious prospect? And why are these individuals drawn to this particular movement? The first two questions relate to the converts themselves, including their family backgrounds, their previous religious affiliation and their state of mind at the time of their conversion. The third question relates to the Watch Tower community and the ways in which its doctrines, internal organisation and social relations appeal to the prospective recruit. Throughout the chapter, I will show how both sets of factors work simultaneously in attracting a certain type of individual. More importantly, I will argue that the Witnesses are able to offer a way of life that is of particular significance at the beginning of the twenty-first century.

Who is the convert?

In general, the reasons for joining any kind of religious movement can be understood only by asking what prospective recruits might be looking for and what the community itself appears to be offering. Motives could include the yearning to feel part of a group of like-minded people, or the need to find answers to questions of a philosophical nature. Some converts claim that the movement they choose to follow helps them to escape from criminal activity, offers them direction at a time when their lives have become aimless, gives them self-respect when they are feeling worthless or frees them from psychological constraints (Beckford 1985).[1] The experiences of the individual and the nature of the organisation cannot be separated if the conversion process itself is to be understood. In the case of the Watch Tower Society, Beckford argues that conversion nearly always takes place in the context of mental anguish manifested in the form of moral indignation that certain values do not exist in the world as it is. Devotees thus perceive a discrepancy between their own values and the majority of the British people:

> The discrepancy was only rarely painful enough to entail demoraliz-ation, but more commonly it led to a state of latent suggestibility to any ideology that might have offered to explain, and thereby to explain away, the anxiety. Given the strength of their Christian background, it is not surprising that our respondents should have eventually responded to a *religious* ideology. But no generalizations can be offered on the relation between type of anxiety and type of ideological relief until adequate control groups can be examined.
>
> (Beckford 1975a: 185)

According to Beckford, the converts' already monistic view of truth made them ready to accept what he calls a 'comprehensive and unambiguous ideology'. This was accompanied by a strong desire for world peace and anxiety about life after death. The most frequent critical event, the doorstep sermon, helped to focus their anxieties around the Witnesses' religious perspective, and this has enabled the movement to gain recruits. Prior to their conversion, most individuals in Beckford's study had taken very little interest in social or political concerns, but claimed that Watch Tower evangelists had helped them to interpret the world in ways they found mean-ingful (1975a: 165–7). Beckford outlines a number of general hypotheses for his analysis of Watch Tower recruitment and conversion. These include *frustration–compensation*, *world-view construction* and *social solidarity* (126–32). The *frustration–compensation* hypothesis states that sects offer compensation for low social status as a result of the unequal distribution of goods and/or the inability to attain goals. This results in the search for alternative goals in compensation. However, Beckford is loath to accept that Witness converts are disprivileged or suffering loss of status.[2] *World-view construction* concerns the notion that belief systems attempt to offer individuals a way of understanding the world which will give them ordered and meaningful lives. Those adopting this perspective argue that people confused about moral standards are more likely to respond positively to religious activists. It is true that, as a world-renouncing organisation, the Watch Tower Society offers a clearly defined view of the world that plays a crucial role in the construction of a closed community. Finally, *social solidarity* is sought by individuals who have had only tenuous association with other people. According to Beckford, such individuals have a tendency to seek integration in political and religious movements. This is mainly because sectarian systems tend to appeal to those who have rejected (or have been rejected by) other social environments. For these people, community-based religion provides an opportunity to celebrate and maintain solidarity with others.

Beckford outlines a number of predispositions, states of suggestibility and critical events that he argues are significant in the conversion process. There was not one respondent in Beckford's sample who had not had a conventional Christian upbringing, and most lacked enduring ties with social groups outside the family and workplace. Recruits were drawn from the lower middle and upper working classes, and, although Beckford provides few specific examples of their occupations (mainly because he categorises the Witnesses' occupations by *strata*), he does tell us that their work involved little interaction with other colleagues or members of the general public. Beckford also found that many Witness converts had encountered the movement through a relative, friend or workmate, although their real interest was more likely to be aroused by a doorstep minister whom they did not know.[3] However the process begins, those who are in association with active devotees are more likely to respond favourably to representatives of the movement and to accept a Bible study than those who are not (Beckford 1975a: 160).[4] Watch Tower conversion is thus a consequence of *learning*, through association with established members.

Though he does not analyse his fieldwork data from a modernity perspective, Beckford suggests that Witness converts tend to be rather isolated individuals who respond positively to communities that are able to offer direction and support. If prospective recruits are indeed people who are prone to feeling that the world is in a state of crisis and that the Witnesses can offer a way forward, then it may well be that the Watch Tower Society is providing solutions to the ills of modern life. But such a hypothesis is altogether too simple, first because it fails to address the specific modern problems to which these individuals have been exposed, and second because it does not explain why they become Witnesses rather than members of, say, Greenpeace or the Socialist Workers' Party. Although detailed analyses of other religious, social and political movements would take me too far away from the principal aims of this book, an empirical analysis of the convert's biographical reconstruction does at least help to account for the current tendency towards Watch Tower recruitment.

Beckford discovered a diversity of occupations among his sample of Witnesses, but most were employed in the skilled sector. Like Beckford's study, my own research in the late 1990s showed that there were indeed a wide range of occupational profiles, but the biggest percentage of those in employment were in clerical and white-collar work (Holden 1999). What ought to be borne in mind here, however, is that the last three decades have brought about enormous changes in Britain's social class composition as a result of the swelling of the service sector and the expansion of clerical and/or administrative work in both the public and private sectors. Though large numbers of the population have also moved into professional and managerial work, this is uncommon among the Witnesses since work of this kind requires an educational training that they are not usually willing to undertake. The Society's expectation of Armageddon means that very few

Witnesses aspire to post-compulsory education or plan successful careers. Indeed, they are more likely to be found in occupations that involve little interaction with the general public, and many are self-employed (this is something devotees often pursue as a result of their conversion).[5] Prima facie, there is nothing about these people's previous occupations that impinges on their new religious status, but closer analysis of the movement's teachings suggests something significant about the nature of the Witnesses' employment. The autonomy often associated with low-profile work enables members of world-renouncing religions to distance themselves from worldly association, and, for this reason, those already in these kinds of occupations are more likely to be attracted to the movement than those who are not. Although the Witnesses are renowned for worldly contact in the sense that they engage in door-to-door proselytising, this is a purely spiritual exercise and one over which they generally have control; but in the world of employment they do not have anything like the same opportunity to recruit, and may find themselves in situations in which they must keep their beliefs in check for fear of ridicule or conceal them altogether in order to avoid hostility. As far as preparing for the post-Armageddon Kingdom is concerned, those who run their own businesses are in a favourable position. Not only are they more likely to have greater flexibility in and control over their work patterns around which activities such as pioneering, doorstep ministry, attendance at conventions and Bible studying might be organised, they are also better able to make use of their time (finances permitting) to carry out voluntary work for the organisation such as building and maintaining Kingdom Halls (for which, incidentally, the Witnesses themselves are responsible – two of the many ways in which the Society substitutes labour for capital) and assisting in the preparation of annual events.

Another significant conversion factor concerns previous religious affiliation. Almost all those who convert to the Watch Tower Society have had some former association with mainstream Christianity. More recently, the Society has managed to recruit members from non-Christian backgrounds (particularly former Muslims and Hindus), but these are in a small minority.[6] Since the Bible is the only source of authority on which Watch Tower beliefs are based, the Witnesses are much more likely to appeal to people who have been exposed to Christian teachings, especially those who have unhappy memories of their religious pasts. This supports Beckford's claim:

> For a variety of reasons they lost their attachment to religious groups and failed to replace the former centrality of Christian teachings in their outlook with an alternative ideological position; their commitment to Christianity became latent. They did not, however, lose all interest in religious affairs but merely ceased to support any particular religious group.
>
> (Beckford 1975a: 172)

The high degree of previous affiliation to other Christian organisations conveys as much about the perceived failure of orthodox Christianity as it does about the success of the Watch Tower Society.[7] Witness converts are people who have never completely abandoned Christian ideals, but who complain that they did not feel well integrated in their previous churches. They are also people who express discontentment with church dogma. One woman in her fifties who had been reared in the Roman Catholic Church explained:

> When I was young I wanted to be a nun, but I think I was more in love with the church than the teachings if you know what I mean. I couldn't relate the idea of hellfire to a loving God, but I never questioned it because we were always told not to because it was a mystery and we had to have faith in the teachings of the church.

Criticisms of clergy who encourage their parishioners to accept Christian teachings unquestioningly are widespread among Witness converts, but by far the most serious concern is that few if any church leaders support their sermons with specific scriptural references. In an interview with a man of a similar age, I learned:

> Before I became a Witness I had a spiritual need which was still hanging over from when I was younger. Obviously I was searching for God, and the Witnesses was one religion I hadn't looked at. For as long as I can remember I have always been conscious of some kind of spiritual need. Even as a wandering little one, I used to go around, unattended, looking at various churches and listening to what they had to say. My RE teacher used to say that I asked deep and searching questions. I was affiliated to the Church of England where I served on the altar, and things like that . . . I found the answers which are given by other religions unsatisfactory; like, for example, if a baby dies the priest might say, 'Well, God wanted a flower for his garden' and 'They're probably in purgatory now, but for a couple of mass cards and a couple of hundred pounds they'll rest in peace.' The problem with other Christian religions is that they just don't use the Bible. They *carry* a Bible, but they don't use it.

This was echoed by a younger, more recent convert who told me 'My only memories of the Church of England are reading one of the Gospels, just saying "This is the Word of the Lord" and that's it! There was no explanation of it. It had no meaning.'

Generally speaking, the Church of England and Roman Catholicism are the two main Christian religions that receive most criticism from devotees, but, as I explained in the previous chapter, the whole of Christendom is presented by the Governing Body as an instrument of the devil. The apparent failings of orthodox Christianity are certainly ones on which the Watch Tower Society has been able to capitalise.

There is, however, one other crucial factor that makes a certain type of individual susceptible to Watch Tower recruitment. By far the most commonly cited experience immediately prior to conversion is the feeling of total disillusionment with the world. This disillusionment is often expressed in terms of complete disaffection with the social, political and economic system and intense disrespect for those in power such as politicians, policy-makers and civil servants. Here are two typical accounts of this, the first from a man in his forties:

> When I read UN reports or watched the news I used to become depressed. There's enough food in the world to feed what would be the population in the year 2000 eight or nine times over but yet there are thousands of people starving in refugee camps all over the world. Listening to this stuck in my throat. I became absolutely frustrated with the political system and whatever other systems mankind has concocted. I became more and more aware of the futile attempts of mankind to govern himself.

Similarly, a woman who had joined the Society in the late 1980s commented:

> Round about 1985–86, I became concerned about all the hungry children in Ethiopia. I used to think it was a shame that there were so many hungry children while there was so much wealth and power elsewhere. This used to worry me.

There are, it must be said, any number of potential reactions to this kind of disillusionment. Few people in the world today do not, at some stage or other, experience feelings of profound sadness when they think about social, economic and political crises, yet most would never join an ascetic, millenarian organisation. Moreover, I must have spoken to hundreds of people who were baptised in infancy, educated in denominational schools, attended churches regularly during childhood and then lapsed in later life, never to return to any religious institution. It would appear, therefore, that although disillusionment is a *factor* in Witness conversion, it is not enough in itself to complete the process, since it does not tell us why these individuals are drawn to this particular movement or why countless millions of others who experience disillusionment are not. Be this as it may, feelings of doom and gloom, dissatisfaction with former religious organisations and the failure to feel comfortable in secular environments (particularly the workplace) often emerge. But there is one very strong clue that helps to explain why people are drawn to the Watch Tower community. The more I analysed my own questionnaire and interview data, the more it became apparent that prospective converts were not just people who could accept the inevitability of social injustice, they were people who needed *explanations for* and *solutions to* it. So how might we make sense of these people's experiences in the twenty-first century, and what kind of 'solutions' do the Witnesses appear to offer?

Out on a limb

Although the prospective Witness convert is not someone who (in crude terms) is *dispossessed*, the Watch Tower Society undoubtedly appeals to isolated individuals with narrow social horizons. These seem to be introspective people who, though disillusioned with humanity, are aroused by questions about the current state of the world and the meaning of life. Such people are potential candidates for recruitment, not only because of their former association with Christianity but also because they are likely to respond positively to those who are like-minded. It is fair to say that most prospective converts are affected by a situation in which goals such as educational attainment, career success, wealth and personal ambition appear to be meaningless, as are the conventional (that is, institutionalised) means of attaining these goals. In sociological terms, one could regard this as the result of a loss of effectiveness in the normative framework that regulates modern life, leading to unhappiness and social disorder – a condition which modernity theorists call *anomie*.[8] Although other theorists have used this concept to explain pathological (or 'deviant') behaviour, as far as the Witnesses are concerned it is the main reason for their lack of ambition and their refusal to aspire to modern goals of success. These recruits are thus responding to a *social* situation. But while anomie may help to explain some of the disillusionment felt by these individuals, there are other aspects of their conversion on which it cannot easily shed light. It would be highly misleading to suggest from personal biographies that conversion is a consequence of the failure to achieve goals. It should not be forgotten that the absence of strong social ties is another factor in Watch Tower recruitment for which conversion may be compensation. Though it could still be argued that this isolation is a feature of the anomic condition, converts invariably speak of a lack of direction in their lives when reflecting on their initial contact with the movement. This suggests that their decision to undertake a Bible study with a Witness evangelist is a response to a deeper-rooted phenomenon. When we add to this their disillusionment with the world and the mental anguish described by Beckford, the overall picture is one of loss of meaning for which modern secular society could be said to be the cause.

Social theorist Meredith McGuire (1987) regards religious conversion as a consequence of rapid social change in a world that is now dominated by *pluralism* (that is, the coexistence of competing worldviews) and *privatisation* – the process by which certain institutions become removed from effective roles in the public sphere. McGuire suggests that these processes (both of which have occurred on a local as well as a national scale) have undermined community and weakened the norms governing social interaction. These are the features of modernity from which loss of meaning and other identity crises stem. This account of social change helps to explain Witness conversion in the particular location in which my own study was carried out. Although Blackburn still had a fairly strong manufacturing base at the time of the study, it was the town's large number of businesses and the growing service sector that provided the people in my survey (that is, those who were not either self-employed or housewives) with work. But, like most other manufacturing towns in the North of England, Blackburn has undergone major clearance programmes over the years and is characterised by declining industries and unemployment. The current picture is one of fragmentation and instability. More generally, the withdrawal of the family and religious institutions from the economy over the last two or three centuries has been accompanied by the division of life into specialised areas and increased contact with strangers. Traditional social structures are being replaced not by others but by a plurality of forces with no single organising principle – a process which Laclau (1990) calls *dislocation*. Indeed, secularisation theorist David Martin (1978) argues that mainstream religion, particularly Christianity, has tended to decline in large urban areas that are dominated by heavy industry, particularly those that have a homogeneous working-class population.[9]

According to theorists such as Laclau, dislocation lies at the heart of discontentment with modern life; hence, the Watch Tower movement can be said to provide a safe haven in a world that is characterised by fluidity and loss of identity. The Witnesses have thus managed to compensate for the difficulties individuals face in maintaining a strong sense of identity and a close attachment to institutions such as the family and the local community. While the Watch Tower Society appeals to unfulfilled individuals with relatively unsuccessful profiles, these are people who often speak fondly of their families but who claim that their parents, siblings and spouses are unable to understand their disdain for the world and/or fail to offer them the emotional support for which they yearn. It is at this point of feeling 'out on a limb' that the Watch Tower movement seems able to offer them a meaningful explanation for their discontentment as well as the support of a caring community. It is as though, at the point of their initial contact with the Witnesses, the prospective recruit is experiencing the psychological effects of dislocation. From a modernity perspective, the ruthless break with preceding conditions, particularly tradition, unhinges the stable identity and leads to anxiety in the human condition. The ties that bind people to the past are unravelling, resulting in self-estrangement, isolation and emotional insecurity – a condition which Berger, Berger and Kellner call *homelessness*:

> The pluralistic structures of modern society have made the life of more
> and more individuals migratory, ever changing, mobile . . . Not only are

an increasing number of individuals in a modern society uprooted from their original social milieu, but, in addition, no succeeding milieu succeeds in becoming truly 'home' either . . . Modern society has threatened the plausibility of religious theodicies, but it has not removed the experiences that call for them. Human beings continue to be stricken by sickness and death; they continue to experience social injustice and deprivation. What it [modernity] has accomplished is to seriously weaken those definitions of reality that previously made that human condition easier to bear.

(Berger, Berger and Kellner 1974: 165–6)

It is this failure to belong to the modern world described so succinctly in this passage that causes some individuals to search for certainty. The Watch Tower movement is able to offer an affective bond to those whom secular society has abandoned. Large-scale commercial enterprise, urban development and the impact of globalisation have undermined the kind of community that the Witnesses have managed to re-create.[10] As never before, people are being forced to operate as free agents in a huge global economy, but this is a world in which not everyone can survive. Lash and Urry (1994) argue that the speed and intensity of modern life with its constant flow of people, money and symbols have dramatically eroded our sense of belonging. The modern world is a world of anonymity in which whole societies become the locus of 'homeless' individuals and where behaviour is monitored by technological surveillance rather than informal controls. Belief systems are no longer considered necessary for social cohesion but are embraced out of choice – a situation that has evolved from the rise of individual sovereignty. Like it or not, identity at the beginning of the twenty-first century is individually constructed.

Heelas's work on New Age religion makes for an interesting comparison with the Watch Tower Society, not least because it conveys different responses to a fast-changing world. In contrast with the exclusivity of the Watch Tower movement, the New Age movement is profoundly inclusive (Heelas 1996). Its message is that we are all essentially one and that there is truth in all religion. Unity prevails within diversity. Heelas suggests that New Age religion derives from individual freedom and the loss of all-embracing communities: 'much of religion – indeed, culture as a whole – has tended to develop in favour of the autonomous, the privatized, the individuated, essentially the assumption that the person should shape his or her *own* values and beliefs' (171–2).

Throughout his book, Heelas stresses that the pluralistic nature of modernity enables New Age converts to explore what he describes as *the inner self*. By this, he means that authority is placed in the hands of the consumer who, while drawing on religious traditions, is at liberty to bypass monosemic dogma. New Agers reject traditional beliefs and put their faith in a wisdom that they argue lies at the heart of a new spiritual domain.

But while some people celebrate individual liberty, others renounce it and seek refuge in absolutism. For the Witnesses, the modern concept of liberty belongs to a world that places greater value on hedonism than on moral duty. Their renunciation of individual freedom is their rejection of something sinister. From the Witnesses' perspective, modernity is a great evil that represents the antithesis to salvation. It is a force they must resist if they are to live God-fearing lives; yet hereby hangs a paradox. Though the Witnesses use the so-called ills of modernity to their advantage, the success of their movement owes a great deal to the rationalism, liberal democracy and advanced technology with which we associate modernity. The Witnesses are thus highly dependent on a phenomenon they condemn in order to sustain their current levels of recruitment. To this issue I will return, but first I must complete my analysis of conversion by examining what the movement itself is able to offer those whom it attracts.

Witnesses to the rescue

The factors I have described so far concern what some conversion theorists crudely call *predisposition* – that is, factors that *push* certain individuals towards the Watch Tower Society at a particular time in their lives. But these factors alone are only enough to produce a potential rather than an actual convert. Other factors need to be considered if we are truly to understand the conversion process from the stage of initial interest to the final point of baptism. These factors concern the movement itself and its appeal to prospective recruits as part of its mission to secure their salvation and distract them from other life options. Conversion theorists often call these the *pull* factors.[11] An examination of the interplay between these two sets of factors raises important issues for sociologists interested in the Witnesses' brand of millenarianism.

In nearly all the conversionist literature on the Watch Tower Society, there is some mention of the Witnesses' skill in integrating new recruits into a tightly bonded community. On the whole, however, the literature provides very few details of how exactly this is achieved. As I have already explained, Beckford suggests that individuals who are drawn towards the movement are often searching for fellowship. He argues that, despite the lack of emotionality and piety among the Witnesses, converts often describe their initial reception as warm and friendly. Although I agree with Beckford that the Witnesses are primarily rational in their approach to prospective recruits, it would be wrong to suggest that they do not also appeal to people's emotions. Devotees claim to offer love and support (which they regard as essential characteristics of 'truth') to the whole of humanity. The problem, as they see it, is that others are simply unwilling to listen to them and to accept their offer of Christian friendship. In order to address this, they spend a great deal of time at their weekly *ministry school* meetings rehearsing their doorstep sermons and learning how to use their personalities to sell their message. Showing the outside world that they are caring people is not something they can afford to neglect.

Fellowship undoubtedly appeals to those who show initial interest in the movement's beliefs. While the Witnesses may not be renowned for *lovebombing*,[12] they always make sure that newcomers are given a warm greeting. One woman who had not long been baptised described the reception she encountered on her first visit to the Kingdom Hall: 'The first time I came to a meeting, I was overwhelmed by the friendliness, the warmth and the love. Everybody was happy when they were here and I came to appreciate that this is the truth. It really is the truth!' This woman's comments show how an affective bond can play an important role in the process of conversion, particularly in a closed community. Affection provides prospective converts with the warmth and security that might otherwise be missing in the environments from which they have come and thus enables them to adapt to a demanding way of life. But over and above all this, 'love' has an important part to play in persuading new members that Jehovah's Witnesses are an *exclusive* people. By presenting themselves as loving evangelists both in their ministry work and at their own place of worship, the Witnesses enhance their recruitment prospects and affirm the view that they are somehow different from the rest of humanity. To the devotees themselves, however, love and exclusivity go hand in hand. For new members, love, fellowship and scrupulous honesty are character-istics of uniqueness. Combined with a world-renouncing theology, the dogmatic adherence to the belief that truth cannot exist without these features is indicative of a movement that claims to be *in* but not *of* the world. While most converts claim that the validity of the movement's doctrines is the real reason for their conversion, references to exclusivity are also common. A young man whom I have already quoted commented, 'Jesus said that the true religion would have love among themselves, they would be a united people. All Witnesses throughout the world are united.'

The bonds successfully created by Witnesses reaffirm the notion that they are different because they are the *only* people in history to have retained their unity. However, there is nothing in Watch Tower theology, unlike Judaism, to suggest that devotees see themselves as *chosen* people; but their belief that their good living along with their commitment to minister the one true word of God reassures them of their eligibility for salvation and helps to maintain their exclusivity. This distinctiveness is a successful means of recruiting new members and fending off the outside world of sin. In short, exclusivity must be demonstrated through social action.

The enforcement of a strict purity code is another means by which the Witnesses are able to achieve exclusivity. Rules about physical and moral cleanliness are used to establish lines of demarcation between good and evil and thus act as a powerful armoury for resisting those aspects of modern life which they regard as sinful. These rules demonstrate to those considering membership that conversion involves a considerable degree of self-sacrifice.[13] When individuals undergo baptism, they are committing themselves to a way of life that has enormous implications for how and with whom they will spend their time in the future. Their loyalty is principally to a community that makes membership difficult to obtain; hence, conversion is presented as a *heroic* act that requires self-sacrifice, courage and conviction. The Witnesses' concept of purity strengthens their pride in belonging to an untainted community and this helps to attract people who see the modern world as awry and permissive. Watch Tower teachings on sexual conduct provide an excellent example of the usage of purity to combat the risk of contamination posed by modernity. The belief that sex is a strictly heterosexual affair which should be practised only within marriage suggests that the Witnesses are heirs of what Jeffrey Weeks calls the *absolutist* model of sexual morality rooted in the Judaeo-Christian tradition (Weeks 1992). This approach regards sex as potentially dangerous and anti-social and contrasts sharply with the *libertarian* position in which sexual desire is seen as benign and life enhancing. According to Weeks, various political movements in Britain over the past 150 years have forced governments to adopt a more liberal position which distinguishes between what *should* be allowed publicly and what *can* be tolerated privately (249–52).[14]

The Witnesses have never been able to accept what most people now regard as a basic human right in an ostensibly liberal democracy – the right to sexual freedom. The 1960s reforms concerning homosexuality, obscenity, family planning and theatre censorship exemplify a certain willingness on the part of policy-makers to come to terms with social change; hence the relative success of modernity in challenging the absolutist approach to sexual mores. Although these reforms were little more than an attempt to regulate behaviour that had been previously subjected to unworkable laws, the appeal of the Watch Tower Society to new recruits in Britain alone over the past century owes much to the Witnesses' persistent condemnation of a world that they believe has become all too tolerant. According to one of their publications:

> We have read in the Scriptures that 'fornication and uncleanness of every sort should not, with improper motive, even be mentioned among us.' (Eph. 5: 3–5) But what if such themes are cleverly accompanied by music that has a pleasing melody, a catchy rhythm or an insistent beat? Might we even unconsciously start repeating lyrics that glorify sex without marriage, use of drugs for pleasure and much more? Or, while we know that we should not imitate the way of life of people who indulge in such things, do we tend to identify ourselves with them by imitating the way they dress, their hairstyle or their way of speaking? How crafty Satan is! How insidious the methods he uses to entice humans to conform to his own corrupted mind! (2 Cor. 4: 3, 4) To keep from falling victim to his sly devices, we must avoid drifting along

with the world. We need to keep in mind who the 'world rulers of this darkness' are and earnestly be wrestling against their influence. (Eph. 6: 12; 1 Pet. 5: 8)

(Watch Tower Bible and Tract Society of Pennsylvania 1983b: 67)

It is interesting how the Society's warnings of sexual impurity in this tract are accompanied by other forms of behaviour that are considered dangerous, including the lyrics of songs, the use of drugs (that is, for hedonistic purposes), the wearing of certain clothes and the style of one's hair. These warnings against the dangers of offensive bodily expression have important implications for the presentation of self. The Witnesses' adherence to beliefs that admit no ambiguity complements their obsession with neatness. Male Witnesses are renowned for keeping their hair clean and short. At meetings and on their door-to-door ministry, they present themselves in tailored suits, formal shirts and ties and polished shoes. Their female counterparts are equally smartly presented in either suits or formally cut skirts, blouses and jackets. Though women rarely wear head coverings, their hair is always tidy and nails well manicured. The Witnesses believe that to be slovenly in dress is to be disrespectful of oneself, since outward appearance is indicative of personal morality. Conversely, smart appearance is symbolic of cleanliness – a virtue attributed to Godliness. Physical appearance is thus a symbolic expression of the pristine community to which the Witnesses pledge their loyalty.

The Witnesses' attempt to avert physical and spiritual contamination is perceived by converts as evidence that the organisation *must* be ordained by Jehovah. The effort expended on keeping purity within and pollution without suggests that devotees are living as though they are already *in* the post-Armageddon world they so eagerly await. Below are the comments of a man who described to me his very first impression of the community at an annual convention:

> I remember going to my first Witness convention many years ago and everybody was clean and well behaved. There was only one policeman and one policewoman on duty that day. The policing of the car park was done by the brothers. The organisation really impressed me. Everybody called each other 'brother' and 'sister', which I could relate to, but the thing that really stuck in my mind was the fact that there wasn't one scrap of paper on the floor. No one was smoking. The Witnesses cleaned the entire stadium; even to picking the grass out of the nicks on the terraces and in the gutters. They painted over the graffiti in the toilets and laid extra drains so that they could put more toilets in and I thought, 'Wow, if there was going to be a new world society then this would be the nucleus of it'. If anyone accidentally dropped something, someone else would pick it up and put it in their bag or their pocket. I was so amazed that I even brought my niece to come and have a look.

The organisation has never ceased to amaze me ever since. We class ourselves as a nation out of nations.

This man's observations reveal how the Witnesses' extraordinary attention to detail is a powerful means of persuading prospective recruits that the movement is the image of perfection, and that conversion is the only step necessary for entry into the New Kingdom. The Witnesses' creation of this kind of community is a seductive invitation to those who are experiencing homelessness. If, as I have already suggested, the identity of the prospective recruit has been attacked by the forces of anomie and dislocation, then it seems reasonable to suggest that it can be restored through meaningful relationships.[15] While the Witnesses' successful recruitment owes much to the cohesion of their community, converts will always insist that it is the impeccable nature of Watch Tower doctrines that sustains their commitment. This cannot be underestimated. The substantiation of every doctrine with biblical references is crucial in convincing the potential convert that the Society is ordained by Jehovah. Not only are the Witnesses' shared beliefs the reason for their coming together at weekly meetings, they are the sole purpose for their public ministry. But it is the millenarian aspect of their theology that has by far the greatest attraction since this is what offers homeless individuals refuge. Converts often cite biblical texts that refer to signs of the end (especially those of Matthew and the Book of Revelation) and these play an important role in persuading them that the Witnesses are able to explain the entire history of the world and offer hope for the future. The following comments of a newly baptised member provide a succinct example:

> When you come to learn about the God of the Bible, you realise that 80 per cent of His promises have been 100 per cent correct, even down to silly little things like throwing a city out into the sea. The scriptures tell us that we are tenants on a planet. Things are happening on an unprecedented scale now, not just worldwide but closer to home such as break up in families and the increase in lawlessness which are all part of a sign that Jesus talked about that when you see these things happening on an unprecedented scale, that's the time when God is going to step in and do something about it.

By matching world events to biblical prophecy, devotees are able to support their promise of eternal bliss in a way that is missing in the more esoteric religions of Christendom. New members often refer to discussions they had with Witnesses who they claim helped them to put some of their previous experiences and general anxieties about life into a new context. To those who find the questions of conscience and articles of faith espoused by Christian churches unconvincing, the Witnesses' explanations of worldly crises and their prescription for everlasting life are a source of inspiration.

There is, however, one remaining feature of the Watch Tower movement that helps to explain its appeal, and this concerns the high level of commitment it expects from its devotees. Once received into the community as a fully baptised member, the individual is expected to contribute to the movement's worldwide success. In other words, conversion means evangelism. The austerity of the Watch Tower regime ensures that commitment is sustained year on year, and that only those who *demonstrate* their millenarian convictions (by attending Kingdom Hall meetings and devoting as much time as they can to the doorstep ministry – details of which will be discussed in Chapter 4) are allowed to remain in membership. Not surprisingly, the Witnesses' renunciation of the world and their success in establishing a close-knit community appeal to those who have difficulty in embracing modern secular society and who feel very much at risk in an age of uncertainty. But it is the movement's propensity to screen out potential time-wasters that is particularly effective in generating and sustaining high levels of religious activity.

There are, of course, limits to how much austerity or leniency is beneficial to a religious community. Movements that are too strict risk losing members in large numbers, as do those that are too liberal. According to Stark and Iannaccone: 'One easily notices groups too strict to expect growth. Strictness must be sufficient to exclude potential free-riders and doubters, but it must also be sufficiently low so as not to drive away everyone except a few misfits and fanatics' (Stark and Iannaccone 1997: 145). No one would deny that the Watch Tower Society is demanding, but its insistence on a compulsory ministerial role for every devotee is hugely successful in providing even the most complacent individuals with a firm evangelistic identity. This instils into the members a strong sense of self-worth. Moreover, there is little evidence from the movement's membership statistics of apathy or resistance. For those whom modernity has abandoned, the prospect of being of service to a community of people who share similar life experiences and objectives can be a very attractive one indeed.

Summary

Through a combination of Bible studies and Kingdom Hall meetings, the Watch Tower movement is able to provide a number of weekly activities that help new members to fill in the gaps which appear to be present in their lives at the time of their initial contact with a Witness evangelist. But it is the movement's millenarian beliefs, strong camaraderie, rules of purity and provision of religious roles that are its real resources for integrating recruits into a new way of life. These resources enable the Witnesses to impart a dualistic view of the world – that is, a view that glorifies their own community and condemns those aspects of modernity of which they disapprove. This system of classification protects new members by means of regular association with like-minded others and the enforcement of taboos that prohibit a whole series of unacceptable activities. Strange as it might seem, such movements provide a home for certain kinds of people in the twenty-first century.

Throughout this chapter, I have argued that Witness conversion involves a number of pushes and pulls. The reasons why people opt for world-renouncing millenarianism cannot be established without some kind of enquiry into their backgrounds, life experiences, cognitive make-up and a range of factors concerning the ways in which movements such as this appeal to potential recruits. Research shows that some former association with Christianity appears high on the list of influences along with low-profile occupations, loose communal ties and a high degree of disillusionment. People with these kinds of experience seem to be susceptible to a dualistic worldview. But I have also argued that these factors alone cannot account for Watch Tower conversion. A complete picture can be attained only by an understanding of how the Witnesses are able to capitalise on these conditions and experiences. Thus, the doorstep sermon or some other contact with an evangelist is crucial in initiating interest, followed by a process of learning doctrines in an environment that the individual finds appealing. Conversion is clearly as much about the kind of community the Witnesses are able to offer as it is the background of the prospective recruit. Push and pull factors must therefore work simultaneously in order to facilitate the psychological and emotional needs of those to whom it ministers.

However we theorise conversion, there can be little doubt that the hierarchical structure and weekly activities of the movement provide the basis for a highly integrated community that appeals to those who join. From the Witnesses' point of view, the way of life prescribed by their Governing Body provides them with a ticket for entry into paradise, and in this way the millenarian dream is kept alive. From a modernity perspective, conversion can be seen as one of many options in a pluralistic world – a world in which people continue to battle against a huge number of forces that threaten their identity. The modern world is a world in which there are no dominant authorities. For the Witnesses, this weakens the prospect of salvation. Anomie, dislocation and the absence of unambiguous moral guidelines lead to confusion, powerlessness and loss of meaning. Wherever there is ambiguity, there is danger. The forces of modernity are those that lead to sin, and in this respect the construction of a closed community is an attempt, consciously or unconsciously, to protect those who embrace it. While the rest of the world drowns in a sea of uncertainty, the Watch Tower Society provides a safe haven for those who yearn to belong.

4 Rational means to rational ends

Those who convert to the Watch Tower Society are gradually resocialised into a new way of life. This involves the reshaping of their identity in order that it becomes consistent with that considered appropriate by other devotees. Group support is particularly important if this transition is to be successful. The bonds provided by any world-renouncing religious community affirm the new self and meaning system as new recruits gradually withdraw from their previous social relationships. Affiliation to the Society requires an analysis of how the individual's meaning system is socially acquired and supported by a wide range of activities through interaction with other members. I explained in Chapter 2 how the Witnesses belong to an organisation that demands a high level of commitment that is strengthened by regular meetings and shared symbols. An effective means of integration is essential if they are to maintain a uniform system of beliefs and reduce the risks posed by secular society. In order for converts to become 'good' members, they must pledge their loyalty to the community by adopting its worldview, participating in its rituals and learning to minister to others. Affiliation begins the moment the prospective convert expresses an interest in the organisation. In order fully to understand the socialisation process, we need to know something about how Watch Tower theology is learned and subsequently 'sold' to non-members. It is this learning and selling that binds the community together and provides devotees with a set of strategies for dealing with a satanic world. This requires them to make use of modern resources both in their ministry work and in their interactions with each other.

Eschewing mysticism

If there was one feature of the Watch Tower community that occupied my thoughts in the initial stages of my fieldwork, it would have to have been the absence of *mysticism*. I had not known what to expect before I sought permission to attend my first Witness meeting, and my Catholic upbringing could never have prepared me for what I was to observe. Though I was well aware from my postgraduate studies of mainstream Christianity that

Catholicism is one of the most renowned Trinitarian belief systems for the advocacy of mystery, what struck me was the stark contrast between the awesome symbols and rituals of a church with which I was familiar and the apparent *rationalism* of the Watch Tower organisation. Communities that operate on rational precepts cannot easily accommodate charisma or individual creativity. Rational systems are generally purposeful and pragmatic, eschewing all arbitrary performances and events. At the same time, religion is, to a greater or lesser extent, a question of faith; and, since this is something that cannot be quantified, it is reasonable to expect a certain amount of tension between these two phenomena. The Witnesses pose a challenge to traditional religions, not least because they use rational means to undermine the beliefs and rituals of established churches.[1] More significantly, perhaps, they adopt rational procedures for induction, the regulation of worship and the dissemination of their doctrines. The contrast between the Watch Tower Society and Roman Catholicism manifests itself in terms of visual images, style of worship and procedures for dealing with wrongdoing. It is the adoption of rational principles that has enabled the Witnesses to recruit and expand in the way they have throughout this century. These principles are in operation long before the individual reaches full membership.

I explained in Chapter 3 how the process of conversion begins with some kind of contact with one of the organisation's representatives, either on the doorstep or more informally through a friend or relative. This is followed by an invitation to undertake several months of Bible study (normally in the recruit's own home) alongside a series of visits to the local Kingdom Hall where the individual will participate in weekly meetings. Only when the individual has demonstrated complete suitability for full membership is his or her dedication to Jehovah symbolised in baptism by total immersion.[2] This takes place at a large public assembly at which multiple baptisms are arranged. New members are then morally obliged to take the message back to the doorstep, though it may be some time before they undertake ministry work alone. Studying the organisation's literature is a crucial requisite for complete membership, which means that there is always a considerable time span between initial contact and baptism.[3] In the course of my fieldwork, an elder informed me that this can take anything between six months and two years, although he did cite one example of a zealous young man who was baptised within eight weeks. He also told me that the organisation will not generally baptise anyone under the age of fifteen. Since the process of initiation is a gradual one, any concept of a new self appears to be absent for quite a long period, although this varies according to how conducive the person's previous lifestyle was to the Society's teachings. New ways of looking at the world may be incorporated into the previous world perspective of the convert without necessarily resulting in any major change. In the early stages, involvement with the Witnesses is likely to be perceived as something which may be broken at any time and could therefore be described as *experimental* (see Lofland and Skonovd 1983).[4] Witness converts claim that it is only when they have internalised the organisation's theology, codes of practice and weekly activities that they recognise the inadequacies of their previous ways of life.

The 'knowledge' required for full membership of the Watch Tower community is fundamentally different from the emotional intensity often associated with, for example, evangelical Christianity.[5] Reading textual material is more intellectually demanding and time-consuming than making a sudden decision to offer one's life to God at a charismatic revival meeting. This is not to suggest that Witnesses do not believe what they 'know' or that evangelical Christian ministers are always sure that those who step forward to be saved have total conviction, but rather that preparation for Watch Tower ministry is largely devoid of supernatural invocation.[6] One indicator of this is the fact that the familiar stories in which born-again Christians declare how lost they were before they saw the light were missing in the testimonies of Witness converts. This confirms Beckford's findings:

> First and foremost we must report the virtual absence of anything which closely resembles the phenomenon of religious conversion as it is customarily understood. Jehovah's witness converts certainly experience no sudden conviction that they have miraculously received God's grace nor that they attained an immediate assurance of salvation. In fact, very few Witnesses can isolate a particular moment in time as a decisive turning point in their religious or spiritual development: certainly none could remember having an overwhelming religious experience.
>
> (Beckford 1975a: 190)

The Witnesses' failure to acknowledge grace or even their own unworthiness reflects their belief that salvation can be earned by taking the time to *read* about God and adhere to the way of life prescribed by the Governing Body of his earthly Society. The people I interviewed referred to the uniformity of Watch Tower doctrines and their complete scriptural basis, but what was particularly interesting (if not altogether unsurprising) about their reasons for joining the movement was the consistency with which they claimed the Witnesses were able to offer them 'facts' that were free from dogma. Here are two examples:

> When I first read some of the literature and started a study with the Witnesses, every question I had ever thought of when I was growing up like 'Why are we here?' and 'What happens to a person when they die?' the Witnesses showed me in the Bible what happens to people when they die and I knew then that other religions had got it wrong. So, that started me thinking. To tell you the truth, when I started studying, I tried to prove them wrong if you know what I mean. I started to read the

Bible for myself then, and when I went for my weekly study, I used to have question after question after question and I tried to pull them up, but I couldn't. They could show me in the Bible the facts.

When I first started studying, I tried to prove it wrong actually. They answered the questions I asked in a reasoning way. The answer was always shown to me from the Bible. I'd never used the Bible before as a Catholic, but the Witnesses always showed me from the Bible.

Although these two converts convey a highly simplistic notion of right and wrong, their claim that they tried to 'prove the Witnesses wrong' demonstrates a certain deference to reason. The Witnesses consult the Bible not only for verification of doctrines concerning everyday life issues but also as a blueprint for conduct. This helps to validate the organisation in the eyes of the convert.[7] Scriptural literalism is a rational means by which the world and its problems can be explained. The Bible confirms to the Witnesses that Jehovah has a rational plan for humankind and that absolute truth (as revealed, for example, in the fulfilment of prophecy) is contained therein. It is this truth, say the Witnesses, that has been perverted by the ungodly and by all other religions.

Rationalism is an essential characteristic of modernity that stems from the Enlightenment tradition. It involves a qualitatively new way of thinking concerned with innate ideas independent of experience.[8] Weber (1970) regarded the rise of science and technology in industrial capitalist societies as evidence of a whole process of rationalisation. He argued that this would manifest itself in the economic distribution of goods and services, in the ordering of work and in social life in general. Weber also suggested that rationalism would lead to tension with traditional cultures in which ordinary people for whom religion had been an important influence would not easily adapt to laws and procedures that were devoid of human emotion. Bruce (1995) argues that the process of rationalisation means that our attention has been taken away from supernatural explanations of the world, and that phenomena of all kinds are now seen to be governed by the principles of cause and effect. He provides an excellent example of this in his analysis of the impact of science on religion:

> Science and technology have given us a notion of cause and effect that makes us look first for the natural causal explanation of an event. When an aeroplane crashes with the loss of many lives, we ask not what moral purpose the event had but what was its natural cause. And, in so far as we keep finding those causes (a loose engine nut, a terrorist bomb), we are subtly discouraged from seeking the moral significance . . . There is no need for religious rites or spells to protect cattle against ringworm when you can buy a drench which has proved over and over to be an excellent cure for the condition . . . Our knowledge of hygiene and our

> possession of tetracycline remove a whole series of occasions for a
> revival of religious commitment.
>
> (133)

Here, Bruce highlights the challenge which science poses for religion. But,
contrary to the expectations held by Enlightenment thinkers that science
might eventually replace supernatural beliefs, Bruce contends that it has
merely changed them. This change, he suggests, began with the undermining
of churches by sects, many of which became denominations. But it will be
recalled from Chapter 2 that, for Bruce, it was the amorphous nature of cults
(driven by the forces of moral relativism as exemplified recently in the New
Age movement) that posed the biggest threat to monotheism as well as to
rationality itself (133–5).

Though I agree with Bruce's analysis, the recent attack on rationalism
has done little to harm Watch Tower doctrines or the ways in which they are
disseminated. Weber argued that, even when theodicies ceased to provide
solutions, problems of meaning could not be addressed by science alone.
But, from a Watch Tower perspective, nor can they be addressed by moral
relativism. Rationalism is one feature of modernity on which the community
has been able to capitalise. It provides devotees with strategies for recruitment and enables them to prove beyond all doubt that their word is the
word of God. Moreover, it arms them with ammunition for demonising the
outside world and protecting their cherished boundaries. The Witnesses
believe that Jehovah created the earth in seven days and intended Adam and
Eve to live in a state of eternal happiness. However, it is as though they
believe that, since the Fall, he has taken a back seat and allowed people to
govern themselves until such time as they reach the point of their own (and
the world's) destruction. This is, perhaps, one of the reasons they spend
little time in prayer. Though they contend that Jehovah loves all people and
cares about what happens to them, their anticipation of Armageddon seems
to prevent them from beseeching him for world peace or good fortune.[9]
Their failure to spend much time in meditation, prayer, healing, and other
such rituals seems to convey their unwillingness to recognise that God will
intervene in human affairs.[10] One woman told me that she and her husband
had recently made an offer on a house with which they had fallen in love,
but were still awaiting a phone call from their solicitor to confirm that
contracts had been exchanged. When I asked the woman if she had been
praying for a successful outcome, she casually announced, 'To be quite
honest with you, I don't think Jehovah minds where we live'. Though this
couple would no doubt have been disappointed had they not managed to
secure the sale, their rational belief system prevented them from beseeching
divine intervention. Another example of the way in which the Witnesses'
rational beliefs influence their daily lives concerns a woman whose Anglican
mother had died some years before. The woman recalled an incident in
which her mother had received a hospital visit from two friends:

she'd had a stroke and she was on this ward. She was unconscious at the time and she was really poorly. Anyway, I remember my mum had two friends who were devout Catholics and they used to bring a little bottle with holy water in it and I remember rubbing my mum's arm with this holy water thinking. 'Oh, God'll make her better'. I laugh now when I think back at it.

Although these could be the thoughts of any non-Catholic, they convey something significant about the Witnesses' approach to suffering and death. The biblical story of Job's plight provides the Witnesses with the knowledge that, since misfortune strikes indiscriminately, it must be endured by those who have faith as well as those who do not. The Society's teaching that death and dying are the inevitable consequences of original sin means that grief is also part of the human condition. The Witnesses are thus encouraged to confront these feelings rather than suppress them. In a pamphlet entitled *Comfort for the Depressed*, the Society informs its members:

> Yes, our loving heavenly Father . . . knows that we inherited sin, sickness, and death and therefore have great limitations. The fact that we feel grieved and vexed with ourselves is in itself proof that we do not want to sin and have not gone too far. The Bible says that we were 'subjected to futility' against our will. So God sympathizes with our miserable plight, and he compassionately takes into consideration our weaknesses. (Romans 5: 12; 8: 20)
> (Watch Tower Bible and Tract Society of Pennsylvania 1992a: 4–5)

This extract seems to acknowledge that human frailty is as much the reason for people's inability to cope with misfortune as it is their tendency to sin. Similarly, the widely distributed magazine *When Someone You Love Dies* (Watch Tower Bible and Tract Society of Pennsylvania 1994) advises devotees that grief is a perfectly natural process which should be released by weeping and sharing memories of the dead person as widely as possible. The magazine goes on to describe the grieving process, which includes shock, disbelief, denial, guilt feelings, anger, memory loss, fatigue and changes in appetite. It then offers practical suggestions about how to deal with the loss. These include confiding in friends, taking care of one's health, postponing major decisions, establishing a daily routine and avoiding excessive medication and alcohol. Were it not for the inclusion of biblical references, this magazine could equally have been published by a counselling service or the medical profession. Although it contains the story of Lazarus's resurrection and a message of hope for the future, its emphasis on practical advice has all the trappings of an anti-mystical belief system. This absence of mysticism in grief is echoed in the Witnesses' explanation of what happens to people when they die. It will be recalled from my earlier summary of Watch Tower doctrines that, unlike more orthodox Christians, the Witnesses do not believe that the souls of the faithful go straight to heaven or that their spirits are still present. Rather, they believe that the dead fall completely asleep and remain unaware of anything until the time that Jehovah establishes his New Kingdom and resurrects them from unconsciousness. The wicked and unfaithful remain dead for ever. According to the Society, the only purpose of the funeral service is to dispose of the body and to honour the words of Genesis 3: 19, 'For dust you are and to dust you will return.' At no point is reference made to the transcendence of the soul.

The Witnesses' rejection of conventional beliefs in the supernatural and in heaven and hell accounts for their claim that dead people cannot yet live on. Devotees maintain that trying to contact the dead is not only a futile but also a highly sinful exercise, and that those who claim to have seen or received messages from their deceased loved ones have been misled by Satan. Those who claim to be able to help the bereaved to contact dead relatives will stand accountable on the Day of Judgement. Although these beliefs may be of little comfort to those who prefer to think that their deceased loved one is close by and experiencing eternal bliss, they are an effective means by which the Watch Tower community is able to keep the Satanic influences of Christendom at bay.

'Studying'

It is not uncommon for Witnesses to ask each other how long they have been in *the truth* or when they first began to *study*. Studying is a term which devotees use when they are referring to the process of learning Watch Tower theology. It also allows them to confirm their allegiance to Jehovah. Since becoming a respectable Witness involves reading large amounts of textual information in preparation for a never-ending series of meetings, studying is a more appropriate term for describing their weekly activities than *worship*. Glossolalia, creed recitation, even periods of silent meditation are so far removed from the Witnesses' activities that someone claiming to have had an experience of a transcendental nature would be most unlikely to find solace in a Kingdom Hall. At no point in meetings is time made available for individual prayer. Unlike charismatic movements, spontaneous prayers and prayers by invitation are absent. Although short prayers are recited, these last no more than two or three minutes and serve mainly to open and close meetings. In a modern age in which social movements articulate expressive identities, the Witnesses stand out as staid and conservative.

The notion of studying is conducive to a community that has no time for superstition. During my first observation, I remember feeling bewildered by what seemed like a numbing dullness of the Kingdom Hall compared with the awesome ambience of a Catholic church. It was as though my childhood memories of penance, rosaries, plenary indulgences, novenas, transubstantiation and benediction belonged to a different world. Here was an organisation that did not just eschew mystery, it openly condemned it. Watch Tower magazines repeatedly warn devotees of the dangers of apostasy by showing pictures of Catholics praying before images of saints (particularly the Virgin Mary) for intercession. Elders impart the view that venerating anything or anybody other than God constitutes false worship and is forbidden in the Bible.[11] This idea is nothing new (it was, after all, one of the arguments that came out of the Protestant Reformation), but what is perhaps significant is that the Witnesses' style of worship resonates with the idea that religious superstition is contrary to the principles of modernity. In his work on the Enlightenment in *The Crooked Timber of Humanity*, Isaiah Berlin writes:

> The rational reorganisation of society would put an end to spiritual and intellectual confusion, the reign of prejudice and superstition, blind obedience to unexamined dogmas, and the stupidities and cruelties of the oppressive regimes which such intellectual darkness bred and promoted. All that was wanted was the identification of the principal human needs and discovery of the means of satisfying them.
>
> (Berlin 1990: 5)

Berlin is suggesting that rationalisation would bring about the death of superstition and the rise of human emancipation. Few people would regard the Watch Tower Society as liberating in any sense of the word, but the Witnesses' attack on saint-cults and their refusal to accept the 'unexamined dogmas' to which Berlin refers could be seen as freedom from the shackles of traditional religion. Though they are religious in the sense that they believe in the supernatural and offer their allegiance to a deity, the Witnesses' one true interpretation of scripture eradicates superstition, drawing instead on the modern forces of reason.[12]

The desire for a rationally oriented system of beliefs is apparent also in the layout of Kingdom Halls and what they contain. Unlike the Roman Catholic tradition in which relics, crucifixes, statues, pictures, holy water and tabernacles are an indispensable part of the spiritual ethos, the Witnesses' place of worship appears sparse and disenchanted. Throughout the course of my observations, I saw no one meditating or lighting candles and the elders never burned incense. Nor did they wear vestments or stand before an altar. The Hall was essentially functional. It was always tastefully decorated, spotlessly clean and well maintained by the members, who seemed to take great pride in its upkeep.[13] The spatial layout of formally arranged chairs and an elevated platform on which devotees delivered their well-rehearsed sermons exemplified the rational nature of the organisation. The three well-groomed elders in the background quietly confirming the order and content of the meeting from their official Watch Tower itineraries enhanced the atmosphere of order and precision.

Witnesses are expected to attend three weekly meetings, two of which are held at the Kingdom Hall. The third meeting (the *Book Study*) is held in a member's home. The two Kingdom Hall meetings each last approximately two hours. The first meeting is held on a weekday evening and revolves around sermons, ministry and discussions of moral and theological issues from various publications. The second meeting (held by most congregations on Sundays) comprises a *public talk* and a *Watchtower study*. Each congregation is responsible for conducting its own meetings. Book Study meetings last only one hour and consist of groups of around twenty people, making several groups to a congregation. Although a number of groups meet at different houses on the same evening, every practising Witness should be able to attend a meeting at a house near to where he or she lives. All meetings begin and end on time with a short hymn and a prayer. The meetings I attended were formal events that followed the schedule of the Watch Tower Bible and Tract Society to the letter.[14] Such standardisation of procedures for conducting meetings undoubtedly adds to the organisation's coherence. Male Witnesses in positions of seniority attend the entrance of the hall at every meeting to welcome the members with the usual handshake. Copies of *The Watchtower* are printed in most languages for Witnesses worldwide, and are used at these meetings in almost every country in the world. So uniform is the Society's theology and content of meetings that, in principle, every Jehovah's Witness in the world will read the same literature during the same week in preparation for the same programme at their local Kingdom Hall.

Watch Tower authoritarianism is highly implicit in the ways in which devotees interact at the meetings and I noticed an unusual degree of subordination among both women and children. The organisation is a patriarchal one in which women are expected to defer to their husbands' authority and children to that of their parents. The Witnesses claim that dynamic roles for women such as convening meetings and organising events are scripturally renounced. The principle of male authority is to be honoured even in cases where the husband is not a Witness. At none of the meetings did I see women leading discussions, although they were allowed to practise their sermons in public (of this issue of the position of women in the organisation, more later).[15] Witness children are expected to demonstrate respect for authority at all times in their lives. Any potentially disruptive behaviour is forbidden at meetings. Parents exercise strict authority over their children's conduct and children from a very young age are encouraged to follow the programmes of the meetings and undertake Bible study. Babies who persistently cry are taken out of meetings (usually by the mother, unless she is absent). Authority to which children are expected to defer is learned not just from parents and elders but also from published literature. The preface to one book for children published by the Society reads:

A person's youth can be one of the happiest periods of life. Unfortunately, for many it is not. Changing standards have created a mixed-up world, and today's problems often rob young people of happiness. This book is published to help them to see the solutions to these problems and so get the best out of life now and in the future.

> (Watch Tower Bible and Tract Society of Pennsylvania 1976)[16]

This particular book is filled with Watch Tower teachings on parental authority and discipline as well as moral issues such as dating and sexual relationships. These publications play an essential role in the teaching of Watch Tower beliefs. Despite the Witnesses' claim that the Bible is their only source of authority, they make constant use of a huge welter of both hard and paperback publications, tracts and *The Watchtower* and *Awake!* magazines. In fact, without these aids it would be impossible for the Society to hold its meetings in their current format. It is also doubtful that devotees would be able to proselytise or to recruit new members. Materials such as *The Watchtower* are almost as significant to the Witnesses as the Bible, since the information is presented as the inspired work of theologians, and they are, therefore, believed to contain as much truth as biblical texts. Of all the literature published by the Society, articles from *The Watchtower* and various extracts from a circular entitled *Our Kingdom Ministry* provide the Witnesses with their weekly reading material. The weekly meetings are structured around these articles, which devotees spend a large amount of their own time reading in preparation. The content of these texts provides an important topic of conversation before the meetings begin and after they have ended. It is not uncommon for devotees to highlight certain paragraphs and key phrases in their tracts, and some even prepare their answers to the attached questions on notepaper. As usual, scriptural references are used to support the discussion.

One of the most interesting features of the Witnesses' meetings is the way that Watch Tower literature is used by officials to impart the tenets and beliefs. The theology is sometimes disseminated by means of the delivery of sermons from key speakers on the platform. Publications serve to enhance the sermons and appended questions are used to invite responses from the audience. These responses are elicited by microphones offered by congregational attendants. Question and answer sessions of this nature seem to be viewed as the most effective way of studying and are analogous to the pedagogic teaching and learning styles commonly employed by teachers in classrooms. Despite the fact that the Witnesses claim to *reason* from the scriptures, their theology is taught in a highly mechanistic fashion, and written publications encourage the members to learn almost by rote. One woman in her early thirties who defected from the community in the early 1990s, had vivid memories of how she was trained to prepare for meetings:

You had to read it through, read it through again, answer the question and then read it through *again*. So by the time Sunday came, you were an expert at it. You were a fully trained parrot! Everybody had their answers underlined. You could see everybody looking at each other's *Watchtower* to check if the answers were underlined. Everybody comes out with the same answer. You virtually repeated the answer out of the book . . . it's like 'learn with mother!'

Midweek Book Study meetings also entail this kind of learning. Although the size of the groups and homely setting of the meetings would suggest that these are informal occasions, chairs are arranged in three or four rows in order that the person convening the meeting can be seen in the usual position at the front. On entering the house, people chat in a friendly manner and supply the host with packets of biscuits and home-made cakes for the refreshment period at the end. Once the meeting is about to begin, the twenty or so people sit attentively with their books opened at the correct page. For the next hour, the selected passage is read from the tract paragraph by paragraph. In a similar way to the Watch Tower meetings, the accompanying questions are read out one at a time by an official who co-ordinates the responses. Personal contributions are discouraged and devotees may volunteer an answer only by raising their hands.

The absence of mysticism does not seem to prevent officials from achieving a high level of commitment from the audience. The rational procedures that the Witnesses have at their disposal for the operation of meetings help to create an atmosphere of uniformity which they regard as a tangible source of truth. But over and above the teaching and learning of the theology, there is another purpose to the meetings – particularly the Book Study – which is of sociological significance. Given that there are no more than twenty people at each Book Study, these meetings make possible more personal interaction and they are also one of the official channels through which the Witnesses organise their door-to-door ministry. Combined, these two 'functions' rekindle the Witnesses' consciousness of their unity and enhance their feelings of solidarity. The reinforcement of the Society's millenarian mission thus attaches the individual to the wider social group in the way propounded by Durkheim (1912). The Witnesses' attendance at annual conventions (often held at football stadia) where they are able to express their allegiance along with thousands of others is visual evidence of this kind of social cohesion. Watch Tower symbols depend upon shared meanings if they are to work effectively, and this requires a shared reality. Participation of this kind produces an experience of unity while separating Witnesses from national collectivities. By sharing a uniform theology, devotees espouse the same values and moral beliefs that form the collective conscience.

There can be no doubt that Watch Tower meetings intensify the Witnesses' sense of belonging to a religious community. This attachment seems to play as important a role as studying in maintaining high levels of commitment.

Meetings constitute the social basis for the continued existence of the organisation's meaning system. Berger (1967) refers to this as a *plausibility structure*. As the term implies, social structures enable the meaning system to remain plausible (that is, *believable*) in the eyes of their members through specific social processes or interactions within a network of people. Berger argues that plausibility structures allow belief systems to become taken-for-granted entities. In the case of the Watch Tower community, the social support provided at the meetings draws devotees into fellowship with the larger group and reinforces their worldview. This plausibility can be demonstrated by examining the effects of the meetings on recent converts. Through interaction with other Witnesses, it is clear that new members learn to adopt a different way of life. Several Witnesses explained how, particularly in their first few months of full membership, they acquired a zeal for their new beliefs and never wanted to be away from their spiritual brothers and sisters. One woman described how she became almost obsessive and jokingly said that she ought to have been locked away for a full six months just after her conversion. The woman went on to say that, although, twelve years later, she still believed that the Watch Tower Society represented the one true faith, she now attended meetings more out of duty than enthusiasm.[17] This would suggest that, once new recruits have fully internalised the Witnesses' *Weltanschauung*, attending meetings becomes a conventional activity.

In the initial months of membership, most converts find their former friends less than supportive of their new found faith. One of the best ways of examining the effects of initiation is to ascertain whether new recruits choose to spend time with non-Witnesses or confirm their allegiance to the community by severing those relationships that support the old self. Over half the converts I interviewed claimed they had very limited circles of friends during the time of initial contact with Watch Tower evangelists, but for the remainder, a considerable degree of adjustment was necessary. One young man who had enjoyed his social life with a wide circle of friends prior to baptism told me:

> Friday and Saturday nights I used to go round town with the lads and I'd be paralytic. We used to go round the nightclubs . . . ten of us went away on holiday, but their thinking was totally different from my own. We used to get drunk, pick women up, and then one night I only drank a couple of pints and then I started drinking coke and my mates said, 'What's up with you?', and I explained that the Bible says that you're not supposed to get drunk, and from then on I lost interest in those things; so when they said, 'Are you coming out?', I just said, 'No'.

Another convert, rather typically, found his answers in the scriptures. He explained how he was able to use the Bible to counter disapproval from his friends once he began studying:

You see, so many people are divided against each other in so many ways and yet they are united in their opposition to Jehovah's Witnesses, which was why I thought, 'Well these people must have something'. If you look in the scriptures, Jesus said, 'You will be hated on account of my name, all the nations will hate you'. So, the political system and the quasi, false religious system are all wrapped up together, and there's one on the outside. But a friend from school got engaged and we used to go out for a drink. Once I started studying with the Witnesses he thought it was a bit strange, but our friendship went back a long way, so we still went out once a week, but as I became more involved with the truth, my drinking became less and less and for years and years he'd been trying to get me to do this, but he went the opposite – he started drinking more and more and he started saying, 'Come on, have a drink', but eventually we just drifted away and I don't have any contact with those friends now.

Like most new converts, these two men expressed difficulty in keeping a foot in both camps once they had internalised Watch Tower beliefs. The greater the involvement the individual has with those already in the community, be it at meetings or outside, the less they appear to want to associate with those they leave behind. The main exceptions to this are those cases in which breaking all ties would either be emotionally too painful (as in the case of Witnesses who convert after marriage and/or whose closest relatives are non-members) or financially too difficult (that is, where devotees are dependent on the outside world for employment) and, even then, such relations need to be carefully negotiated.

By attending meetings on a regular basis, converts adopt the idea that reality consists of the two irreducible modes of good and evil described earlier. These two opposing principles become the Witnesses' frame of reference for managing their relations with the outside world. Reading the Society's literature is one of the ways in which new members learn that Satan has misled the whole of humankind and that they are involved in a cosmic struggle for salvation by siding with good forces.[18] At one of the meetings I attended, Satan was mentioned no fewer than twenty-six times. Such constant reference to Satan is effective in persuading devotees that, if they leave the community or stray from its teachings in any way, they are failing to surrender to the will of Jehovah. It also serves as a reminder that evil is present in every other system of beliefs and worldly organisation. Demonising the world in this way enables the Witnesses to construct a unique version of risk from which they then claim to provide protection. This version of risk contrasts sharply with that of scientific and academic communities which attempt to explain in secular terms crises such as global warming, toxic residues in food, AIDS and HIV, the fear of physical violence and the breakdown of law and order. While theorists such as Beck and Giddens argue that the heightened consciousness of risk is a response to the dangers of modern living, the Witnesses see it as evidence of human torment which signifies the tragic consequences of original sin in a world that is becoming predictably worse.[19]

Though literal biblical interpretation may not constitute rational thinking to outsiders, it is, in fact, a rational means by which devotees make sense of the cosmos. Their avoidance of mysticism, their objective search for truth and their ability to run meetings in a businesslike fashion all display a willingness to make use of modern resources in order to create a mood of certainty and protect the community from dangerous forces. It is not difficult to see how this is appealing to those who have less than happy memories of orthodox Christian dogma. The Witnesses are able to present their monosemic beliefs in a way that appears reasonable to those who are prepared to listen, and Kingdom Hall meetings provide an appropriate setting for this to take place. It is here that they can affirm their affection for each other as well as their anger against the rest of humanity, whom they consign to destruction in the eagerly awaited holocaust. Meanwhile, they must try to persuade the rest of us that they have a message that cannot be ignored.

Learning to minister

One of the peculiarities about the Watch Tower Society is that faith in its millenarian position is not enough in itself to constitute being a Witness. Belief in the doctrines must also be expressed in religious participation, and in this sense Witnesses are not just believers, they are also activists. Those who take the step to become full members of the community and publicly acknowledge this in baptism are automatically ordained as ministers. This means that they have a moral obligation to disseminate Watch Tower doctrines as evangelists of 'the truth'. Devotees claim that ministering and believing must coexist if their principal mission of accelerating the New Kingdom is to be achieved.[20] Door-to-door proselytising is the most appropriate means of alerting the rest of the world to 'the signs of the end'. The Witnesses regard their presence in every country as the fulfilment of Matthew 24: 14.

Evangelism can be a great source of inspiration for millenarian movements. For the majority of Witnesses, recruiting others can be challenging and rewarding; yet there were some quite different reactions from converts. Some are keen to proselytise, not only because of their desire to share their new found faith but also because they feel the need to contribute something worthwhile to their religious community. Others are more circumspect, mainly because of their lack of evangelistic experience; but even these individuals are convinced that ministering to others is what Jehovah requires of them. Their immediate status as servants of Jehovah means they can no longer hide behind missals or listen to what is being said from a pulpit. Witnessing means knocking on doors with the sole purpose of recruiting more members.

The capacity of the Society to stir devotees into action is achieved mainly through its delegation and calculation of religious activity. The Governing Body centralises the worldwide ministerial effort of devotees and publishes annual reports (including statistical information) on the success of door-to-door proselytising in gaining converts. Thus, the onus is on every congregation in the world to improve its previous year's recruitment performance and is the reason for the large amount of time spent at the Kingdom Hall in the practise of effective ministry. Each member has a personal responsibility to spread the good news and to monitor their performance by recording the total number of monthly hours allocated to the ministry, the specific amount of literature left with the householder, the number of return visits made to a prospective convert's home and the number of home Bible studies conducted. These details are submitted on a monthly basis to the congregational secretary. Those who fail to devote a satisfactory amount of time to doorstep evangelism (currently around seventeen hours per month in the United States) soon lose the respect of their co-religionists and may even be disfellowshipped. The Witnesses are thus forced to think quantitatively about their salvation. Though the Watch Tower authorities acknowledge that factors such as old age, ill health and family responsibilities may mean that some people are unable to devote as much time to the ministry as others, *all* Witnesses are expected to contribute to the recruitment effort. Those whose activities might be impaired for any of the above reasons are encouraged to write letters for the organisation to publish or to Witness by telephone. This is an extremely resourceful movement in which every member is a missionary. There is no place for anyone wishing to tag along as a free-rider.

The Witnesses' determination to bring forth the Millenarian Age is epitomised in the industry with which they approach their evangelistic mission. Their endless ministerial efforts (vis-à-vis the scepticism with which their message of salvation is often received) echo the work ethic of the Calvinists in the sixteenth century. Weber's famous work *The Protestant Ethic and the Spirit of Capitalism* conveys how Calvin's high regard for the virtues of self-discipline, purity and industry encouraged a rational, efficient and highly committed approach to work. Weber argued that these virtues sowed the seeds for the development of modern capitalism (Weber 1930).[21] But the Protestant ethic did not produce only a spirit of capitalism, it also produced a new spirit of labour which is reflected in the Witnesses' dedication to their ministry. The precise calculation of the time spent by devotees in their door-to-door proselytising and the planning and rehearsing required for success bear all the hallmarks of Calvinist rationalism. Ministering to the general public at their homes and out on the streets is something the Witnesses are ever trying to improve. There is no shortage of Watch Tower material encouraging devotees to sell their theology to others. Photographs of Witnesses from all ethnic backgrounds happily evangelising to prospective converts appear in a large number of Watch

Tower publications and demonstrate an unreserved anti-racist stance.[22] Some of this literature also contains pictures of the huge buildings in which the organisation's tracts and magazines are printed and from which they are distributed. These images suggest continuous expansion and portray the movement as fast-growing and successful. The Witnesses' annual *Yearbooks* are packed with information about the various activities that have taken place since the last edition, including the number of Kingdom Halls built around the world (making a grand total of 89,985 in January 2000), the tens of thousands of books printed in various branches, the number of baptisms conducted, the millions of dollars spent on overseas travel and the total number of hours recorded for missionary work (1,096,065,354 in 1995 alone). While success of this kind confirms the fulfilment of prophecy, it serves also to remind devotees that this work must be complete before the arrival of Armageddon and that no one can afford to rest on their laurels. Doubtless, the Witnesses face rejection upon rejection at the majority of their house calls, but it would be wrong to think that their doorstep proselytising is fruitless. On present performance, if the number of world-wide annual Witnessing hours is divided by the total number of new recruits, each publisher would need to devote an average of only twenty hours per month to achieve a 7 per cent growth rate. Although this means that it would take the collective effort of fourteen evangelists per annum to produce just one baptism, the end result is nevertheless impressive. How, then, do the Witnesses go about learning to minister, and how do they deal with the indifference of all those householders who have no desire to be one of the 7 per cent?

In one guide published by the Society (Watch Tower Bible and Tract Society of Pennsylvania 1989b), there is a whole chapter on how to begin conversations on the doorstep. None of the suggestions refers to scriptural texts or to the fact that the visitors are Jehovah's Witnesses. Instead, the evangelist is advised to select a global catastrophe, current affair or social issue to win the attention of the householder. The chapter contains 'conversation starters', which are presented under the headings of current events, employment/housing, family/children, future/security, injustice/suffering, life/happiness, old age/death and the example which I have used below – crime/safety:

> Hello. We're talking with folks about the matter of personal safety. There is a lot of crime around us, and it affects our lives. Do you think the time will come when people like you and me will be able to walk the streets at night and feel safe?
>
> (Watch Tower Bible and Tract Society of Pennsylvania 1989b: 10)

In this way, the Witnesses are able to present the householder with a vision of a world in which crime will cease (that is, the post-Armageddon Kingdom) without even a mention of the Bible or the Watch Tower organisation. No doubt there are hundreds of thousands of householders who, familiar with the doorstep sermons of Jehovah's Witnesses or on realising that briefcases, suits and colourful literature mean religious sectarians, politely (or impolitely) terminate the conversation. In the next part of the guide, however, the evangelist learns how to respond to 'conversation stoppers' by following a series of householders' potential responses such as 'I'm not interested', 'I have my own religion', 'We are already Christians here', 'I'm busy', 'Why do you people call so often?', 'I'm a Muslim' and 'I'm not interested in religion'. Each weekly Ministry School meeting includes one full hour of platform role-play where devotees hone their missionary skills in front of an enthusiastic congregation. Every possible reaction which householders might produce is met with Watch Tower rhetoric. Role-play activities cover doorstep sermons, street proselytising, home Bible studies and workplace ministry – all contexts in which devotees are encouraged, should the opportunity arise, to share their faith. At the end of each activity, the congregational officials assess the quality of the rehearsal and provide the individual with comments on which he or she is expected to reflect. Criteria such as 'fluency', 'pronunciation', 'use of biblical references', 'audibility', 'speed' and 'eye contact' ensure that the Witnesses make a constant effort to fine-tune their deliveries.[23] An assessment sheet is then given to the evangelist at the end of the session as an indicator of his or her performance.[24] These ministerial strategies show how, despite the Witnesses' constant verbal attacks on modern society, they nevertheless make efficient use of the resources that it has to offer. The training involved in effective communication for the sole purpose of winning recruits is not dissimilar to that undertaken by sales personnel in the secular world of business.[25] The close attention paid by the members to style and presentation exemplified in the wearing of suits and the carrying of briefcases characterises a rational, professional people who know exactly how to sell their message. In this sense, it is not difficult to see that the Witnesses' way of ministering is conducive to their belief that magic, miracles and superstition do not belong to the twenty-first century.[26] It is also clear that the analytically separable processes of instruction and affiliation are closely intertwined.

Over and above the formal assessment of presentations at Kingdom Hall meetings, individual Witnesses are expected to evaluate their evangelistic skills *informally*. The success of presenting Watch Tower beliefs to the general public might, for example, be measured by considering the effect of the sermon on the recipient. The willingness of the householder to listen to the sermon and accept a copy of *The Watchtower* is regarded as a fruitful first visit. Ministers who manage to persuade their host to agree to a further visit can commend themselves on having made real progress, for it is at this point that a prospective convert beckons. Ultimately, the aim of every Watch Tower minister is to make a series of visits to the same householder in the hope that it will result in a Bible study and a subsequent invitation to the

Kingdom Hall. As one might expect, however, doorstep proselytising meets its fair share of enmity. Several pioneers (who are expected to work more hours on the ministry than publishers) regaled me with stories not only of aggressive householders who had slammed doors in their faces but also of incidents such as dangerous dogs being allowed to threaten the zealous visitors with menaces! While, on the whole, devotees are either politely turned away or their literature accepted with some degree of scepticism, their difficulty in finding new recruits on ministry work, and the hostility they sometimes encounter, lead to feelings of despondency. Several members told me that they preferred to partake in those aspects of Witness life such as Bible study and attending meetings rather than ministry work because of the rejection from large numbers of uninterested sceptics. Whatever the length of membership, degree of fervour or organisational status of the individual, congregational officials stress the importance of erring on the side of politeness in the face of doorstep hostility. This became apparent in a conversation with one elder who told me:

> We went out on Saturday. We were working in Blackburn and the people were curt and sharp. They said, 'We don't want that!' So we said, 'Thank you. Good morning!' So the point is that the ministry is really doing a dividing work – those who want and those who don't want.

These comments suggest that the Witnesses' zeal for their mission is balanced with a certain degree of temperance when they realise that they are fighting a losing battle, and this helps to reaffirm that they are Jehovah's people. Hundreds of thousands of devotees continue to evangelise every week despite the insults they incur. Consider, for example, the following comments from three evangelists with several years' ministerial experience; the first from a woman who had been a member of the community for fourteen years at the time of the research:

> When you knock on the door and give your presentation, some people can be really quite aggressive. You do get people swearing at you and shouting at you, telling you where to go and you just have to walk away. That side of things don't really bother me because that's exactly what they did to Jesus isn't it really?

A man in his seventies who had been a member all his life told me:

> Jesus said, 'If you go to a city and you call at a house and they say "peace be with you", stay there and talk to the people; but if they don't want you, just shake the dust off your feet and go somewhere else'. We're looking for people who are hungry and thirsty. Jesus said, 'My sheep hear my voice', but he didn't say the goats would listen! There are some nice 'goats' around, but they don't listen.

The final story came from a woman who had had an unpleasant experience only the previous week:

> There's a vicar from Saint Martin's church who lives on Burnley Road. Anyway, last week I was out with another sister and we called at his house. He was a really nasty piece of work. He said to us, 'Go away! Go away! I don't want Jehovah's Witnesses round here', and before we could answer, he said it again, 'Go away!' So I just said, 'OK, we're going, but do you know that's what they did to Jesus?!'

There is something far more important about what these three Witnesses are saying than their mere awareness of the distinction between the just and the unjust. Their comments reveal that, ostensibly, they are on a mission to save others, but actually, they are confirming to themselves their own worldview. When the Witnesses cannot even persuade a householder to accept a free pamphlet or a copy of *The Watchtower*, they concede to the knowledge that rejection is a sign of people's unworthiness. Doorstep rebuffs are regarded by the Society as the fulfilment of New Testament prophecy; namely, that 'Christ's true followers will be the objects of hatred on account of his name' (Matthew 24: 9). Hostility of this kind merely confirms the Witnesses' negative perceptions of the outside world and supports their rational biblical logic. The third evangelist's story of rejection by an Anglican clergyman is particularly significant since it affirms the Society's teaching that Christendom is in league with the devil. This no doubt strengthens the devotee's sense of exclusivity. Doorstep rejection is perceived in terms of persecution – an essential feature of the Last Days, when the good news will have been preached throughout the earth. Thus, while unsympathetic householders may be bad for recruitment, the Witnesses continue their proselytising ministry, if only because its failure to win converts confirms their belief that the New Kingdom is imminent:

> The message that would be preached is that God's Kingdom in the hands of Jesus Christ has begun to rule in the heavens, that soon it will put an end to the entire wicked system of things, that under its rule mankind will be brought to perfection and earth will become a paradise. That good news is being preached today in over 200 lands and island groups, to the most distant parts of the earth. Jehovah's Witnesses devote hundreds of millions of hours to this activity each year, making repeated house-to-house visits so that everyone possible is given the opportunity to hear.
> (Watch Tower Bible and Tract Society of Pennsylvania 1989b: 238)

By drawing similarities between their own experiences of hostility on the streets and Jesus's persecution in the city of Nazareth, devotees can draw comfort from the millenarian promises made to those who suffer persecution for the sake of righteousness. This message is as meaningful to the Witnesses at the beginning of the twenty-first century as any other time in history. Their expectation of disapprobation is a sound mechanism for reinforcing social cohesion at the Kingdom Hall, and yet, as I have shown above, the Society's expansion since the days of Russell owes more to the rational tenets of modernity than to its members' humility.

Protecting the sacred

In all closed communities, dangers and punishments attached to wrong-doing are effective in producing conformity. Durkheim argues that one of the essential characteristics of the sacred is the danger involved in its transgression. The sacred is constructed by individuals who are bound together in accordance with agreed rules and it must be protected from the profane by interdictions which are reinforced with sanctions for dealing with the danger of crossing forbidden territories (Durkheim 1912). For the Witnesses, danger lies in acts that offend the moral fabric of their community, and for this reason they have devised an effective system for dealing with offenders. The Witnesses' definitions of right and wrong cannot be compromised. Whenever individuals violate Watch Tower injunctions, they automatically offend the whole congregation and put their own salvation in jeopardy. There is nothing like a wrongful act for reaffirming the sacredness of Watch Tower doctrines.

The Society has an established set of rational procedures for reconciling and penalising those who stray from its teachings. For this reason, concepts such as *sin, holiness* and *sacredness* are not part of the Witnesses' discourse when they are referring to the effects of the damage done by offenders. Nor are words such as *penance, healing* or *reconciliation* used to describe absolution. Rather, there is an administrative system with clear guidelines for dealing with transgressions. Only congregational elders have the juris-diction to enforce the appropriate sanction and to notify the congregation of the action taken. One of the most common ways of dealing with minor wrongdoing is by what the Society calls *counselling*. This is not, as in the case of welfare workers who conduct counselling sessions with their clients, therapeutic, but a mechanism used by officials to reproach the wrongdoer and to warn him or her (with the aid of biblical texts) of the dangers of further transgression. Counselling entails a series of meetings between the individual and the elders, either after congregational gatherings or at the offender's own home. This is often followed by a formal announcement from the platform at the next meeting that the person concerned has been reproved. From what I learned from the elders, counselling plays an important role both in chastising members for their wrongdoings and in keeping any further transgressions at bay. The elders themselves consider counselling to be an act of love and concern for offending Witnesses who have sinned through their humanity:

Because we are all sinners, changes in our attitude, our speech and our conduct are required in order for us to reflect the personality of our God . . . Counsel and discipline help us to identify areas where adjustments are needed and then to see how to make these . . . Jehovah does not leave us to struggle alone with matters that may be a special problem for us. With loving concern, he makes provision for personal help. Millions of persons have benefited from such help by means of home Bible studies. Parents have a special responsibility to discipline their children in order to safeguard them against conduct that could cause much heartache later in life. (Prov. 6: 20–35; 15: 5) Within the congregation, too, those who have spiritual qualifications bear responsibility to use the Scriptures to readjust others when they discern a need, but doing so in a spirit of mildness. (Gal. 6: 1, 2) In these ways Jehovah counsels and disciplines us so that we might worship him as a united people.

(Watch Tower Bible and Tract Society of Pennsylvania 1983b: 130–1)

Although this passage states that counselling helps those who have strayed to make 'adjustments', in Durkheimian terms it is a disciplinary strategy – a symbolic weapon used by the community to protect itself from risk. This shows that boundaries are not just perceived but acted upon. Douglas argues that the damage caused to social order by pollution offences can be diminished, even scrubbed out, by ritual:

Some pollutions are too grave for the offender to be allowed to survive. But most pollutions have a very simple remedy for undoing their effects. There are rites of reversing, untying, burying, washing, erasing, fumigating, and so on, which at a small cost of time and effort can satisfactorily expunge them. The cancelling of a moral offence depends on the state of mind of the offended party and on the sweetness of nursing revenge . . . Rites of reconciliation which enact the burial of the wrong have the creative effect of all ritual. They can help to erase memory of the wrong and encourage the growth of right feeling.

(Douglas 1966: 135–6)

According to the Witnesses, counselling is primarily a preventative strategy. This means that congregational elders may use counselling as a means of rebuking unacceptable conduct before it reaches a level which cannot be redressed other than by disfellowship. Counselling is thus part of a moral appeal to the offender who, with the help of an elder, is asked to examine his or her conscience. This is an effective way of reinforcing a dualistic worldview, since those who violate official tenets are being asked to consider their behaviour in terms of the organisation's *Weltanschauung*. The 'spirit of mildness' mentioned in the previous publication is undoubtedly a euphemism for a disciplinary strategy which is rather less formal than disfellowship. The formality of the discipline enforced by the elders reflects the severity of the transgression. While mild misdemeanours such as idle gossip, occasional lying, failing to attend meetings regularly and excessive contact with the world can be dealt with informally through counselling, major transgressions such as adultery, slander, homosexuality, apostasy and continual drunkenness call for greater punity which may result in disfellowship. Disfellowshipping is, however, much less common than informal discipline such as counselling. One elder whose responsibilities included disfellowshipping wayward members told me that, in his own congregation of nearly a hundred people, there had not been a case of disfellowship for seven years. He explained that, within the previous ten years, there had been an annual average of forty thousand disfellowshipped members worldwide; but, since there were around eighty thousand Watch Tower congregations at the time of the interview, this figure is very small indeed. He also informed me that disfellowship does not mean permanent exclusion, and that, upon repentance, the majority of disfellowshipped members are allowed to return to the congregation.

Disfellowshipping is the ultimate sanction against those who wound the collective sentiments of the congregation and is therefore one of the most effective means by which the Governing Body of the Society is able to reinforce sectarian boundaries. The elder with whom I spoke pulled no punches in explaining the concept to me:

> The Bible says that we have to be a clean people, and that means morally clean. How can you be if you've got someone unclean in your midst? If, for example, someone is committing adultery, he is really breaking God's law because he shouldn't commit adultery; therefore if that practice continues, he has gone outside the rule of law. If he won't come back and repent, then we say to him, 'Right, the door is shut, you can't come back until you put the matters right'. Now if he is disfellow-shipped, he is invited to come to the meetings, not to converse with people because he is no longer a brother, and he may try to persuade others to go his way if he is still weak, and if he needs some help with his personal matters he may approach the elders. He is treated as an outcast and therefore we would not seek conversation with him. So disfellowshipping is like a cutting off from association.

Although disfellowshipped individuals are still free to attend Kingdom Hall meetings, it seems strange that they should choose to do so, since they are shunned by the congregation. The 'cutting off' described by the elder is not manifest spatially, but communication is limited if not non-existent. It seems that the purpose of shunning is to ensure that the exclusivity of the community is preserved. This confirms Douglas's argument that those who exist on the boundaries (or, in this case, cross them) are treated as peripheral, since they are emanating danger to others. Disfellowshipping is the ultimate means of ridding the congregation of pollution, and it is very likely that, for disfellowshipped individuals who continue to attend meetings, shunning will induce feelings of guilt and shame. Such feelings are considered an important requisite for the eventual reinstatement of the offender. Devotees believe strongly in penitence as well as purity, and they triumph at the prospect of reconciliation with their brothers and sisters who have been excluded. Though disfellowshipping can in no way be regarded as inexorable, it is considered necessary not only for the sake of protecting the sanctity of the community but also in order that the sinner may eventually be redeemed. This scenario of a hopeful return was explained by the elder in the following way:

> The disfellowshipping is to make the person see the seriousness of their sin, show them what there is outside and what they've lost inside and make them want to come back. Like Jesus said, he came to find the lost sheep of the house of Israel, he didn't worry about the flock, he said, 'Hey you, little lamb, come back'. The prodigal son is a situation where the son went off to riotous living, but while he was there feeding on the pigswill, he started thinking about home – what he'd left, what he'd lost, the depravity he'd come to – he was filthy, he was dirty, he realised that he'd made a mistake, so he decided to go back and ask for his father's forgiveness, and, when the father could see that he'd gone back with a changed attitude, a repentant attitude, he welcomed him. Now we treat them just the same. If someone comes knocking at the door, so to speak, we watch him for a while as he comes to the meetings, humbly and quietly. We find out that he really is repentant, he asks for forgiveness, the elders meet with him and find out that it's from the heart and we say, 'Right, we withdraw the disfellowship' and we announce from the platform that he's now back again.

The combination of appeal for forgiveness, attendance at meetings, Bible study and visits from congregational elders all serve to reinstate the 'sheep that has been lost'. At this point, relations with the other brothers and sisters are once again unfettered as the reinstated member is free to converse with other members and to knock on doors preaching the good news. The acts of shunning, disqualification from ministry work and a public announcement from the platform that the person has been disfellowshipped show that, while penitence is considered an important requisite for forgiveness, absolution from sin is not in any way regarded as a sacrament or even a form of spiritual healing. Rather, it is something that must be earned as part of the formal procedure for reinstatement. Whether the offender is counselled for a minor misdemeanour or disfellowshipped for serious wrongdoing, the rational Watch Tower protocol enables the elders to keep a tight rein over the conduct of those for whose spiritual welfare they are responsible. In the same way that bureaucrats gain promotion on the basis of their administrative training and experience, elders earn their positions from their years of dedication and number of hours served in ministry. This ensures that the duties of an elder are subject to impersonal regulation rather than personal behest. When counselling or disfellow-shipping dissident members, elders must follow the official procedures laid down by the Governing Body, which means that they can never be appeased by charisma and are certainly not amenable to bribes. This shows how the rational criteria that are used to determine the Witnesses' suitability for entry to the organisation apply also to their expulsion.[27]

These procedures reflect a community that operates on the basis of what Weber called 'technical reason'. Weber argued that, in the post-industrial period, Western societies had become governed by rules and regulations deriving from legal-rational authority, and he regarded these as an important feature of modernity (Weber 1922).[28] However, despite the fact that some devotees find the Society's demand for loyalty difficult to satisfy, it would be a mistake to suggest that they find these boundaries oppressive. Far from being a source of resentment, the rational-authoritarian nature of the movement seems to produce both the conformity and the strong feeling of unity that enable it to function. The unambiguous definitions of right and wrong that are internalised and acted upon on a day-to-day basis confirm the unquestionable nature of Watch Tower beliefs. Notwithstanding the apparent tension between faith on the one hand and reason on the other, the Witnesses are remarkably successful in utilising rational procedures for their ultimately religious ends. Biblical references confirm the inevitability of an apocalyptic finale and play a key role in validating beliefs. Studying textual material requires skills of literacy, reason and learning by rote. The Witnesses' initiation of new recruits, their criteria for good practice, their meticulous collation of a huge range of statistical data on ministry and recruitment and their strategies for averting risk confirm an indubitable dependency on modern rational principles. This suggests that Watch Tower evangelism succeeds *because of* modernity. In other words, the modernity the Witnesses oppose is the modernity they also mimic. In the next chapter, I consider how the Witnesses use other modern resources to promote their millenarian message.

5   Returning to Eden

In Chapter 2, I argued that the Witnesses' view of the cosmos and sense of spiritual mission puts them in tension with secular society. Their world-renouncing beliefs mean that they are at once abandoned by modernity, yet they succeed by offering an affective bond to those who are rejected, isolated, disillusioned or unfulfilled. The Witnesses recruit by offering hope, self-confidence, support and direction to those who are prepared to listen to their message. In this chapter, I examine some of the cultural dynamics that play a part in sustaining membership and validating the Witnesses' *Weltanschauung*. This requires an understanding of the world as the Witnesses themselves see it and an examination of their future vision.

This too will pass away

The Mormons, the Seventh-Day Adventists and the Witnesses all belong to movements that espouse remarkably similar millenarian doctrines. All three communities are renowned for their unequivocal evangelistic messages concerning the end of time, and all see their mission as an essential part of the fulfilment of biblical prophecy. Although the belief in the Second Coming of Christ is steeped in the Judaeo-Christian tradition, orthodox Christianity has very little to say about how the event will occur, or when it is likely to happen. Consequently, those who belong to established churches and denominations are generally much less vociferous in their eschatological ministry than are world-renouncing sectarians. Indeed, one of the main sources of tension between Christian millenarians and modern secular society is the expectation of things to come. Like the Witnesses, Mormons believe that their proselytising efforts are essential for the inauguration of the Messianic Age. The gathering of the people of Israel from other nations, the return of the Jews from Jerusalem and the restoration of the lost tribes prophesied in Isaiah 2: 2–3 will, according to the Mormons, be brought about by their current worldwide missionary activities, after which Christ will return in glory and exact vengeance on the wicked. Similarly, the Seventh-Day Adventists believe that Christ's Second Coming will consign the unbelieving to destruction on earth, while the righteous will be taken up to heaven. The Adventists predict the annihilation of Satan and the subsequent transformation of the earth into a place of eternal bliss.

These millenarian prophecies are based on a salvation narrative of past, present and future. According to the Watch Tower Society, human misery was triggered long ago when Adam and Eve ate of the forbidden fruit. This literal interpretation of the Book of Genesis enables the Witnesses to explain every kind of human experience in an unambiguous fashion. Though they acknowledge that life can bring happiness as well as sadness, the success of their ministry lies in their ability to persuade the rest of humanity that good fortune is arbitrary and shortlived. Biblical mythology thus pervades the Witnesses' thoughts and provides them with an explanation for why life does not always run smoothly, as Margaret explained:

> What you've got to remember is that the world is imperfect and we're imperfect, because Jehovah never intended it to be like this. We've inherited our imperfection from Adam and Eve. Jehovah wanted us all to be happy, but we decided to be disobedient and we'll never be truly happy until he steps in and we go back to what he wants it to be like.

Margaret's analysis of life's struggles derives from her concept of original sin that the Witnesses believe we have all inherited from our ancestral parents. This doctrine is an essential part of all Christian theology; but, unlike those who follow more orthodox Christian teachings, the Witnesses still accept the Genesis story as a factual event rather than a myth which is intended to introduce humankind to a creator God and/or to the idea that God gives us free will. The Witnesses' acceptance of the Fall as a literal story is an important part of the foundation on which their millenarian tenets are built. As I have argued elsewhere, the Society's uniform literal beliefs help cement the Witnesses into a worldwide community. Moreover, substantive doctrines such as these enhance the authenticity of the belief system as a whole, and, since Watch Tower evangelism is an essentially rational exercise, these doctrines help devotees to achieve a sense of coherence and purpose justifying their ultimate religious ends. The success of the Society in promoting its millenarian message depends mainly on whether the prospective convert is willing to accept its account of sin and salvation. In other words, people must be ready to listen to the Witnesses' version of the end of the world and share their hope for the future:

> No other generation has heard so much talk about the end of the world . . . Has a world ever ended before? Yes, a world did end. Consider the world that became very wicked in the days of Noah. The Bible explains: 'The world of that time suffered destruction when it was deluged with water.' The Bible also says '[God] did not hold back from punishing an ancient world, but kept Noah, a preacher of righteousness, safe with seven others when he brought a deluge upon a world of ungodly

people.' – 2 Peter 2: 5; 3: 6 . . . So we need to learn God's will and do it. Then we can survive this world's end to enjoy eternally the blessings of God's new world.

(Watch Tower Bible and Tract Society of Pennsylvania 1992b: 1–6)

Although this publication revolves around the story of the flood in Genesis, the underlying message is that God will punish all sin, whenever it takes place. Witnesses throughout the world make reference to people's wrongdoing – a message that is premised on inherent wickedness, but which always ends on an optimistic note. Like the other millenarian movements mentioned above, the Watch Tower organisation promises eternal salvation to those who are prepared to lament their sins, preach the good news and wait patiently for Jehovah's intervention. The idea that the renunciation of wickedness can help to win everlasting life is part and parcel of the Witnesses' appeal to human logic. As I have already shown, Watch Tower evangelists depend on rational explanations of human frailty (mainly through the usage of biblical texts and the Society's own published literature) in order to entice new members. Tom, a former member of the organisation, described the appeal of the Witnesses' theology as follows:

> This guy came to the door and he spoke about a time of peace on earth and it appealed to me. I had a wife and a child and for the first time in my life I was actually thinking about other people. I still had a lot of problems in my life. I was drinking a lot, I was gambling and I was very violent. I was violent in my imagination in the sense that I was a strong supporter of the republican cause, and it had been getting me into trouble. But then I began to change and see that God had a purpose for the earth and that he was going to bring an end to all the world's injustices. Everything this guy said was in the Bible and he persuaded me that his organisation was the only place to be, because soon Armageddon was coming.

Tom's comments clearly confirm that he was discontented with his life at the time the evangelist called on him. Tom provided me with examples of how the evangelist's references to the Books of Genesis, Daniel and Revelation seemed to persuade him that human weakness would soon be transformed into perfection – a message that he claimed enabled him to see his life through a different perspective. Tom's story demonstrates the skill with which the Witnesses are able to use the salvation narrative of past, present and future to construct a seductive message. Tom went on to explain how the evangelist's millenarian message combined with the subsequent Christian fellowship at the Kingdom Hall were to have a profound impact on his life for the next fourteen years. The pursuit of an ultimate religious goal – namely, to inaugurate the post-Armageddon Kingdom – is one of the most powerful mechanisms which the Society has at its disposal for strengthening the ties of its members. But this is not all. Tom's testimony also tells us something about his relationship with the world at the time of his conversion. The promise of the end of all wickedness seemed to provide him with spiritual ammunition with which he could defeat those who had previously done him harm. It would appear that Watch Tower millenarianism is at its most persuasive when there are a series of negative forces at work in the lives of individuals at the time they came in contact with the movement – a point I have already made as part of my discussion of the conversion process.

Although the Witnesses' utopian vision can appeal to people like Tom who are experiencing personal difficulties, it also has a tacit role to play in enabling people to cope with some of the insecurities and uncertainties that modern life presents. This is particularly true for those who are inclined towards pessimism. Indeed, the Witnesses' vision of the future reinforces the pessimistic orientation in its presentation as the perfect antidote to the worst conditions of modern secular society. This contrast of repugnance and splendour is a dominant feature of Watch Tower theology, and is probably most likely to influence those who have an uncertain view of the world in which we live. This became apparent in an interview with Kelly and her non-Witness husband, Steve, who worked as a paramedic. Kelly explained:

> As the scriptures say, we obey God as our ruler rather than man. There's only one government that the Bible talks about and that's the heavenly government. I worry about my child because it's hard for kids these days, having a *supposedly* good time going to nightclubs when these young girls dress up in really short skirts. I mean, they're asking for trouble . . . and then they go off with young lads and they're jumping into bed and things. We really do feel that things are getting worse in the world. This country is on a par with America for its sex and its crime and its violence and its drugs . . . all the other prophecies in the Bible have happened; so we feel the urgency of Armageddon. I know it's hard for a lot of people to believe there's anything better, but you just have to keep your faith. Does living for ever not appeal to you without the fear of violence?

Clearly agitated by his wife's comments, Steve retorted:

> You see, I don't agree with her! I believe that life's good . . . 99.9 per cent of the population of the world and what goes on in the world is good. You see, I'm an optimist. I *could* look at the world in a bad light if I wanted to. It's like football hooliganism, you get fifty thousand people at Old Trafford on a Saturday afternoon, and about *five* of them will get into trouble and fight; now what percentage is that?! It's only about 0.1 per cent, and that's what Friday and Saturday night in town is like. Ninety-nine point nine per cent of the people are having a good time.

People are basically good; but what percentage of these people end up in bed together? About one per cent! When these girls go out in short skirts showing everything they've got, it's just the way things are. It doesn't mean they're bad people or that they're looking for anything in particular; but when I talk to these people on a Friday and Saturday night – and I do meet a lot of them – more often than not, they're nice people. There's optimism and there's pessimism, and the Witnesses are pessimistic. I see people using drugs and I see fights and domestic disputes and all sorts, and I could easily come home from work and think, 'It's terrible out there', but I don't!

This heated dialogue demonstrates two contrasting versions of reality. Steve explained how his atheistic belief system prevented him from accepting the Witnesses' vision of the Last Days or their doctrines of life after death. His optimistic view of secular society enabled him to regard scantily dressed teenage girls entering nightclubs as young people in pursuit of fun. Steve believed that, although crime existed, it was carried out by only a small number of wayward individuals who he later suggested would be best incarcerated. Notwithstanding this, his secular outlook allowed him to embrace the modern world in positive terms, despite its discontents. Like most other secular thinkers, Steve believed that life should be lived to the full because there was nothing after death. Kelly's perspective, on the other hand, is based on the view that the world has deteriorated *because* it has become secular. She was emphatic in her belief that young people who entered nightclubs had questionable motives and that such places were reprehensible. She expressed grave concerns about the influences to which her twelve-year-old daughter could later be exposed and hoped earnestly for the arrival of Armageddon before it all happened. As far as Kelly was concerned, whatever small concessions the world could offer – success in careers, material wealth or a happy marriage – real contentment could only be achieved and sustained in the Eden-like realm of Jehovah's New Kingdom. For Kelly and her co-believers, Armageddon is the beginning of the end of risk and uncertainty. It marks the final stage of an ongoing battle that will be resolved once and for all by supernatural forces. The millenarian tenets of the Society are thus based on an ancient mythology which devotees claim represents the imperishable word of God. The Watch Tower vision of Jehovah's victory assumes a deeply cynical view of the world in its past and present forms – a view which puts its adherents in tension with those who do not share their faith.

Demonising the world

Although the Witnesses are by no means the only millenarians to believe in the dualistic entities of good and evil,[1] they have a somewhat distinctive way of using recent historical events to undermine their opponents and propound their religious convictions. One of the most interesting examples of this is the Society's frequent reference to the persecution of its members in the Nazi concentration camps during the Third Reich. The suffering and martyrdom that took place throughout this period serve as an example to contemporary Witnesses of how 'the truth' cannot, under any circumstances, be compromised. This is reflected in their strict neutrality and adherence to pacifism in Germany in the 1930s and 1940s – an issue that has been researched in some detail by historian Christine King. King argues that, of all sectarians under the dictatorship of the Nazis (for whom neutrality was not acceptable), the Witnesses adopted the most intransigent line in making clear to all concerned that, while they would do no harm to anyone, their allegiance could only be to Jehovah-God (King 1982). King goes on to describe the persecution which they endured as a result of this declaration.[2] This involved imprisonment, torture, the separation of parents and children, transportation to concentration camps and, ultimately, execution:

> By 1936 the police were devoting an inordinate amount of time to the pursuit of Witnesses and the courts were soon to become so choked with cases against them that they were either tried, *en bloc*, by special courts, or detained without trial. By 1935 there were so many Witnesses in camps that they constituted, for administrative purposes, a separate category. In 1933 there were twenty thousand Witnesses in Germany; by 1945 ten thousand had been imprisoned and some four to five thousand executed. The relative scale of this operation can only be compared to the war against the Jews.
>
> (132)

King documents the Witnesses' bravery in stepping up their work as the pressure of the Nazis increased against them. This included door-to-door preaching and delivering vast amounts of smuggled Watch Tower literature through letterboxes. The fact that the Witnesses heightened their campaign at the very time when several thousands of their brothers and sisters were a special target for the brutality of the Nazis is no small indicator of their millenarian conviction. King argues not only that they were unwilling to compromise but that they were unable to do so without undermining the authority of their Governing Body. For them, serving in the army or saluting Hitler would have meant acknowledging that the claims of this world were dominant over the will of Jehovah, and this was tantamount to appeasing Satan.

Stories of eschatological battles with authorities in Eastern Europe, Germany and Africa, in which martyrdom was allegedly most common in the 1930s and 1940s feature regularly in Watch Tower literature. The Witnesses literalise and intensify their beliefs by demonising their enemies, as exemplified in the following article written by a group of alleged Holocaust survivors:

> They shot Brother Dickmann and told us that we would all be shot if we didn't sign the declaration renouncing our faith. We would be taken to the sandpit thirty or forty at a time, and they would shoot us all. Next day, the SS brought each of us a note to sign or else be shot. You should have seen their long faces when they went away without a single signature. They had hoped to frighten us with the public execution. But we had more fear of displeasing Jehovah than of their bullets. They did not shoot any more of us publicly.
>
> (Watch Tower Bible and Tract Society of Pennsylvania 1993a: 6)

Although there is no way of knowing the extent to which poetic licence is at work here, such stories reach a worldwide audience of over six million members in what constitutes obligatory reading material. It is a sociological axiom that one of the optimal conditions under which world-renouncing movements thrive is persecution. All the Witnesses with whom I have ever spoken hold the view that the suffering endured by their ancestral brothers and sisters adds weight to the belief that those who carry their crosses like Jesus will be rewarded with eternal salvation. Physical persecution is seen as Satan's way of turning individuals against Jehovah, and, like many other aspects of their lives, the Witnesses' experiences of it are dealt with by reference to scriptural texts that provide an explanation of why it occurs. The promise of a Messianic Age for those who are faithful symbolises the prevalence of good over evil. Separation is a key theme in Watch Tower literature and is regarded as an essential requisite for salvation:

> There are also other significant events that Jesus prominently associated with the conclusion of the system of things. One of these is the separation of the 'sons of the kingdom' from the 'sons of the wicked one.' Jesus spoke of this in his parable about a wheat field that an enemy oversowed with weeds. The 'wheat' in his illustration represents true anointed Christians. The 'weeds' are imitation Christians. In the conclusion of the system of things the 'weeds' – those who profess to be Christians but who prove themselves 'sons of the wicked one' because they cling to the world of which the Devil is ruler – are separated from the 'sons of [God's] kingdom' and marked for destruction. (Matt. 13: 36–43)
>
> (Watch Tower Bible and Tract Society of Pennsylvania 1983b: 179–80)

The passage goes on to describe the defilement of the clergy of Christendom *vis-à-vis* the integrity of Witnesses. Anyone fearing or doubting Watch Tower teachings is reminded of Satan's power to corrupt the faithful; hence, life is portrayed as a cosmic struggle in which siding with good forces will secure a place in the New Kingdom. By contrast, Christian clergy support the forces of evil – a belief that acts as a closed system of legitimation, affirming the boundaries between the Witnesses and the demonic world, and providing the ultimate mechanism for dealing with both internal and external conflict.

Watch Tower literature is riddled with text, images and captions all condemning Christendom for idolatrous worship, false teaching and the infliction of suffering and torture of the worst imaginable kind. To take only two of countless numbers of tracts about the role of Satan as the guiding force of all other Christian faiths, we read:

> Thus, by what they have taught and what they have done, the religions of Christendom have demonstrated that their claim of believing in the Bible and of being God-fearing and Christian is a lie. They have betrayed God and the Bible. In doing so, they have disgusted millions of people and caused them to turn away from belief in a Supreme Being.
> (Watch Tower Bible and Tract Society of Pennsylvania 1993b: 19)

> Satan has used verbal and physical persecution to turn individuals away from true worship. But he has also employed more subtle means – cunning acts and sly devices. He has cleverly kept a large proportion of mankind in darkness by means of false religion, letting them think, if they so desire, that they are serving God. Lacking a genuine love for truth, they may be attracted by mystical and emotional religious services or be impressed by powerful works. (2 Thess. 2: 9, 10)
> (Watch Tower Bible and Tract Society of Pennsylvania 1983b: 64)

Conflict between the Watch Tower Society and Christendom is the result of two deeply opposed systems of belief, both of which are vying for the monopoly of divine truth.[3] Evil can be averted only by self-abnegation as demonstrated in the act of religious conversion and the heroic sacrifices of the Witnesses' predecessors. However, the Society's accusations of heresy act also as a means of control. As with many systems of belief, fear of destruction looms large among communities with a small membership. Without the ability to discredit other religious movements, such communities might fall apart. The Witnesses have thus been successful in dealing with hostility from orthodox churches by adopting a series of offensive rather than defensive strategies, including undermining the symbols of other religions and desacralising their rituals. Heroic mythology is an important part of the Witnesses' worldview, and they use these ideas to confront the evils of injustice and inequality that the modern world has failed to eradicate. The solemnity with which the Witnesses narrate the heroic actions of their ancestors echoes the movement's disillusionment with modern secular society. As far as devotees are concerned, heroism signifies victory over the forces of evil, danger or any other undesirable entity that poses a threat to salvation. But heroic acts neither begin nor end with martyrdom.

Belief systems which embrace the notion of evil remind their adherents that self-abnegation is part of carrying one's cross. The Witnesses show others that they are willing to do this by renouncing their allegiance with the world.

The Witnesses' refusal to support worldly causes is also exemplified in their failure to revere secular symbols. In the same way that they refused to salute Hitler in the Third Reich, the Witnesses continue to abstain from saluting flags – an activity which they regard as a form of idolatrous worship. This belief is taken from Exodus 20: 4 which reads, 'Thou shalt not make unto thee any graven image, or any likeness of any thing that is in heaven above, or that is in the earth beneath, or that is in the water under the earth'. The Witnesses also cite examples such as Mordecai, who refused to bow down to Haman, contrary to the authoritarian rule of the land (Esther 3: 2) and Shadrach, Meshach and Abednego, who were cast into a fiery furnace for refusing to revere a golden image (Daniel 3: 10–30). Moreover, their refusal to salute national flags led them into a considerable amount of legal trouble in the United States in the 1930s and early 1940s, when the practice was compulsory in many state schools during assemblies. Inevitably, failing to honour the flag posed difficulties for Witness children who found themselves in the unenviable position of wanting to defy neither their teachers nor their parents. Historian Jerry Bergman documents the traumatic experiences of children as young as seven who refused to salute the flag. Schools' reactions included public criticism of the child's beliefs, humiliation in front of the whole class, corporal punishment, physical coercion of children to salute the flag and referring children to reform schools. Bergman argues that most children still found the ritual traumatic, even when pressure to participate was relaxed (Bergman 1987: 179–81).[4]

If Witness children experienced persecution for their resistance to the flag salute in the USA, so too did older members. Bergman records how the Witnesses' opposition to the flag salute seems to be the chief reason for their persecution in several states, which caused them to be mobbed, shot, tarred and feathered and driven out of their neighbourhoods. It was not until 1943 that the Supreme Court ruled that flag saluting was to be optional:

> The flag salute cases involved a long and bitter struggle, but one which culminated in a decision giving concrete meaning to the Pledge of Allegiance itself. These cases and others that the JWs have taken to the Supreme Court are now heralded as establishing important precedents which preserve the freedoms of speech, press, and worship for all Americans. The bitter and eventful history of conflict between religious minority groups and the state is centuries old and is not yet over, even in the United States. The flag salute has been only one of many problems which have surfaced in this conflict, but it touches on the very heart of religious worship.
>
> (Bergman 1987: 192)

Like most other aspects of Watch Tower theology, the Witnesses' position today concerning saluting flags has not changed. Elders and other members with whom I spoke told me that, on the odd occasions that they had attended concerts or school pantomimes at which the National Anthem was sung, they refused to partake either by singing or standing. While one might think that this would be far from easy in public places where there might be hundreds of people, the Witnesses gather inspiration from the far greater price paid by their ancestors and from their unquestionable belief that patriotic behaviour is offensive to God. Moreover, their knowledge of the widespread suffering and persecution of their predecessors would make any modern-day violation of these principles by contemporary devotees little less than sacrilege of the most unforgivable kind.

The ultimate act of devotion for the Witnesses is, of course, their refusal to receive blood. As I have already explained, the Witnesses maintain that blood transfusions violate Jehovah's law, and they interpret Psalm 16, Leviticus 17: 11–12, Deuteronomy 12: 27, 1 Chronicles 11: 17–19 and Acts 15: 19–21 to mean that blood should not be taken into the body in any way. The Society teaches that, if devotees are sincere in their convictions, then their refusal to receive blood into their bodies is a small enough price to pay for everlasting life. The Witnesses believe that, since the end of the world is imminent, their dying now will secure their entry into the New Kingdom.[5] It would appear that, by offering their lives for a deeply held religious principle, they are able to prove to each other that they can combat wrong-doing in the same way as their forefathers in the Nazi concentration camps. Heroism of this kind accentuates the Witnesses' idealism and strengthens their conviction.

These examples convey how the Watch Tower organisation demonises all outside forces that threaten its doctrines, and this helps to reinforce its exclusivity. Knowledge of the history of persecution exists in the conscious-ness of the Witnesses, reminding them that the world is their enemy. Conventional Christianity, particularly Roman Catholicism, is the 'Beast' *par excellence*. This mythology helps them to remember that the warring forces of good and evil are still battling it out, and that Jehovah's law must be placed before that of the secular state. By emphasising the prevalence of evil outside the Kingdom Hall, the Witnesses exalt their own harmonious community and commend those who have already died for it. Heroic self-sacrifice and the resistance of evil thus affirm the boundaries between the inside world of safety and the outside world of risk.

The symbolic construction of millenarianism

Conquering evil is the one theme that locates the Witnesses' experiences into a framework of order and meaning. Over and above their involvement in public events such as Kingdom Hall meetings and annual conventions, the Witnesses conceptualise their relationship with the world by evoking symbols such as artefacts, modes of dress, speech patterns, ceremonial rites, purity codes and bodily expression, all of which are an important part of membership. Though I have already discussed some of these, the Watch Tower symbols to which I will refer here include visual images, metaphor and linguistic exchanges between devotees themselves. The representations in the Society's published materials suggest that the world is about to undergo a dramatic transformation.

The Witnesses use language and imagery to construct social boundaries, and, as I have shown above, these boundaries accentuate difference between members and non-members. Symbols enable devotees to draw around themselves a kind of mental map to affirm who belongs to the community and who does not. Since symbolic representations help to reinforce millenarian beliefs and carry with them a message of hope for the future, they are both a repository of meaning and a frame of reference for the Witnesses' identity. These images are used in most of the Society's literature to support the theology. In addition to the photographs of Watch Tower evangelists actively announcing Jehovah's Kingdom which I described earlier, every copy of *The Watchtower* and *Awake!* and nearly every tract and hardback publication shows positive pictorial images of Witnesses in a variety of forms. Other pictures are fictitious (sketched by artists), portraying visions of the beautiful world of post-Armageddon and characters from the Bible for the illustration of parables. Whether the pictures are real or drawn, the images are always idealistic and utopian. Deliriously happy faces with surrounding emerald green slopes, clear blue skies and bright sunshine set the scene in the delineation of the world of Jehovah's Witnesses. All drawings are presented in vivid colour and are designed to present the theology in the most positive visual form. Some pictures show devotees in the New Kingdom reunited with their deceased loved ones, while others portray animals such as lions and tigers (presumably once wild and ferocious) at play, at rest, or being caressed by children. Future-oriented symbolism reminds Witnesses everywhere of their millenarian vision and impresses upon them the need to minister to others. This exaggerated version of contentment conveys a subtle but powerful message to all who peruse the literature – that infinite happiness, justice and peace can be achieved through membership of the Watch Tower organisation.

If positive images promote millenarian doctrines, negative ones warn of the presence of evil in the world. The same publications are filled with pictures of people being murdered, thieves breaking into houses, heretics worshipping idols and couples acting promiscuously – all of which show life outside the organisation as debased and riddled with moral danger. Unlike the pictures of millenarian bliss, these images are presented in dark colour and portray characters with unattractive features. This contrast of salvation on the inside and risk on the outside implies not only that there can be nothing in between the two systems but that morality cannot exist beyond the Watch Tower community. More importantly, this portrayal of sin contrasts sharply with millenarian idealism, emphasising the doctrine of salvation. These images which contrast post-Armageddon and sin help to provide for the Witnesses the authenticity for which modernity theorists tell us people yearn in a fast-changing world. This echoes Hall's analysis of the representations deployed by patriots in the construction of national identities (Hall 1992). Like nationalism, millenarianism is dependent on a narrative that emphasises *origin, continuity* and *timelessness* – all of which are essential features of the *imagined community*.[6] Since it would be impossible for all the Witnesses in the world to know each other (as it would all people in a nation), the Watch Tower community can only be imagined. Imagery enables the Society to romanticise the evangelistic activities of Witnesses everywhere, and at the same time offer its devotees a glimpse of what life will be like when the present world no longer exists. The uniformity with which these symbols are presented adds to the authenticity of the community in much the same way as national emblems authenticate patriotism.

It could also be argued that the Witnesses' romantic vision of the future is a response to one of the most widely documented features of modernity; namely, *disenchantment*. Weber's theme of the ever-increasing rationalisation of the modern world was based on the more general argument that the Enlightenment failed to produce the happiness for which people had hoped. The application of instrumental reason robbed the world of mystery and excitement, and this led to the increasingly pessimistic view that the costs of modern civilisation outweighed the benefits. In his analysis of cultural change since this period, sociologist Robert Bocock argues:

> The project, set in motion by the Enlightenment, of increasing progress, wealth and happiness through the application of science and technology, first to industry and then to social life as a whole, and the weakening of the hold of custom, magic, superstition and other supernatural taboos over which the *philosophes* rejoiced, has been put in question. In the traditional culture of Europe before the Protestant Reformation, religion provided the moral framework for everyone. Everyday life was punctuated by saint's days, fairs, pilgrimages, festivals, seasons of feasting, atonement and celebration. The culture of ordinary people was saturated with folk customs, magical spells, rituals and religious occasions. Springs and wells provided healing waters, the relics of saints offered safe journeys or protection to relatives and friends.
>
> (Bocock 1992: 261)

If Bocock's analysis is correct, utopian thinking can be seen as a reaction to the demystification of culture (part of what modernity theorists suggest has given rise to secularisation) which has existed in various forms since the Reformation. In this sense, utopian expression is a cultural resource used by the Witnesses to counter the soullessness of the modern rational world. But this poses a paradox. I have already shown how, although Watch Tower literature is full of utopian imagery, the Witnesses belong to a movement that promotes calculable doctrines and recruits prospective members by essentially rational means. This combination of romantic idealism and rational calculation adds to the Witnesses' distinctiveness. Could it be, therefore, that rationalism and idealism are not necessarily as incompatible as the modernity literature (particularly that which addresses the post-Enlightenment period) suggests? The simultaneous usage of the rational and the romantic has greatly contributed to the success of the Watch Tower Society since both resources allow the Witnesses to appeal to emotions as well as intellect. Thus, it should come as no surprise that, in their visual presentations of the post-Armageddon world, they make little use of mystical imagery. Though they are utopian, Watch Tower tracts do not produce transcendental symbols such as angels, heaven, mist or haloes. Instead, they show scenes of lush valleys and flowing streams.[7] These images portray an *earthly* rather than a mystical afterlife, illustrating the Witnesses' belief that the overwhelming majority of the faithful will return to Eden – the place that God originally created for humankind. They support this with scriptural references such as Daniel 7: 13 which they claim foretells the eternal worship of Jehovah on paradise earth. The usage of scripture to substantiate a millenarian vision of the future seems to suggest that, like the rationalists of the eighteenth century who continued to believe in God, Witnesses synthesise faith and reason. Bland though they might seem compared with mystical representations, illustrations of earthly beauty allow the New Kingdom to be imagined without much difficulty. The Witnesses' association of a beautiful landscape with eternal peace exemplifies their preoccupation with tranquillity; and yet they are able only to offer a glimpse of what they imagine life to be like in the future.

In addition to pictorial representations, metaphor, allegory and analogy are also part of Watch Tower symbolism. These linguistic props help to create an impression of an authentic community united in Brotherhood, and play a subtle role in the Witnesses' evangelistic mission. Sociolinguists George Lakoff and Mark Johnson argue that everyday language is full of metaphors which give meaning to the world. Metaphors deepen an experience by imbuing it with all the connotations of the concept with which it is compared. For example, when we talk of the snow being a blanket, we view it as a cover as well as infuse it with associated feelings of warmth and softness. Metaphors are powerful because of the inferences that are drawn from them and the actions that may be sanctioned as a result (Lakoff and Johnson 1980). Metaphors and allegories are clearly part of the Witnesses' *Weltanschauung*. The most pervasive metaphor is, of course, *The Watchtower*, which provides a caption for published literature as well as the official name of the organisation. The term is central to millenarian ideology and prompts devotees to be both vigilant and active; and yet little is written explicitly about this concept. Nevertheless, the Witnesses' general usage of metaphor, allegory and analogy is another means of reaffirming conviction. The following passage provides a good example:

> Sometimes a young person may say that he or she associates with another of questionable ways and reputation so as to help that one. To want to help others is a fine thing. But if you go along with them in their selfish pleasures, how much help are you giving them? For example, if you saw a child in a mud puddle, would you take some soap out into the puddle and try to clean the child with it? You would only get yourself dirty as a result. You would first have to try to encourage the child to come out of the mud puddle before you could hope to do anything about cleaning him up at close range. Actually, to accept a person with bad habits as a close associate will often have a bad effect on that person (as well as on yourself). Why? Because it may encourage him to keep on in the same way, feeling that he can always rely on your backing him up. Wouldn't it be of far greater help to limit your association to times when you can really aid the person by pointing out good counsel and by inviting him to accompany you to places where that counsel is explained?
>
> (Watch Tower Bible and Tract Society of Pennsylvania
> 1976: 64–5)

Other metaphors and analogies could have been used to illustrate the Witnesses' desire to purify the impure, but what is particularly interesting about the analogy of the mud puddle is the way in which it is used to warn against *self*-contamination. Equally important is the suggestion that 'good counsel' and 'places of good counsel' can be provided by Jehovah's Witnesses. The scenario of the casualty of evil being delivered to salvation by the righteous illustrates to devotees the need to seek friendship of only those already in 'the truth', or prospective recruits who are willing to be cleansed.

Metaphor plays a key role not only in the Witnesses' written publications, but also in their verbal utterances. In one interview, an elder used metaphor to illustrate how people who join the community 'grow' at different rates and how they vary in their response to Watch Tower teachings. New recruits were equated with horses being drawn to water, trees bearing fruit and athletes preparing for a race. Devotees use figurative speech interchangeably with biblical parables both to win converts and to renounce the world outside. Such language is used frequently by speakers from the platform at the Kingdom Hall. Indeed, among the titles of the sermons for the Annual District Convention held in the summer of 1997 were 'Walking by faith, not by sight', 'Considering the daily text builds faith', 'Put up a hard fight for the faith' and 'Keep your eye simple'. All the speakers who delivered these sermons made constant use of metaphor and aphorism to impart their messages. Romantic concepts thus pervade the Watch Tower community.

The Witnesses identify themselves with 'the New World' as opposed to secular society, with which they claim they have little affinity. Not surprisingly, they also use certain concepts to emphasise differences between themselves and those who do not share their beliefs. Sprague (1946) examines some of the various contexts in which these concepts are used:

> 'worldly' authorities are contrasted with the Bible; the 'worldly employ-ment' of brethren is contrasted with the life of a pioneer in full-time Kingdom service; attendance at motion picture theatres and the like are described as a stepping outside of the Lord's organization and into the world, and such worldly pleasures are contrasted with the joys of serving the Lord on witnessing expeditions. In fact, applying a procedure analogous to a Paretian residue-derivation analysis, we may recognize in the witnesses a tendency to organize their experience in terms of dichotomies of contrasting 'principles,' of which tendency the two contrasting 'worlds' constitute but a single manifestation . . . Each set of contrasting concepts differs from the others in emphasis and in the contexts to which it is appropriate. Thus, where the emphasis is on individuals, especially as they reveal themselves by their reaction to the Kingdom message, we have the contrast between 'goats' and 'sheep,' 'persons of good will,' or 'Jonadabs'; or between 'religionists' or 'Devil-worshippers' and 'persons devoted to the truth' or 'followers of Christ Jesus.' Where the emphasis is on systems of belief and practice, we have the important contrast between 'religion' and the 'truth,' closely associated with which is the characteristic contrast between the 'word,' 'teachings,' or 'authority' of God and those of 'imperfect men.'
>
> (139)

Sprague's commentary on the ways in which devotees use language to demarcate 'the truth' and 'the world' inadvertently draws attention to their ability to romanticise their doctrines. When the Witnesses refer to outsiders as 'goats' and 'devil worshippers', they exaggerate the unworthiness of 'the other' and in so doing, they present their own belief system as harmonious. Concepts like these are used frequently by devotees in their social time spent together as well as at the meetings. By showing a genuine interest in Watch Tower theology and never criticising it, I was invited to a country pub by some members of the congregation on two or three occasions. It was here that I came to appreciate the value of participant observation. Conversation often centred on recent articles in *The Watchtower*, sermons at meetings and experiences on the door-to-door visits. References to 'the world', 'the Kingdom', 'the ministry', 'Armageddon' and 'the truth' were frequently used, as were scriptural quotations. Equally, the terms 'brother' and 'sister' are dominant terms of reference during door-to-door ministry and at the Kingdom Hall. These personal references enhance the authenticity of the community and affirm the boundaries that set it apart. Images, metaphors and verbal exchanges lend themselves to the Witnesses' ultimate objective of preparing for the New Kingdom. Language, visual imagery and metaphor are the tools used by the Witnesses to disseminate their millenarian beliefs. These cultural resources enable the Society to present itself as an authentic community. The creation of authenticity is a response to a disenchanted world in which chivalry is regarded as a thing of the past. The symbolic construction of the perfect community in a world of risk and uncertainty is part of the Society's appeal.

Temporality: apposition or anachronism?

Modernity theorist Peter Berger (1977) argues that one of the most profound and least contentious changes in human experience over the centuries is the way in which time is conceptualised. This has been marked by a shift away from concern with the past and present towards a preoccupation with the future. According to Berger, transformation of time has taken place on three levels. The first of these is what he calls *the level of everyday life*. Here, clocks and wristwatches are used both to arrange and measure the length of all life activities. The second level is *the level of biography*, on which the individual perceives and actively plans his or her life as a 'career'. On the third level, the level of an entire society, national governments and other large-scale institutions construct their long-term plans, examples of which might be 'the transition to communism' or 'the stages of economic growth'. Berger suggests that these three levels of transformation present ways of experiencing time that contrast sharply with those preceding modernity. These *futuristic* ways of conceptualising time are precise, measurable and, in principle, subject to human control. Since time governs the functioning of the whole of modern life from employment to military strategy, it has become something to be mastered. Scientists, intellectuals and technical experts (that is, those who claim to 'know' the future) will make life and death decisions by employing allegedly objective methods. But, above and beyond this, Berger argues that we have become time engineers in the most intimate aspects of our lives such as family planning, guidance counselling and sex therapy (1977: 104–6).

There are, however, issues of a philosophical nature about this modern futurity that Berger brings to our attention. We may, for example, need to weigh our preoccupation with time against the detrimental effects of the pace of modern living on our mental and physical health:

> Futurity means endless striving, restlessness and a mounting incapacity for repose. It is precisely this aspect of modernization that is perceived as dehumanizing in many non-Western cultures. There have also been strong rebellions against it within Western societies – a good deal of both youth culture and counterculture can, I think, be understood as insurrections against the tyranny of modern futurity, not to mention

the current vogue of 'transcendental meditation' and similar mystical aspirations towards a liberating, timeless 'now'.

(ibid.: 105)

Berger provides some interesting ideas that can be used to explain why the Witnesses are the subjects of biblical eschatology rather than futurity. Although the Watch Tower Society must plan future events such as public assemblies and conventions months ahead of schedule, the Witnesses regard time only as a short-term entity. As individuals, they conceptualise everyday life time in much the same way as any other Western citizen, in that they live in accordance with the twenty-four-hour clock, but their belief in the imminence of the end of time as we know it prevents them from making advanced plans for the future. Several long-term members told me how the organisation's prediction of Armageddon in 1975 had profound implications for how they planned their lives. Some made a conscious decision not to have any more children and to cancel all voluntary pension premiums and insurance policies. Others continued to enter into marriage and apply for mortgages, but, since the Society prevented them from thinking that 1976 would arrive, most of these individuals did not expect to see ripe old age or watch their endowments mature. To this day, most Witnesses think along these lines.

The 'striving, restlessness and a mounting incapacity for repose' to which Berger refers are among the more negative features with which people associate futurity. But modernity theorists also claim that people's reluctance to face the future derives from their discontentment with the present and a pessimistic view that things are becoming progressively worse. This pessimism often manifests itself in the form of concern about moral decline and a lamentation that the orderly, peaceful past has gone for ever (Pearson 1983, Sked 1987, Bailey 1988). Nostalgia of this kind often results in moral entrepreneurialism and an attempt to restore tradition.[8] Consequently, Christian fundamentalists engage in political affairs, demanding the 'return' of law and order and the legal condemnation of homosexuality, abortion, pornography and any other activity which they believe undermines the sanctity of the family. In addition to this Beck (1992) and Giddens (1990, 1991) argue that anxiety about the future has been exacerbated in recent decades by the threat of environmental catastrophe on a global scale. But while secular society has jettisoned religious versions of temporality that offer millenarian hope for the future, the Witnesses have clung to their eschatological interpretations of world events. Although nobody with whom I spoke bemoaned the loss of a great golden age (not least because the organisation teaches that Satan has led humankind astray ever since Adam and Eve's expulsion from the Garden of Eden), concern about worsening morality was widespread. Unlike more orthodox Christians, however, the Witnesses are prevented from lobbying their MPs and organising public demonstrations because of their belief that true devotion to God is apolitical. Consequently, they remain deeply pessimistic about the present and about people's ability to bring about future change. Until such time that the world will be transformed by divine intervention, they maintain that the future holds bleak prospects. During the 1980s, Watch Tower evangelists referred frequently to the threat of nuclear war as a means of disseminating their belief in the inevitability of self-destruction and the arrival of the New Kingdom. The Witnesses are thus prevented by their own doctrines from romanticising the past and the present, but they do romanticise the future. In his discussion of movements that work towards the dawning of a New Age, Wallis argues:

> The world-rejecting movement expects that the millennium will shortly commence or that the movement will sweep the world, and, when all have become members or when they are in a majority, or when they have become guides and counsellors to kings and presidents, then a new world-order will begin, a simpler, more loving, more humane and more spiritual order in which the old evils and mistakes will be eradicated, and utopia will have begun.
>
> (Wallis 1984: 9)

Wallis's commentary suggests not only that millenarian movements are romantic in their vision of the future but that they are precise about the conditions that will transform their dreams into reality. These movements are in constant dialogue with time inasmuch as they reflect on past events such as wars, famines and earthquakes in their prediction of the Last Days. It is this temporal view of the cosmos that enables millenarians to sustain their utopian visions. Temporality is therefore crucial to the Witnesses who, in their hunger for Armageddon, use the Book of Revelation to predict the demise of all other religions and worldly institutions. According to the Governing Body, the prophecies in Matthew 24 have all now been fulfilled. Watch Tower literature persistently claims that Armageddon will come within the generation of those who were alive in 1914, when Christ returned invisibly to establish Jehovah's Kingdom. The Witnesses have thus already inaugurated the post-Armageddon period.

This Bible-like scientific approach to prophecy is used to encourage devotees to keep in mind the dawning of the New Kingdom. In a section entitled *Keep Close in Mind Jehovah's Day* from the publication *United in Worship of the Only True God*, they are advised:

> the apostle Peter counseled all who have true faith to 'await and keep close in mind the presence of the day of Jehovah, through which the heavens being on fire will be dissolved and the elements being intensely hot will melt.' The nearness of 'Jehovah's day' is a fact that none of us should ever minimize. The visible governmental heavens and wicked human society are soon to be replaced by 'new heavens and a new earth'

of God's making, and all the 'elements' that go along with the present worldly system – its independent attitude, its immoral and materialistic way of life – will be brought to their end in the destructive heat of 'Jehovah's day.' (2 Pet. 3: 10–13) We need to keep alert, being aware that these world-shattering events could begin at any moment. (Matt. 24: 44)

(Watch Tower Bible and Tract Society of Pennsylvania
1983b: 177–8)

Constant references to keeping alert have a huge impact on the minds of the members. In several of the meetings I attended, articulate speakers delivered sermons urging the congregation to be vigilant and to keep up the good work of door-to-door evangelism; for only when this work is complete will the end arrive. This exemplifies the symbolic influence of Armageddon and the way it impacts on the Witnesses' concept of time. So convinced were devotees that 1975 would mark the end of the world that in that year many of them abandoned their houses and pitched tents in remote areas in eager anticipation of the opening of the heavens! Cohn (1955) argues that it is this theological emphasis on the forthcoming Kingdom that plays the most important role in uniting the Witnesses. In its anticipation of the cataclysmic end of the world and Jehovah's victory over Satan, the Society is able to instil a fanatical rejection of the present world and the belief that they really are a people set apart (Cohn 1955: 287–9).

The twentieth century was characterised by feelings of hope, tension and revival, and this was reflected in the Witnesses' commitment to ministry and recruitment. Most of the meetings I attended stressed the significance of aggressive evangelism in preparation for the New Age, and yet there are differences between devotees in how this knowledge of the end of time affects their daily activities. One lifelong member aged seventy-four told me:

I once remember visiting a brother in 1975 to talk over some congregational matters, and when I arrived, he was patching up his house. He said, 'I'm only giving this a lick of paint 'cos it's no good giving it a thorough job.' I said, 'What do you mean?' He said 'Well, it's 1975', but I still burnt the paint off my house when it needed it and I still bottomed it and sanded it. I thought, 'Why should I do a botch job, I like doing things well'. Now then, I went to see him in '78 and there he was taking the plaster off and putting a new damp course in! We work with a double split mind. One is, it could start tomorrow, two is, it might be years, so we've a split mind . . . so each day has its anxieties and you cope with them; you plan to continue, but you also realise that if half-way through building another extension on the house Armageddon comes, don't cry about it! The society is living by the same principle. They're putting up buildings galore all over the world, and they're not worried about whether Armageddon's going to come this year, next year; they're just going to go on allowing for expansion as long as the world continues. We are a progressive, forward-looking organisation and our time, our efforts, our energy, our thinking and our finance all goes into carrying out Jehovah's work until he is ready for stepping in.

Thus, the Witnesses' expectation of Armageddon is not incompatible with pragmatic activities such as erecting headquarters and ministering to the world. This part alertness, part denial shows how millenarian beliefs must coexist with evangelism if the principles on which the community operates are to be fully acknowledged. It is as though the Witnesses are living in a twilight world of transition between an unworkable present and an eagerly awaited future – a future that is conceptualised in terms of timelessness and continuity. The significance of temporality can be illustrated also by examining how the Society views the death of its members. For non-believers, death signifies the end of time for the individual, but for the Witnesses it is merely a rite of passage into the New Kingdom. The Witnesses believe that, since Armageddon is imminent, they are soon to see the resurrection of their former brothers and sisters who are meanwhile asleep. The following passage from a Watch Tower tract provides a succinct description of this future event:

> Can we really believe the resurrection promise? Yes, there is no doubt that Jehovah and his Son are both willing and able to fulfil it. What does this mean for you? You have the prospect of being reunited with dead loved ones right here on earth but under very different conditions! Jehovah God, who started mankind off in a lovely garden, has promised to restore Paradise on this earth under the rule of His heavenly Kingdom in the hands of the new glorified Jesus Christ. (Genesis 2: 7–9; Matthew 6: 10; Luke 23: 42, 43) In that restored Paradise, the human family will have the prospect of enjoying life without end, free from all sickness and disease. (Revelations 21: 1–4; compare Job 33: 25; Isaiah 35: 5–7.) Gone, too, will be all hatred, racial prejudice, ethnic violence, and economic oppression. It will be into such a cleansed earth that Jehovah God through Jesus Christ will resurrect the dead.
> (Watch Tower Bible and Tract Society of Pennsylvania 1994: 31)

This vision of the resurrection challenges some of the key principles of modernity. From a modern rational perspective, death is not a sacred event, but rather one that marks the end of all life opportunities. The twenty-first century encourages a secular image of time by reifying it as a resource that contains no special meaning. Millenarians, on the other hand, maintain that time promises immortality and that death is the fulfilment of a romantic narrative. The events of one's life such as birth, adolescence, employment, marriage, parenting, ageing and finally death are all part of a large cosmic drama, the finale of which millions now living hope to see.[9] But although the

Witnesses' millenarian dream is based on rational biblical interpretation, their escape from the present and their romantic vision of the future violate the whole meaning of rationalism in a modern secular world.

Summary

In this chapter, I have shown how the Witnesses deploy a variety of cultural resources to promote their millenarian doctrines. The Watch Tower organisation uses ideas such as love, heroism, persecution, self-abnegation and temporality, all of which have contributed to its international success. I have also argued that the Witnesses' narrative of past, present and future contains both optimism and pessimism. The combination of millenarian beliefs and pragmatic activities raises some interesting issues about the Witnesses' response to risk and their relationship with modernity. Their plans to erect more headquarters all over the world are not as incongruous with their belief in the Final Days as one might think; for, if they are to fulfil their eschatological mission, they must find some way of embracing the modern world. Their willingness to engage in long-term building projects is thus part of their zealous international ministry, the completion of which will aid the fulfilment of prophecy. This exemplifies what the Witnesses themselves refer to as 'the split mind' – a psychological strategy that enables them to plan a future they do not expect to see. Their belief that nothing can be done by outsiders to solve the world's problems means that long-term planning gives way to immediate concerns; hence, they remain trapped in the present. Their refusal to embrace the future in modern secular terms (as, for example, in the way described by Berger) is indicative of a people who feel permanently at risk. No doubt, modernity poses anxieties for everyone, but, while others approach the twenty-first century and all its uncertainties with optimism, trepidation or indifference, the Witnesses retreat into their own world of safety – a world in which time is suspended and fear suppressed. Despite all this, the Witnesses are very like moderns. The evidence suggests that they are mainly rational people with a highly romantic imagination. The fact that they pivot between the rational and the romantic demonstrates their versatility in expressing their beliefs, as well as their ability to make use of a wide range of resources in a world they find repugnant.

6 Inside, outside

Throughout this book, I have suggested that Watch Tower theology is a weapon used by the Witnesses to avert the risks posed by modernity. But what happens in practice? I now turn to the issue of how the Witnesses operate between two systems – their own closed system (or 'the truth') and the open system of the outside world. This raises a number of questions that need to be addressed if the Witnesses' status in so-called secular society is to be understood. For example, how easy is it for the Witnesses to remain within the parameters of the Watch Tower Society when in the company of non-members? How do they respond when outsiders with whom they are associating openly flout Watch Tower teachings? How do they distinguish between acceptable and unacceptable behaviour in situations where official teachings are absent? And do they all share the same notion of acceptability? In this chapter, I argue that the Witnesses cannot be entirely private in their religious behaviour and that, although they are in certain respects compatible with modernity, they are also unsuited to it. Despite their world-renouncing beliefs, the Witnesses do not separate themselves completely from the wider society. They live in neighbourhoods alongside non-members, send their children to state schools, hold jobs in secular environments and even occupy the same households as those who do not share their faith. Unlike separatist groups like the Hutterites, who primarily seek their own salvation, the Witnesses have never lived communally, although the organisation discourages unnecessary contact with the outside world. This is not to suggest that differences do not exist among devotees in the nature and amount of worldly contact, but what it does mean is that Witnesses everywhere are likely to spend part of their time with those who may have little sympathy with their worldview.

The chapter is in four sections. In the first section, I offer a brief summary of a phenomenon which has been of some concern to modernity theorists; namely, *the privatisation of religion*. This theme has important implications for how world-renouncing millenarians manage their identity in public places and thus helps to contextualise the subsequent discussion. In the second section, I examine how the Witnesses distinguish between per-missible and non-permissible behaviour. Some of the people I interviewed offered accounts of previous events that had pushed them into closer contact with the world than the Society might otherwise be willing to sanction. Others preferred to talk only about fictitious situations which, in their own view, would require careful management. In both cases, the scenarios convey certain discrepancies between the official teachings of the Society and the actions of its members. The third and fourth sections address substantive areas of life in which there is tension between members and non-members. The two institutions on which I focus my analysis are the family and the workplace, both of which pose challenges to devotees and provoke a range of responses. I also use some of the data to discuss the various ways in which the Witnesses conceptualise and avert risk in their everyday lives.

Privatising belief

One of the most important aspects of secularisation theory is the contention that, in modern societies, religious beliefs become privatised. This idea was first presented by Thomas Luckmann (1967), who maintained that religious institutions have been progressively forced to withdraw from the modern capitalist economy and occupy a peripheral position in a world that is abstract, impersonal and narcissistic. Luckmann's thesis centres on the claim that non-religious roles, which are both specialised and functionally rational, now dominate the public sphere. This has led a great many people to adopt a secular worldview, while those who continue to embrace religious *institutions* find themselves moving from secular to sacred activities in routine fashion. Whatever the consequences, people are left to negotiate their way through a whole series of conflicting ideas and demands. In short, religion has become an increasingly private matter.[1]

Erving Goffman was one of the first sociologists to take seriously the relationship between the public and the private. Goffman maintained that everyday life requires the careful management of self across both public and private spheres. For Goffman, 'the field of public life' includes the entire realm of face-to-face interaction when people come together in social settings. Conversely, the private sphere is the 'backstage', in which the individual can relax unobserved before preparing for the public theatrical performance of interaction rituals (Goffman 1959, 1963, 1967, 1971). Goffman's ideas are profoundly important for those interested in religious behaviour. The gradual separation of religion from social, political and economic life means that those who hold religious convictions must manage their beliefs between public and private spheres. What makes this all the more demanding is that, as societies in the West have arguably become more secular, references to the supernatural have come to be regarded as inappropriate and anachronistic, except among people who are like-minded.

As far as Christianity is concerned, the shrinking role of mainstream churches has resulted in the *individuation* of the relationship between God and humankind.[2] The single sacred canopy (to use Berger's phrase), has given way to self-empowerment (a situation which has arisen from religious pluralism). Religion has thus become a personal quest for meaning rather than a collective act of worship. Bellah *et al.* illustrate this by quoting a woman who had named her faith after herself: ' "I believe in God. I'm not a religious fanatic. I can't remember the last time I went to church. My faith has carried me a long way. It's Sheilaism. Just my own little voice" ' (quoted in Bellah *et al.* 1985: 221).

Although the 'cult of the individual' has not fully replaced institutional religion, few sociologists would disagree that it is becoming a pervasive feature of the modern world. It has long been acknowledged that, even where people continue to attend conventional places of worship, they still reserve the right to allow their own consciences to decide which aspects of faith are truly essential.[3] The 'privatisation of belief' thesis provides a useful perspective for a sociological analysis of the Witnesses' relationship with the outside world. Unlike other world-renouncing movements which express their beliefs through political activity (like, for example, Protestant fundamentalism in the United States), the Watch Tower Society refuses to use official public channels to promote its cause on the basis that it is not of this world. At the institutional level, therefore, the Witnesses' insistence on religious detachment assigns them a marginal position that prohibits any social or political activity to which they are entitled by citizenship. Needless to say, it also prevents them from partaking in ecumenical worship with other religious organisations. Yet, paradoxically, this reservedness is highly characteristic of an exclusive organisation that is staking a claim to one of the many constitutive freedoms of modernity – the right to privacy.[4] Privacy is far from easy for those with world-renouncing beliefs to maintain, particularly if they are avid evangelists. The Witnesses' moral obligation to proselytise in a secular world exposes several contradictions. The strength and uniformity of the Watch Tower community means that the Witnesses have difficulty in accepting the notion of private belief, yet they are compelled to accept it if they are to participate in public life. Given that they make use of schools, hospitals and the welfare system, are employed in many different kinds of institutions and live in secular neighbourhoods, they spend a considerable amount of time in the company of non-Witnesses. How, then, do they manage their beliefs in the public sphere?

It might seem rather incongruous that a movement which does not enforce communal living and is in fact *dependent* on the outside world should continue to advise its devotees to keep a low public profile. It is, after all, the public that provides the organisation with new members as acknowledged in 'street-witnessing', door-to-door ministry and evangelism in the workplace. Nevertheless, it would appear that, once prospective converts reach the point of baptism, they take great care in managing their relations with the world from which they have come. At the individual level, the Witnesses often find themselves on the periphery of public life, and it is here that they are acutely aware of risk. If they are to demonstrate their worthiness to outsiders, they must be confident that their behaviour in public would meet the approval of a movement that continually reminds them that they are *in* but not *of* the world.

Transgressing boundaries: who decides?

Most of the time, the Witnesses' millenarian perspective enables them to deal with the incompatibility between their own values and those of outsiders. Tension between the Society's officials and representatives of the state (headteachers, medical practitioners, public sector administrators, judicial officers and the like) often stems from the Witnesses' refusal to violate Watch Tower injunctions. The Witnesses know only too well the conflict, potential and actual, between public mores and private belief, and recognise that, where certain behaviour is prescribed or prohibited, their loyalty is to the Society. There is, however, another dimension to the public and the private. Sometimes, the public tenets of the Watch Tower community may conflict with the *privacy* of the devotee. On a day-to-day basis, it is quite possible that those Witnesses who have some association with outsiders find themselves caught between the dynamics of a social setting and the constraints of their community. These are situations in which transgressions can occur. Even a movement as circumspect as this one cannot maintain control over its members in the course of their everyday lives. Nor can it produce a checklist of taboos covering every conceivable life scenario for devotees to consult in their moments of doubt or uncertainty. Those who step outside the Society's boundaries, either wittingly or unwittingly, may never be found out by those who have the power to discipline them. In most cases, these situations are not likely to be ones that allow the individual time to seek guidance from congregational elders or co-religionists.

Considering the authoritarian nature of the movement, it is not surprising that I had some difficulty in encouraging devotees to talk about transgression, more so persuading them to provide me with examples. I did, however, interview a woman (Diane) who shared with me a story about how, some years earlier, she had made contact with a disfellowshipped member:

> I did once have a meeting with a disfellowshipped person because I thought a real lot about this person and I know all the circumstances as to why she had been disfellowshipped and I cared a lot about her, and because I got high minded about it I felt she'd been unjustly dealt with so therefore I felt justified in talking to her. I felt guilty about doing it but looking back on it now I realise that what I felt I should do overrode what Jehovah said I should do. My own viewpoint came before Jehovah, but I wouldn't do it again.

The Governing Body's teachings regarding contact with those who have been disfellowshipped are unambiguous. Disfellowshipped members, though free to continue to attend meetings, are to be shunned by the rest of the congregation. Other members are instructed to avoid such individuals who are now considered to be in a state of unworthiness. Relatives, if they are also in 'the truth', are advised by the elders to keep only tenuous contact with the offending Witness until such time that he or she is reinstated. Diane's meeting with her disfellowshipped friend did, therefore, constitute a transgression against the community. Her story is significant for two reasons. First, it illustrates the fact that rules governing behaviour are not always strictly adhered to, even by those who claim to be faithful, and, more importantly, it confirms that Watch Tower beliefs can never be regarded as a private concern. Nevertheless, the dualistic nature of the movement cannot tolerate mavericks, and it has no way of taking into account personal motives for wrongdoing. When Witnesses allow ideas contrary to those of their religious community to influence their actions, they are entering forbidden territory. This supports Douglas's contention that people who cross boundaries are symbolically matter out of place and provoke feelings of disapproval:

> people really do think of their own social environment as consisting of other people joined together or separated by lines which must be respected. Some of the lines are protected by firm physical sanctions . . . But wherever the lines are precarious we find pollution ideas come to their support.
>
> (Douglas 1966: 138–9)

The fear of polluting the Watch Tower congregation does not only prevent Witnesses from adopting private beliefs, it also emphasises the presence of risk. Living within boundaries is conceived as release from bondage. The 'truth as safety' metaphor can be illustrated in a conversation I had early on in my fieldwork with a woman who explained to me that living as a true Witness was like being at the very centre of a roundabout which was rotating at great speed. The edge of the roundabout, she explained, must be avoided at all costs, since it was here that the individual ran the greatest danger of being thrown off. Only the centre was absolutely safe. The edge of the roundabout was the space occupied by people who were not living as devout Witnesses – these might be baptised members whose faith was only lukewarm, or those who were in *the world* (that is, outsiders). Her argument was that by attending meetings regularly, ministering to others faithfully and accepting the Society's tenets, one's place at the centre of the roundabout was secure.

Where rules are clearly laid down by the Society, transgressions are dealt with by disfellowship; but, where lines are blurred, ideas about whether an individual is in a state of moral danger vary from member to member. In an in-depth interview with Mary, who came from a family of Witnesses, I learned:

> Several years ago I was at a very low ebb spiritually because I'd been undergoing some personal problems within my marriage and I'd let my spirituality slip by attending less meetings, not praying as I should and relying on Jehovah and not studying – if you don't continue with these three things, your spirituality is going to ebb away. I did start doing things I shouldn't have done. I started going out enjoying myself up nightclubs and things like that with my sister. I came very close to needing some strong counselling then, but I thought, 'Blow it, I'm going out there to enjoy myself because I've had enough', because at that time I didn't care if my marriage survived or not. I felt like I was completely taken for granted. My husband was very up and down with his spirituality. I really felt for a lot of years that he didn't have hold of Jehovah at all. I can't say I gravitated to what we term as 'worldly people', and when I went out I couldn't fully throw myself into it because I kept saying to myself, 'You shouldn't be doing this, this isn't going to help you', but I just wanted an escape from the pressure and neglect I felt at home. I thought, 'Well, John has had a slice of the cake, why shouldn't I?'

Unlike Diane, who knew that her behaviour violated official teachings, Mary's actions are not strictly forbidden. She hints at her husband's lack of religious conviction during a period in which she claims he took her for granted; but what is particularly significant is the way in which she wrestled with her conscience when venturing to nightclubs with her sister who was not a member. Mary never ceases to be aware of the Society's moral code and felt vulnerable because she was in a place of worldly orientation. This does not mean that when Witnesses make *voluntary* contact with the outside world they are necessarily acting in defiance, but it does suggest that they are teetering on the edges of boundaries and this always carries risks. It is here that Douglas argues ideas of pollution come into play. So do Witnesses become matter out of place when they undertake an activity such as entering a nightclub? Douglas writes:

> Danger lies in transitional states, simply because transition is neither one state nor the next, it is undefinable. The person who must pass from one to another is himself in danger and emanates danger to others. The danger is controlled by ritual which precisely separates him from his old status, segregates him for a time and then publicly declares his entry to a new status.

> (Douglas 1966: 96)

Although Douglas is referring to people who are passing from one category to another because of birth, death, puberty or marriage,[5] her idea of people emanating danger when occupying the interstices between social categories can be applied to Witnesses who come close to flouting Watch Tower principles. This is the point at which the purity of the individual (and hence the community) might be perceived to be under threat. In this respect, voluntary contact with unbelievers carries more potential risks than involuntary contact because of the perceived lack of control imputed to the individual's behaviour. At best, an act such as entering a nightclub is considered unfavourable; at worst, it pollutes both the individual and the Society. The threat of pollution controls the Witnesses' relations with outsiders since it affirms acceptable behaviour. This means that there are tacit rules by which devotees must abide in every social context. The people I interviewed claimed they were highly selective about the kinds of venues they frequented and with whom they associated outside the weekly meetings. Leisure time was mainly spent visiting relatives, going to local pubs for drinks, eating out and holidaymaking (sport was particularly popular among the brothers). Though these social activities are common among countless millions of people every day, when Witnesses engage in them it is nearly always in the company of other members of their congregation.

Like all other aspects of the Witnesses' behaviour, risk is portrayed through literature. Outside contact which is likely to impinge on Watch Tower tenets is, as one might expect, categorically discouraged. In one tract, the Society warns its members of the danger of worldly influence in leisure and cinema:

> Another thing to consider is the associations to which playing organized sports may expose you. Locker-room talk generally has the reputation for being sexually immoral. Furthermore, when a team takes a trip to play another school, one may for an extended time be in the company of persons who have little regard for faithfulness to God . . . The type of movie and TV entertainment we choose can also affect our relationship with God. Some movies and TV shows are delightful entertainment; some may even enhance our appreciation of our Creator's marvelous handiwork. But no doubt you have noticed that many shows have exploded with stories featuring adultery, fornication, lesbianism, homosexuality, violence and mass killing . . . In effect, many of today's films shout out: 'We're going to engage in badness! We're going to break all laws, even God's!' Is that the kind of influence you want working on you?
>
> (Watch Tower Bible and Tract Society of Pennsylvania
> 1976: 119–21)

Having created a moral panic to warn against danger, the passage continues with a series of 'safer' suggestions for entertainment, including hiking in woods, handball, badminton and table tennis. The Witnesses are highly selective in their choice of television programmes for their children, who are often prevented from partaking in extracurricular activities at school. What outsiders might regard as marginal differences in the type and extent of worldly contact between any two Witnesses, may, in fact, be highly significant to the brothers and sisters themselves. Since all Witnesses are responsible as individuals for managing their contact with the outside world, close scrutiny from inside the movement might reveal differences in how this is achieved. Only an understanding of the world through the Witnesses' own perspective would make this kind of analysis possible. In a very long conversation with Maureen who, along with her husband, had been in membership for over twenty years, I learned:

> We use our own consciences in a lot of matters. This year, we were supposed to be going on holiday with another couple who, the wife's a Witness but the husband isn't, but he's not opposed in any way; he goes out socially with the Witnesses and so on. Anyway, we found out that this other couple whom they are friends with also wanted to come on holiday with us. They told us that this couple were very nice but it threw me and my husband into a quandary. So I had to say that we would think about it. So when we discussed it, my husband didn't feel right about it because we'd never laid eyes on this couple before and we only had Jennifer's say-so that the couple were all right. But some of the things that Jennifer will put up with, I wouldn't put up with myself. So we decided we wouldn't go on holiday with them. But it turned out that we left it till about six weeks before we went on holiday to book, and we ended up only a few minutes' walk away from them, so we were with them quite a lot on holiday and it turned out that this other couple *were* generally all right – they didn't swear, they weren't rowdy, they weren't into being around immoral circumstances or anything like that, so it turned out all right; but you would find some Witnesses who would definitely have said, 'No, I'm sorry, they're not both Witnesses'.

Maureen proceeded to inform me that other Witnesses would have refused completely to engage in unnecessary association with *anyone* who was not a member of the community. Although it is impossible to generalise about the level of voluntary contact with the non-members in every social situation, Maureen's comments reveal something significant about both the perceived and the actual difficulties experienced by some Witnesses when they negotiate their lives with those in the outside world. For Maureen, the real difficulty seemed to lie not so much in the fact that one couple in her story was unknown, but rather that they were not fellow members.[6] Interestingly, she does mention that one of the original couple was also a non-Witness. This shows that, despite Maureen's misgivings about going on holiday with a couple she did not know, there are outsiders who meet the tacit criteria for worldly association. These outsiders may even be married to Witnesses. It would appear that someone with sympathy for and sensitivity towards Watch Tower principles would be in a much stronger position to qualify for regular contact with the brothers and sisters than those who do not. There is, however, another aspect of Maureen's story that is worthy of mention, and this is the issue of how the Witnesses distinguish between acceptable and unacceptable behaviour when their brothers and sisters are absent. Maureen alludes to this when she says, 'some of the things that Jennifer will put up with, I wouldn't put up with myself'. I have searched long and hard for evidence of uniformity in the Witnesses' perceptions of Watch Tower transgression where official teachings are vague and have come to the conclusion that this is a nettle they do not like to grasp. But one thing that is clear is that the tolerance levels of devotees vary, as does their frequency of contact with outsiders.

Although *some* voluntary contact with the outside world is permissible, the Witnesses are advised to err on the side of caution when forming friendships with those who do not share their beliefs. Maureen informed me that, in the early 1980s, sport had taken up much of her spare time and that she had once befriended some non-Witnesses at her local squash club. When I asked whether her own definition of acceptable worldly contact had changed over the years, she told me:

> Obviously the Bible would be endless if every single thing had to be written in; so a lot is left to conscience. What one person might feel is OK, another person wouldn't. I wouldn't join a club as such. I would go and *play* squash. I used to be a member of a squash club, but that was at a time when my spirituality wasn't what it should have been. I go to step classes and I've also just joined a slimming club. Some Witnesses would look at that and say I was wrong for having any contact with worldly people at all; but just as there are some people who are very narrow-minded about things and some people are very broad minded, when you become a Witness these things don't just drop off you. I'd been attending less meetings, not praying as I should and not studying. I came very close to needing some strong counselling from the elders.

So while certain behaviour may not be deemed offensive or deserving of counselling, it could be viewed as inappropriate. Be this as it may, there is no consensus among devotees about where the lines should be drawn to determine with whom in the outside world they are safe to associate, in what capacity and for how long. It may well be that Witnesses who are experiencing what my earlier interviewee (Mary) described as a 'low ebb' in their spiritual lives have more voluntary contact with the outside world than those who are not, but this is highly speculative. I did, however, find significant differences in the amount of time individual Witnesses spent in congregational activities such as delivering doorstep sermons and attending weekly meetings. There were also various degrees of hostility towards outsiders, despite the unanimous agreement that Satan governs the world. But these differences could be a reflection of personal circumstances and experiences rather than indicators of conviction. It is only when Watch Tower teachings are defied or the individual is exposed to risk that worldly contact becomes an issue for the Society.

One of the main components of the privatisation of belief thesis is that people are allowed the freedom to construct their own religious identity. This assumes an erosion of institutional religion both politically and in terms of its ability to provide an official blueprint for human behaviour. The evidence suggests that, although the Witnesses spend some of their time in worldly situations and with 'worldly' people, they are unable to withdraw psychologically from the Watch Tower community. Certain Witnesses demonstrate their conviction by keeping contact with outsiders to a minimum. Others, though they may befriend non-members and maintain amicable relations with people in their neighbourhoods, make their status known to those with whom they associate. For these individuals, *some* voluntary contact is acceptable, even desirable, so long as it does not mean that their religious principles must be compromised. This suggests that, although the Witnesses are products of the privatisation of religion, it is often at the cost of their own *individual* privacy.

Tensions within the family and marriage

So far, I have discussed the Witnesses' voluntary contact with the outside world, and I have used the term *voluntary* to refer to those times when they associate with non-members by choice. On the relatively rare occasions that the Witnesses spend time away from other members of their congregation, it is usually with friends or relatives who are fully aware of their religious convictions. The evidence suggests that this time is most frequently spent on leisure activities such as playing squash, visiting social venues and going away on holiday. I now turn to two social spheres – the family and the workplace – in which the Witnesses' contact with outsiders creates problems of a rather different nature. Domestic settings and work environments sometimes present devotees with more difficult dilemmas than when they are socialising with non-Witness friends. Unlike places of leisure and entertainment, these venues cannot be avoided. So how do the Witnesses react when their beliefs are challenged, even assaulted, by those with whom they live and work?

Although it is impossible to say exactly how many Witnesses are reared in families in which both parents are members, it is still clear that a large number reside in households in which Watch Tower beliefs are pervasive. It is also true that people who voluntarily join sectarian movements often do so at the expense of their family's happiness. I asked several Witness converts what kind of tensions this created and how they managed their relations with their non-Witness kin. Some of them had interesting stories to tell. The following comments are those of a retired woman who lived on her own, but was still very close to her son and daughter:

> Not being able to celebrate Christmas with them or sending them a birthday card was terribly difficult for me. In fact, it got to the stage where I started to think, 'Is it really worth it?', but then in time things began to get a little easier. I spent the day before Christmas with two people from the congregation last year and that helped; but even now my son doesn't invite me round at celebration times because he knows I don't want to say 'No'.

Another woman gave a more traumatic account of family tension:

> When I first started a Bible study with the Witnesses, my family were violently opposed. My eldest son even said he would rather I was dead than become a Jehovah's Witness. He threatened me with violence, tried to bribe me with money; but the more people fought it, the more I thought, 'There must be something in this'. But now they all support me and don't want me to give it up.

A young man who had been brought up an Anglican but still lived with his parents at the time of his conversion told me:

> When I first started studying, my family were totally against it. They said that if I had any questions about the Bible I should go to my own church. I told this to the brother I was studying with and he just said, 'Well, you know enough now to go to your old church. Go with your parents and confront your vicar.' My parents told me that if I was going to become a Witness I would have to move out. They didn't want the neighbours to think I was a Jehovah's Witness. So I carried on studying without attending the meetings and, when I managed to save up enough money for a deposit, I told them that I was going to become a Witness. Once they could see that it hadn't sent me round the bend they came round to it. They understand it much better now. From my point of view I want them to come into the truth . . . I buy my sister's children presents at other times of the year to compensate for Christmas.

These stories demonstrate the emotional difficulties experienced by families when someone they love decides to study with the Witnesses. The behaviour of these individuals pulled hard at the heart strings of their relatives, who seemed to think that Jehovah's Witnesses were religious fanatics who had the potential to destroy family life. But there is an ideological force at work that enables the convert to counter this disapproval. It should not be forgotten that religious movements all over the world have grown and prospered on outside hostility, real or putative. Biblical texts such as Matthew 12: 48, where Jesus puts the work of salvation before family relationships, are used by the Watch Tower community to prepare new converts for opposition from their nearest and dearest who may try to hinder their salvation. The three accounts can thus be seen as mythic autobiographies of conversion. Once again, this shows that becoming a Witness is perceived as a heroic act that may require subjugating one's closest relatives to the realm of the devil. The failure of sceptical relatives to understand Watch Tower doctrines stands in opposition to the convert's belief that the movement is able to offer hope in a world on the brink of chaos.

The testimonies of these converts show how difficult it can be for devotees to prevent their faith from affecting their non-Witness relatives. Remaining silent about their new-found convictions defeats the whole purpose of evangelising to others. Furthermore, the Witnesses' heterodox theology and the intransigence with which it is adhered to is bound to impact on family life. The Witnesses' rejection of annual celebrations is something which is impossible to conceal, however close the family might be. For one young woman (Donna) with whom I chatted casually at the end of a Kingdom Hall meeting, this had posed a dilemma several weeks earlier on her mother's birthday. Donna explained how she had spent a considerable amount of time thinking about how she might acknowledge the occasion without offending Watch Tower teachings. Her saving grace was the fact that the Society does not renounce social gatherings, and on this basis she agreed to attend the party. Donna explained to her mother that she would not be able to buy her a present or sing 'Happy Birthday' along with the rest of the family, but she did promise to treat her to lunch and buy her a gift later in the year. In this case, Donna had to balance her religious principles with her affection for an outsider. Like the woman I quoted earlier (Mary) who visited a nightclub, Donna's actions pushed her perilously towards the edges of the Society's boundaries.

Some of the most poignant accounts of tensions within the family concern mixed marriages – that is, marriage between a Witness and an unbeliever. These marriages are unsurprisingly rare, but, where they do exist, they raise some interesting issues. In the congregations in which the research was carried out, I came across only five people (all of whom were women) who were married to non-Witnesses. I was curious to learn how these women were able to deal with disapproval (if indeed they encountered it) within what is arguably the most intimate of all human relationships. Four of the women told me that their husbands had at some stage or other undertaken a Bible study, but could not quite make the move to become baptised members.[7] All claimed that, despite some initial opposition, their husbands had now reached the stage of acceptance. Two said that although their husbands agreed with the organisation's teachings, 'stubbornness' prevented them from continuing their study.[8] Officially, the Society warns devotees in mixed marriages of the dangers of excessive contact with the outside world.[9] I asked a congregational elder what advice he would give to those with unbelieving spouses. He explained:

> In the Bible it says that if you're married to an unbeliever, and if the unbeliever is happy to stay with you, you the believer should stay with him or her – it's called an 'unbelieving mate'. The first book of Corinthians chapter 7 says that if the unbeliever is happy to stay with you in that state – because it may be that later on he's won to the faith without you speaking a word because of your conduct; so stay put – so we recommend that wives or husbands who come into the truth stick to their mate.

Since the Witnesses are duty-bound to be ministers of their theology, it would be impossible to imagine that those in mixed marriages would not live in hope of their partners' conversion. More often than not, Witnesses with non-Witness spouses join the Watch Tower community after they marry. This seems to suggest not only that those already in membership are unlikely to marry outsiders but that there is little chance of a non-Witness partner also converting. Nevertheless, it would be wrong to assume that conversion inevitably destroys marriages or that it is necessarily responsible for mixed marriages that do fail.[10]

In an account of her husband's reaction to her announcement many years earlier that she was joining the movement, Margaret told me:

> I came home and told Paul about it and he said, 'You're crackers! If you have anything to do with it I'm going to leave you.' But I've never been one to go out on my own or go out with the girls on Friday night or any-thing. I'm loyal and faithful and I wanted to try to be a better person. Anyway, things got from bad to worse and I'm not exaggerating when I say weeks would go by without us speaking. He didn't like me going for my Bible study because I used to go straight from work. To this day we don't talk about our experiences years ago. He's a lot better than he was, now, but he would never listen and he was rude and aggressive when the Witnesses came. He wouldn't even say, 'Hello'. He'd just walk out. His dad never spoke to me for two years. But I got the strength and the determination to carry on because I knew what I was doing was right.

Margaret went on to explain how, despite her efforts in not mentioning Watch Tower beliefs or the content of the meetings, Paul left home for a period of six weeks and went to live with his parents. Margaret and Paul then reunited, but the marriage ended several years later. Their fifteen-year-old daughter, Katie, had recently been baptised when Paul moved out of the family home for the second time. Despite previous opposition from both Paul and his father, Margaret is clear in her account that she was not prepared to sacrifice her new way of life, but her willingness to remain silent about her beliefs no doubt enabled the marriage to survive for as long as it did. This shows that, in domestic settings where emotional tensions may rise, there is a point at which Watch Tower beliefs must necessarily become a matter of individual privacy. Margaret proceeded to tell me that, over a long period of time, Paul had become less hostile:

> It was no issue once he got used to it, although it couldn't have been easy for him. He came round and came to terms with it. His mum had always been quite amenable to 'the truth' really. His dad was quite aggressive when you got him talking about it but we got on quite well. They did come round for a meal one night and Paul stuck up for us! He said, 'I'll tell you what, if we were all like the Witnesses the world would be safe and if I ever turn to a religion it would be the Witnesses', which was very interesting because he'd been so opposed over the years. But Katie's baptism was the final straw!

I did wonder whether Margaret's silence had played some part in winning Paul's respect. Although Paul was an unlikely candidate for conversion, his willingness to accept his wife's conversion suggests that he had found certain Watch Tower principles commendable. This corresponds with Wilson's study of parents whose children had joined the Unification church:

> Almost always, parents were expectedly apprehensive about a son or daughter joining the Moonies. In some instances, their opposition diminished as time passed, but this appears almost invariably to have been because personal parent–child relationships improved, or, more marginally, because parents found the calibre of other adherents impressive, and their activities laudable, and not because they were attracted to Unification doctrines or to the Revd Moon.
>
> (Wilson 1990: 266)

The Watch Tower Society and the Unification Church are only two examples of world-renouncing religions, but it seems that, once unbelieving relatives start to understand something of the way of life upheld by the movement, the doctrines become less reprehensible and the anger and bewilderment begin to subside. According to Barker, some religious organisations even publish literature which contains testimonies from their members confirming that the conversion has brought the family closer together (Barker 1989: 87).

Mutual tolerance seems to be the key to survival when a person becomes a Witness, but this takes time for both parties. Tolerating the outside world is a lot to ask of someone who has internalised Watch Tower doctrines, particularly in the initial stages of membership when enthusiasm for a new way of life is difficult to quell. That said, Margaret's efforts to undertake door-to-door ministry only when her husband was at work, to keep discussions about her beliefs and activities to a minimum and to prevent her co-religionists from ringing and calling round unless absolutely necessary suggest that, while the Society's prescription for salvation is inviolable, devotees are not always able to minister to those with whom they are emotionally involved. By remaining silent about her religious convictions, Margaret was able to appease her husband and honour the demands of the movement.

There are dozens of domestic scenarios in which the Witnesses could find themselves having to balance their religious principles with family obligations; and what might be an acceptable level of worldly contact to one member might not be acceptable to another. Conversely, what one unbelieving spouse might be willing to tolerate, another might find burdensome. If there is one aspect of Watch Tower theology that could impinge heavily on family life, however, it is the celebration of Christmas. Christmas, perhaps more than birthdays and Easter, involves contact with close relatives and the exchange of gifts for those who celebrate it. But what happens in the case of the Witnesses, who do not? How do *they* conduct themselves when the rest of the family are trimming the house and exchanging presents? And are the teachings of the Society so inexorably binding that individuals who find themselves in this situation must sever all contact with their families? When I asked the same elder I quoted earlier how devotees with unbelieving relatives should negotiate Christmas, I learned:

> If it's a woman with an unbelieving husband and he wants a Christmas tree and his children to hang up stockings and turkey and Christmas pudding, then the wife should support him in providing what he needs, even though not celebrating it. In other words, if he says, 'I'm going to put a Christmas tree up and put flashing lights on it and I'm going to buy my kids some presents and I'm going to buy a turkey and a plum pudding and I want you to cook it', then she will provide that meal and sit down and have it because he's the head of the house. He wants it for his family and he has the right to it, so she will be supportive, although in her heart not celebrating Christmas because she knows that Christ wasn't born on Christmas day. Now then, if it was the other way round and a woman wanted it all, the husband would say 'Well, if you want to do that out of your housekeeping money, then that's up to you but I won't help you to prepare for it.' She can get the tree, she can buy the turkey and she can cook it.

What lies at the heart of the elder's advice is the Society's teaching of the wife's subservience to the husband within marriage; a teaching which the Witnesses claim is supported in the first book of Corinthians which he quoted previously. This provides a possible explanation of why mixed marriages in which the believing spouse is female have a reasonable chance of survival. The patriarchal nature of the community dictates that, whatever the religious convictions of the spouses, the husband is the head of the household and the wife must defer to his authority. Interestingly, this rule empowers an unbelieving male to overrule Watch Tower injunctions. It also explains why, in most mixed marriages, the believer is female. It would be difficult if not impossible for an unbelieving wife to acquiesce to a husband who is imbued with the paternalistic values of the movement unless these are the values she also upholds.

Another reason for those successful mixed marriages of Witnesses is the difficulty that the Governing Body imposes on its members for obtaining a divorce. According to the Society, the only acceptable motive for the legal termination of marriage is in the case of adultery; and, even then, divorce is optional. Here we have another paradox. On the one hand, the Governing Body advises devotees to keep their contact with outsiders to a minimum, yet, on the other, they are encouraged to remain with their unbelieving partners. It could be that the reason for this somewhat contradictory advice is that Watch Tower officials fear losing members as a result of family tension. Alternatively, mixed marriages might, as the elder's earlier comments suggest, be another way of winning recruits. Ultimately, there is no way of knowing whether the Governing Body's general hunger for new members lies behind its advice, but what is clear is that Witnesses with unbelieving spouses do not always follow official advice when negotiating their marital relations. One woman who was divorced from her husband told me of the tensions which studying had created in her previous marriage. Although I am uncertain about whether this was a significant factor in the termination of the marriage, she did inform me that, during the last Christmas they spent together, she had refused to decorate the Christmas tree and trim the house. The other women mentioned earlier, however, told me that they did manage to negotiate Christmas in ways that they did not feel were detrimental to their religious principles. All these women followed the Society's general rule of thumb and helped their husbands with the Christmas preparations, although they claimed to have retreated from the celebratory aspects of the event such as going to parties and visiting friends. Margaret claimed that her husband had reached the point where he had been prepared to sacrifice Christmas celebrations at home, though he did visit his own family during the festive season. It would appear from all this that Christmas, while having the *potential* to cause conflict, can be managed by Witnesses in mixed marriages on the basis that they may spend time with their unbelieving spouses as long as the celebration itself is eschewed. To outsiders, this is an exercise fraught with difficulty, since Witnesses who help their husbands (or wives) and children to prepare for Christmas and who partake in the meal along with other relatives (none of whom may be members of the movement) are, to all intents and purposes, celebrating Christmas; yet, those who find themselves in this position insist that this is not the case. These individuals claim to compensate for Christmas by buying their relatives presents at other times in the year.

These scenarios expose tensions between Watch Tower doctrines and family relations; and it is evident that the lines of demarcation between acceptable and unacceptable behaviour are blurred. The fact that the Witnesses vary in their perceptions of 'good conscience' seems to suggest that, as far as family life and marriage are concerned, the requisites of the movement are by no means unequivocal. The tolerance thresholds of non-Witness spouses may easily counter Watch Tower tenets, but the emphasis placed by the Governing Body on family harmony means that, in practice, members are left to work out their own solutions to moral dilemmas. Family relations belong to the private sphere of life and, for this reason, there is a tendency on the part of the elders to temper their authority. This is not to say that the Witnesses' way of thinking does not penetrate deeply into family life, but there is no knowing what compromises they might make in the absence of their brothers and sisters. Reliable data would, I suspect, reveal a number of inconsistencies if it came to checking for possible dissonance between the injunctions of the Society and the actions of its devotees, though it is hard to imagine that such data could be easily obtained. On the other hand, rejection from loved ones might be the price the Witnesses have to pay for adopting a zealous concept of risk and for making private beliefs a public matter.

Managing the millenarian identity: paid employment

The absence of a communal lifestyle and the tendency for most Witnesses to live in conventional households dictate that they work for a living. I suggested in Chapter 4 that ascetic doctrines of the Society lend themselves to a strong work ethic. From an employer's point of view, people who condemn idleness and are willing to work at unpopular times of the year, particularly around Christmas and Easter, are model employees. Although the Witnesses are industrious people, their commitment to 'seeking first the Kingdom' means that, in principle, the accumulation of personal income beyond a modest level ceases to be important.[11] Their general view of employment is that it is a means to an end – a way of earning a crust until the arrival of Armageddon. This prevents most Witnesses from pursuing successful careers. But the impersonal world of work is very different from the emotional sphere of the family, and people do not always deal kindly with members of millenarian communities.

I have already indicated that there are certain occupations which, for conscientious reasons, Witnesses refuse to undertake. Such occupations include work in munitions factories, designing machines for blood transfusions and serving in the armed forces. This is hardly surprising since these occupations involve duties that contravene Watch Tower principles.

There are, however, aspects of working life in occupations in which Witnesses *are* employed that present a challenge for someone with a millenarian outlook. Consider, for example, the following account from a young man who made a conscious decision to change his job as a result of his conversion:

> I worked five and a half days for my dad. My dad has his own company building chemicals and I was the foreman. I was in charge of some of the lads who used to be effing and blinding, and their way of talking affected me. I decided I didn't want to be in that environment. I know that Jehovah didn't want me to be involved with these people and I decided to find some other way of making a living. I decided to put the Kingdom first. The Bible says it is pointless pursuing material possessions and a career in the world. I saw the futility in it all. I now run my own carpet business.

Another man told me about the relief he felt when he left the civil service on the grounds of ill health:

> I wouldn't have liked to have kept that job because of my conscience. The ethos of lobbying, politics, pressure groups and trade unions were things I wouldn't have wanted to be involved in because they are all part of the world. The way I view it is that I am now apolitical as far as the world is concerned, but hyper-political as far as the theocratic government is concerned. I've simply changed governments!

These two men clearly found themselves in situations that were incompatible with their religious convictions. The first man's comments show how difficult it can be for Witnesses to work alongside those who offend their concept of purity, while the second man's dilemma was caused by internal political affairs which rode against the politically neutral status of the Society. Both these scenarios convey tension. In the world of employment, Witnesses must communicate with those who do not share their beliefs and who are under no obligation to defer to a religious code of practice with which they have no affinity. This means that people working in secular environments are free, perhaps with a few exceptions, to use language which the Witnesses find offensive, subscribe to trade unions, organise Christmas parties, discuss political affairs and so forth. Unlike the examples cited in the previous section, the workplace is one social arena in which the Witnesses find they have less control over the agenda and are unable to rely on the support of their close kin. Where conflict ensues as a result of the incompatibility of work culture and religious beliefs, negotiation may not be possible at all. I use as an example of this an extract from my interview with Diane, who had previously worked as a nurse in a residential home for the elderly:

The home was in three units and they were always short-staffed. They wanted me to work overtime but I didn't want to. I needed the time off to do my ministry and attend meetings but the matron didn't like that so she moved me to another unit where the sister, I know what I'd like to call her, she wasn't nice at all. I made my stand clear that I would like Wednesdays and Thursday evenings off and all day Sunday for the meetings. Well, she wasn't a bit obliging. She said, 'Oh I can't accommodate all you different religions. I've got a unit to cover!', so she was awkward. She would deliberately put me on Sundays and Wednesdays and Thursdays so I wouldn't get to the meetings.

Consequently, Diane left the nursing home and went to work in a large hospital, where she continued to experience problems. She told me:

The novelty of me being a Witness has worn off now, because I got lots of stick about it at first – some funny, some not – but now that I'm part of the team I find that they're watching me and I'm thinking, 'I've got to be on my best behaviour – I'm a Witness to Jehovah'. Sometimes it's really hard, because I'm a Witness and they know that Witnesses have standards. It's like the Bible says, you're a public spectacle – you feel like you're on a stage.

Diane went on to cite some examples of the hostility she faced, which included general teasing, caustic remarks about the Witnesses' attitudes towards sex and shunning by colleagues because of her refusal to mix with them socially. While she found all this stressful, her comment about being a public spectacle confirms her sense of loyalty to the Watch Tower organisation and her constant awareness that she was one of its representatives. Witnessing is thus analogous to a theatrical performance. But like some of the examples I have used in previous chapters, it is difficult to tell whether Diane's sense of loyalty is to Jehovah or the movement itself, since devotees see no distinction. What is important is that, like her two brothers above, she never lost sight of her religious status. Although Diane found hostility from her colleagues distressing, the Watch Tower Society never left her consciousness. This suggests that, when confronted with hostility *as individuals*, the Witnesses' awareness of risk intensifies. Their allegiance to the community remains strong in the absence of other devotees because their theology is reinforced so frequently at meetings and through contact with those who share their convictions that their self-concept becomes impossible to detach from that of the group. Loyalty to a community they cherish becomes much more important for Witnesses in the workplace because they are trying to manage their millenarian identity in a secular environment. This incompatibility often results in ridicule and contempt. The principal reason the Witnesses experience tension at work is not so much that they hold religious convictions but that they are emphatically

world-renouncing, and this has profound implications for their participation in work activities. While their renunciation of the world is not in
itself a source of hostility, it spills into certain work practices that can affect
relations with colleagues. Throughout the course of my fieldwork, I met
several Witnesses, particularly those who worked in factories and public
services, who had experienced some hostility in their workplaces because of
their refusal to join trade unions. Some claimed they had, in the past, been
'sent to Coventry' by their colleagues in situations which required the full
co-operation of *all* workers, as in the case of industrial action. Others
explained how, in the 1970s, they had found themselves in legal battles with
companies that operated on the closed-shop principle.[12] I also spoke with
two civil servants, two nurses and a factory worker who had all experienced
animosity from their co-workers at some stage in their careers because of
their refusal to take part in strike action. This animosity included shunning
and public rebuke.

There can be no doubt that the Witnesses' heterodox belief system
causes tension in the workplace, but their unusual degree of politeness and
deference to civil law makes me wonder whether some of their colleagues'
frustration is not also tempered with a certain amount of respect. The
Witnesses' unwillingness to engage in aggressive discourse, both at work
and outside, is to them an essential requisite for godliness. Thus, when
they are beset with hostility from their workmates for crossing a picket line
or refusing to clock out the minute the supervisor has gone home, mental
references to the crucifixion or the stoning of the disciples for acts of
bravery offer them consolation. By virtue of their beliefs, the Witnesses are
compelled to accept hostility as a test of their faith and to endure it with
dignity. Like those who renounce their families in order to honour Jehovah,
accepting hostility at work for the sake of righteousness becomes an act of
heroism.

There is, however, one incident of which I am aware involving a factory
worker in his early fifties who experienced so much hostility at work that
he chose to resign. This happened when the workers agreed to remain silent
after they discovered that the company had made an error in allowing them
an excessive amount of overtime pay. Not wishing to offend Watch Tower
principles, the faithful Witness decided to render unto Caesar what was
Caesar's. Inevitably, all the other workers were forced to surrender their
surplus amounts to the wages clerk. After several weeks of being ostracised
by his colleagues, he left the company to start his own window-cleaning
business. Though they are ideal employees, this story shows how the
Witnesses are ironically unsuited to secular working conditions. Like
domestic settings, workplaces present them with moral difficulties that must
be carefully negotiated. Strange as it might seem, confrontation with other
workers is an important part of modern evangelism – a test of endurance
rather than something to be shirked. The evidence suggests that, by meeting
confrontation rather than avoiding it, the Witnesses are able to demonstrate

both to themselves and those with whom they work that 'the truth' is something that can never be compromised.

Summary

I began this chapter by suggesting that the privatisation of religious belief is one of the consequences of modernity. Throughout Europe, the cultural landscape has undergone enormous changes since the Enlightenment, not least of which involves the removal of religious institutions from public life. On close examination, it is clear that, while religious expression may have become a private matter for those who have abandoned mainstream churches (it may even be so for those who have not), it is far less easy for millenarians such as the Witnesses to exercise privacy. Their constant mental reference to Watch Tower doctrines in *all* spheres of their lives shows that, contrary to Goffman's assertion, they are unable to separate the self into public and private entities.[13] The fact that the modern world does not allow millenarians to occupy centre stage means that the Witnesses are always likely to be marginalised. Where complete separation is impossible, social interaction with unbelievers requires careful management. But each scenario is unique, and the Watch Tower Society is unable to prescribe a definitive course of action for every conceivable situation. This is indicated by the fact that Witnesses who find themselves in the company of outsiders respond in different ways. Where official doctrines are open to interpretation, moral conduct becomes a matter of individual conscience. One important issue that emerges from this chapter is that Witnessing is, in many respects, the repugnant other to modernity. But the Witnesses regard the outside world as equally repugnant – a place of moral contamination which has allowed sin to become a perfectly respectable feature of everyday life – hence, whenever individual members take issue with their adversaries, they are, in fact, securing their own salvation. This suggests that the so-called individual freedom brought about by modernity is not something they are able to exercise in the sense in which it is theorised.

My fieldwork also offers some insights into how members of the Watch Tower movement conceptualise and avert risk. Risk perception varies in accordance with the social setting and the personality of the individual. While there is no doubt that the Society's teachings impact on private life, relationships in which there is an emotional bond between insiders and outsiders expose all the incongruities of principles and practice. I have shown how Watch Tower rhetoric sometimes gives way to competing loyalties, and it was probably only the sensitivity of this issue that prevented me from uncovering many more examples. Social context thus plays a crucial role in how devotees manage their relations with the outside world. Insiders are under considerable pressure from the Society to show outsiders that they are people of high moral fibre. This is why, in the public world of work, they tend to follow official Watch Tower teachings to the letter. In the private sphere of the family, the outsiders are those whose lives they share in the most intimate ways, and it is here that peace and conflict hang in the balance. Whatever strategies other millenarian movements adopt for dealing with the outside world, one thing remains clear – the Watch Tower movement cannot easily accommodate unbelieving parents, estranged spouses and dishonest factory workers. In the end, the Witnesses may be forced either to temper their zeal or to concede to the will of their opponents.

7   Honour thy father and thy mother

Some of the best examples of the Witnesses' opposition to the modern world are those concerning the socialisation of second and subsequent generation members. Not surprisingly, most Witness couples introduce their children to Watch Tower principles very early on in life in the hope that this will result in baptism. Taking young children to Kingdom Hall meetings serves two essential purposes. First, it is an easy way of recruiting new members to the Society, thereby enhancing conversion statistics for the future and, second, it is a means of protecting what are arguably society's most vulnerable people from the snares of the devil. Year on year, the Witnesses circulate millions of tracts containing information for young people about welfare, morality (that is, social and sexual conduct) and personal happiness. The organisation also publishes a large number of tracts advising parents how best to educate their children in a world that is largely unsympathetic to its doctrines. Perhaps more interestingly, there is a growing amount of material which aims to help parents deal with children who rebel against the Watch Tower regime. The movement's teachings on both childhood and parenting provide the ethnographer with rich information for an analysis of millenarian religion.

Nurturing the innocent

The Witnesses are conscientious people who devote time and effort in educating their own children in accordance with the principles of the Watch Tower regime. Young boys and girls throughout the world are involved at a very young age, often from the point at which they have just begun to walk, in the spiritual activities of the Society. The introversionist outlook of devotees and the difficulty in attracting new members to which this gives rise means that children are a crucial resource. The effective socialisation of children is the Witnesses' strategy for survival. It would, however, be wrong to suggest that there is a uniform approach to parenting, whatever guidelines might exist. I have already shown how devotees deal differently with tensions between personal feelings and ascetic principles, and that there is no response to the modern world that could be regarded as typical. This also applies to the nurturing of children. While it is the hope of all Witness parents that their sons and daughters will continue to fight the Watch Tower cause, there are some quite significant differences in parenting. Examples of these differences include the enforcement of discipline, the degree to which children are allowed to associate with non-Witness children (other than at school) and, perhaps most surprisingly, the extent to which children are obliged to partake in Watch Tower activities. This last example is particularly true of mixed marriages.

The socialisation of children into the milieu of the Society occurs at both macro and micro levels. The macro level concerns the official precepts, particularly written precepts, issued by the organisation and communicated from top downwards, mainly in the form of tracts and articles.[1] Some of these are written specifically for children and contain advice about how best to achieve happiness in a world in which it is (allegedly) becoming increasingly difficult for them to grow up; while others are aimed at parents, offering support and encouragement in times of trial and tribulation. Micro socialisation is about everyday parenting and the scenarios to which this gives rise at grassroots level. The Governing Body propounds the view that well-mannered children are the products of good adult example, and this means the constant monitoring and surveillance of their behaviour. Responsibility for this is considered to rest largely with parents. The nature of children's activities, the dynamics of parent–child interaction and the various levels of discipline are the empirical measures against which micro socialisation can be examined.

The two major texts published by the Society for Witness children are *Your Youth: Getting the Best Out of It* (Watch Tower Bible and Tract Society of Pennsylvania 1976) and *Questions Young People Ask: Answers that Work* (Watch Tower Bible and Tract Society of Pennsylvania 1989a). Both books contain information and advice about issues such as sex, sexuality and dating, peer pressure, relationships with family members, education and leisure, drugs and alcohol, physical appearance and several others. The books are presented in readable but authoritarian style and the latter contains colour photographs for the purposes of illustration. Most children have their own copies of these tracts. One issue of which a great deal is made is that of respect for adults, with particular emphasis on honouring one's father and mother. Interestingly, the Society stresses the importance of child subservience even in those cases where parents may not be setting the best example of Watch Tower principles:

> Parents who are hot-tempered or immoral, who are drunkards, or who bicker with each other – are they really worthy of honor? Yes, for the Bible condemns holding any parent 'in derision.' (Proverbs 30: 17) Proverbs 23: 22 further reminds us that your parents have 'caused your birth.' This alone is reason to honor them . . . Though they are less than perfect, your parents have also made many sacrifices for you.
> (Watch Tower Bible and Tract Society of Pennsylvania 1989a: 13–14)

The acknowledgement in this passage that family life is sometimes far from happy is tempered with a conservative appeal to children to defer to authority. This reveals something important about the Witnesses' concept of childhood; for although it would be wrong to suggest that the Society adopts the Victorian view that children should be seen and not heard (Witness children are, after all, encouraged to take part in door-to-door proselytising), it is clear that it does not welcome dissidence or even mild questioning. This makes it very difficult for young Witnesses, especially those younger than sixteen, to refuse to undertake Bible study or to go along with their parents to the Kingdom Hall.[2] As with fully baptised adults, the Society is relentless in urging children to attend all Watch Tower meetings and to give them maximum priority:

> thousands of youths are finding the meetings at the local Kingdom Hall of Jehovah's Witnesses to be different from dull church services. These meetings provide one with a real opportunity to grow spiritually. Nevertheless, simply attending these meetings does not mean one is really benefiting from them.
> (Watch Tower Bible and Tract Society of Pennsylvania 1988: 11)

The article proceeds with a series of simple instructions for how best to prepare for meetings in order to avert boredom and to achieve maximum spiritual fulfilment. The children I met showed an earnest willingness to honour their parents' wishes by reading the Society's literature and agreeing to attend meetings. All claimed to enjoy studying and said that they looked forward to seeing their friends again the following week. On the whole, young Witnesses display an extraordinary degree of politeness towards adults and a profound respect for Watch Tower doctrines. Only subsequent generations who lapse in later life are usually prepared to say that they had found studying laborious, but had acquiesced during childhood, not only because they had had little other choice but also to keep the peace with their parents and with the congregational authorities.

Children's involvement at both Kingdom Hall and Book Study meetings cannot go unnoticed. Those as young as four or five can be seen volunteering answers to some of the officials' questions, but more active involvement increases with age. Long before their baptism, children partake in the role-play sessions (usually with adults) in preparation for door-to-door evangelism. Another member of the congregation or a close relative usually accompanies the child when he or she is involved in doorstep ministry. Parents, aunts and uncles are the driving force behind children's participation, but close ties between the child and his or her siblings and/or more distant kin help to sustain motivation. Studying is, by and large, a family affair. The Witnesses' dependency on blood relatives is crucial if children are to be effectively socialised into the Watch Tower belief system and if the movement itself is to survive in the longer term. In the short term, it would appear that, by subjecting their children to the serious study of Watch Tower tracts and to the endless activities that take place in the Kingdom Hall, devotees are able to exercise control in a remarkably different way to that of other parents. Witnesses are, to all intents and purposes, strict disciplinarians who do not allow misdemeanours to go uncontested or their authority to be challenged by those for whom they are morally and legally responsible. It is not uncommon to see children who step out of line at Watch Tower meetings being verbally and sometimes physically reproached by parents. One former member told me how, in his earlier years as a practising Witness, he had taken his two sons outside the Kingdom Hall and beaten them when they had become 'disruptive'. Although this might be the exception rather than the rule, parents frequently chastise their children verbally for becoming restless or allowing their minds to wander off a sermon. The macro socialisation of children only can work if parents are prepared to act as policing agents on behalf of the Society to achieve the compliance of those whom they are seeking to protect from the outside world. Hegemonic control over children is, *ipso facto*, hegemonic control over parents.

At the micro level, devotees go to considerable lengths to ensure that their children abide by the Society's rules. While not all parents prevent their sons and daughters from forming tenuous friendships with other young people who do not share their faith, every baptised adult has a responsibility to ensure that Jehovah's theocratic ministry is never compromised; and this means steering children towards activities (that is, leisure and other free time activities) that are compatible with Watch Tower teachings. Large groups of Witness children are often taken to tenpin bowling alleys, ice-skating rinks and the cinema. These pursuits usually take place at weekends and are arranged by parents who form their own transport and supervisory rota. Although teenagers are never allowed to go away on holiday alone with a boyfriend or girlfriend, they are generally free to join other Witness families on trips abroad with adults acting as chaperones. Inevitably, young Witnesses form their closest ties with their siblings, cousins and friends of a similar age with whom they are already in regular contact at Watch Tower meetings; hence, no matter how wide-ranging and well organised the holidays and leisure activities in which these children engage, peer association is nearly always supervised.

But children's leisure is not the only thing that parents like to vet. The Society is all too aware that, once very young children learn to read, the world is their oyster. Parents usually take great care to ensure that, where possible, reading materials, television programmes and, more recently, data that can be downloaded on computers meet the approval of the Governing Body. From an early age, children are weaned on infant reading schemes that contain the Society's own version of creation, the purpose of life, the path to salvation, the causes of suffering and what happens to us when we die. As one might expect, these books contain biblical stories, illustrations, puzzles and simple questions, all of which are designed to make children aware of the errancy of other systems of belief and the wickedness of the world. Perhaps the most subtle characteristic of Watch Tower literature for small children is the absence of conventional make-believe which one finds in non-religious books sold in the West. One mother told me that, although she bought her young son toys, she would not allow him to read books that contained references to witches, fairies or magicians because her religious beliefs condemned superstition. Her rejection of Christmas also meant that, by the age of four, her little boy was aware that Santa Claus was a fictitious character and would not, therefore, be bringing him any presents. There is no knowing whether all devotees are as painstaking as this in their efforts to safeguard their children against acquiring a surreal imagination, but one could be forgiven for thinking that, if the tenets of the Watch Tower are to be fundamentally upheld, no Witness child would ever become familiar with the vast array of nursery rhymes and adventure stories that are embedded in modern culture. In reality, however, child mythology pervades the public sphere (especially in school books), and this means that, no matter how committed to the tenets of the Watch Tower adult Witnesses might be, the censoring of the reading materials to which their children have access is something they will never be fully able to achieve.

Older children, because they are generally allowed more freedom and are exposed to secular adolescent culture (particularly at school), soon become aware of adult literature. There is nothing more alarming to parents who hold ascetic religious beliefs than an inquisitive thirteen- or fourteen-year-old growing up in a world in which traditional authority and moral boundaries have weakened. At the same time, preventing children of this age from hanging around on street corners does not necessarily curtail their interest in teenage magazines, romantic novels and a whole host of other publications that contain fictitious stories as well as factual information pertaining to the modern world. Literature of this nature is widely available in public libraries and local bookshops. In its anxiety over the so-called dangers of this material and the relative ease with which it can be obtained, the Society has little other option than to appeal to the moral integrity of youngsters in their congregations who might be tempted to read it:

> You should be particularly cautious about reading anything that expounds a philosophy of life. Teen magazines, for example, are full of advice on everything from dating to premarital sex – not always advice a Christian should use, however . . . Creating sexual fantasies is indeed the intent of some authors . . . Obviously, reading such material would not help one to follow the Bible's admonition to 'deaden, therefore, your body members that are upon the earth as respects fornication, uncleanness, sexual appetite, hurtful desire.' – Colossians 3: 5 . . . Before reading a book, examine its cover and book jacket; see if there is anything objectionable about the book. And if in spite of precautions a

book turns out to be unwholesome, have the strength of character to put the book down.

(Watch Tower Bible and Tract Society of Pennsylvania
1989a: 284–8)

But, however willing young Witnesses are to heed the moral precepts of their elders and betters, there is one resource that has given children more freedom than ever before to access written and visual text; namely, the internet. This revolutionary technology has enabled young and old alike to search for information ranging from gardening to pornography – a prospect that fills many parents with horror. The Society's response to the worldwide web is ambivalent. At its most sanguine, Watch Tower literature has applauded international electronic communication – a facility from which the organisation itself has benefited. Not only does the internet provide devotees with the opportunity to proselytise through their own websites, it also enables them to e-mail their brethren abroad and to keep abreast of what is happening thousands of miles away. But the Governing Body also has misgivings. At no other time in history has there been so much electronic data available at one click of a mouse button and so little control over what can be found. At the moment, there is little to prevent anyone from establishing their own website address and from supplying potential browsers with whatever information they might request. For this reason, internet surfing is dangerous business. This is one occupation parents are unable to police, and any attempt to do so might encourage a curious child to download illicit material. While some Witness households are connected to the net, the versatility of this technology is a source of great concern for the Society's Governing Body.

On a more prosaic note, it is less difficult for devotees to control their children's television viewing. Although Witnesses are by no means the only parents to worry about the possible effects of television on children's behaviour,[3] the Society still issues an authoritarian warning against unsuitable television programmes and makes some suggestions for how they can be avoided:

> take a hard look at what shows you've been watching. 'Does not the ear itself test out words as the palate tastes food?' asks the Bible. (Job 12: 11) So use discernment (along with the advice of your parents) and test out what shows are really worth seeing. Some determine in advance what shows they will watch and turn on the TV *only for those shows*! Others take sterner measures, establishing no-television-during-the-school-week rules or one-hour-a-day-limits.
> (Watch Tower Bible and Tract Society of Pennsylvania 1989a: 294)

Although this passage is vague in its recommendations of daily viewing and in its description of what constitutes a 'worthy' programme, the tract goes on to list a series of undesirable consequences of too much television, including slipping grades, poor reading habits, diminished family life, laziness and exposure to unwholesome influences. But, unlike written text, televisions are audible items that occupy corners of rooms in which adults are usually present; thus, parents are in a much stronger position to dictate proceedings and can send their children to bed when things get out of hand. Moreover, adult members are themselves bound by the Society to exercise caution in their television viewing in order to ensure that those programmes into which they tune do not offend Watch Tower authorities. One couple explained that they were willing to watch only programmes that would be suitable for their own children and that portrayed behaviour that they, the parents, would allow to take place in their own homes. Consequently, programmes that contained offensive language, the use of drugs, violence or sex were switched off. But no matter how acceptable the content of a programme might be, Witness children are seldom allowed to watch much television because of the number of congregational activities that must be fitted in around homework. Added to this is the parents' disdain for media content and their fear of its ability to lead young people astray. Although there are variations from household to household, it is not uncommon to find whole families of devotees engaged in a study of *The New World Translation* or *The Watchtower* on those evenings when they are not at meetings. On one occasion, having been out for a drink with some people from the local congregation, I was invited back to a member's home for coffee, only to discover that her husband and thirteen-year-old daughter had spent the whole evening learning biblical references in preparation for a role-play activity at the Kingdom Hall the next day. Although this may not necessarily be typical, it serves as an example of the lengths to which this teenager was prepared to go in pursuit of the post-Armageddon Kingdom. For young Witnesses with as much zeal for their faith as she, home entertainment is a small sacrifice for everlasting life.

It would be remiss of me to end this section without commenting on how parents deal with older children who begin to express an interest in the opposite sex. Naturally, Witnesses in their mid- to late teens often form an attraction for someone of a similar age either in or outside the organisation and yearn for a relationship. But, unlike many of their counterparts in 'the world', these young sectarians are not given the approval of those who are responsible for their well-being. The Governing Body is critical of parents who allow children unlimited freedom, and premarital sex is forbidden. In turn, parents have deep reservations about nightclubs, city-centre pubs and other social arenas that encourage hedonism, even if their children are of a legal age to enter them. The Witnesses' approach to romance is regarded by many as old fashioned. Dating while still at school is frowned upon, partly because of its possible effects on educational attainment, but mainly because those of school age are considered far too young to enter into relationships. It is every Witness parent's dream that their child will marry within the community and bring his or her own children up as committed members.[4] Although the Watch Tower authorities see nothing wrong with platonic friendships between young people of the opposite sex, encounters that can stimulate sexual appetite are condemned on the grounds that they can lead to sinful behaviour. Parents who suspect that their son or daughter may be physically attracted to another young member of the congregation are inclined to keep a watchful eye on proceedings.

Notwithstanding the Society's objection to unsupervised romance, it would be more than a little surprising if the Governing Body were to issue an official age at which serious dating could commence. In general, young couples in their late teens are free to meet each other without a chaperone. By this age, the tacit rules of dating are the same as for anyone else in the organisation. But courting couples have a moral responsibility to show the rest of the world that chastity is not dead; hence, while they are free to meet each other in public places, they must take all necessary steps to avoid being alone together in private. Moreover, Watch Tower guidelines for young people stress the importance of sexual purity before marriage, and urge those who are dating to resist situations that may lead to temptation. Witnesses in romantic relationships, including those engaged to be married, can face serious disciplinary action if there is any reason to suspect that they may be involved either in sexual activity or in immodesty such as petting or heavy kissing. Engaged couples who buy houses in preparation for marriage must make every effort to ensure that, should they need to carry out repairs or do some decorating, a third party such as a friend or relative is always present. There is one case with which I am familiar involving a young woman who, because of a dispute with her family, had already moved into the bungalow that she and her future husband had bought some weeks before. In order to demonstrate the purity of their relationship to the neighbours, she arranged to meet her fiancé outside the house when he visited. She even prepared his evening meals which he ate in the car. Though reminiscent of a bygone age, chivalry of this kind is an outward sign of what the Witnesses regard as clean living.

Parents in the organisation often talk to their children about the importance of sexual morality and are scathing in their condemnation of premarital pregnancy. It is not surprising, therefore, that sex is an issue that devotees prefer to keep within their own families. The large body of Watch Tower literature with its persistent stress on the importance of celibacy outside and fidelity within marriage approaches sexual issues from a moral perspective that does not allow for deviation. Although there are sections in this literature on puberty and hormonal changes, there is no mention of birth control. Some parents with whom I spoke were vehemently opposed to sex education in schools since they believed it would encourage even more teenage pregnancies, the rate of which they already considered reprehensible.[5] The Witnesses' unabated attacks on homosexuality and adultery serve also to inform their children that restrained heterosexual sex between married couples is the only acceptable form of sexual expression, and one on which their continued membership of the organisation as fully baptised adults in future years depends. In the meantime, it would take a courageous child to argue.

Growing up in the Watch Tower Society is not something non-Witness children would envy. While the effects of childhood socialisation vary from one individual to another, there is little doubt that the movement's *Weltanschauung* has a huge impact on the ways in which young Witnesses view the world. This may also be true of mainstream Christianity and other systems of belief, but former members who were reared in the Watch Tower community have spoken to me at length about how, although they were far too young to question anything their parents told them at the time, they felt that they were somehow different from other children. This is seldom something Catholic, Anglican or even Muslim children tend to experience, not so much because there are more of them in the mainstream British education system but rather because their beliefs do not prevent them from doing things that most other children are able to do. This is not to say that Witness parents do not buy their children toys, games and learning aids, but I have offered several examples of how conventional childhood – regular play time, escapism and adventure, watching anything other than a small amount of television and writing letters to Father Christmas – is rejected by the Witnesses because of the sectarian and essentially rational nature of their beliefs and the effects of these on their way of life. To the sceptical outsider, this is a childhood devoid of enchantment and frivolity. Whatever one's position, children who are brought up in accordance with a strict religious code such as this have little other option than to honour their fathers and their mothers.

Lambs to the slaughter: young Witnesses at school

Like the workplace, the education system does not allow the Witnesses to avoid the outside world; yet, for all their antipathy towards secular forces, few educate their children at home. Nor does the Society have its own schools. This means that young devotees are committed to state education until they are sixteen; unless, that is, they have been given special exemption as in the case of children with severe learning difficulties or some such disability. This raises a number of interesting issues. I have already shown how the Witnesses go to considerable lengths to discourage their children from having too much contact with non-members for fear of secular influences. I have also argued that parents are duty-bound to ensure that their children are protected against textual and electronic media that undermine Watch Tower theology. What, then, is the Society's general advice to children regarding participation in school life? What happens when young Witnesses are asked to take part in school activities that are incompatible with their religious convictions? How do schools respond when Witness parents request that their children be exempt from certain educational activities? And how do Witness pupils negotiate their interactions with their unbelieving peers?

The Witnesses' approach to education is marked by an unusual combination of resistance and compliance. In 1983, the Society published a detailed pamphlet entitled *School and Jehovah's Witnesses* (which it revised in the mid-1990s) outlining its position on education. The pamphlet was intended mainly for school authorities and began with a summary of the organisation's main beliefs before going on to discuss youth morality, national celebrations, the school curriculum, extracurricular activities and the role of parents. Although the pamphlet was written in a very courteous manner, it contained a large number of objections to much of what went on (and still does) in the modern education system, and these had huge implications for pupils with a millenarian orientation. In addition to this pamphlet, the Society also addressed children of school age through its youth tracts from which I have already quoted. These contain specific chapters that address educational issues (Watch Tower Bible and Tract Society of Pennsylvania 1976, 1989a). The more recent pamphlet *Jehovah's Witnesses and Education* (Watch Tower Bible and Tract Society of Pennsylvania 1995) appears to adopt a much more conciliatory approach than this earlier literature, giving little mention of the 'dangers' of extracurricular activities or of the Witnesses' general disdain for further and higher education. This pamphlet applauds the efforts made by teachers to instil discipline and learning in schools, but continues to make known the Society's millenarian objectives. It must be borne in mind, however, that, since the Watch Tower organisation is a worldwide movement, it cannot hope to offer anything other than general advice to parents or to children of school age. It is certainly unable to respond to specific policy initiatives adopted by some local authorities or by schools themselves other than through its regular publications. Parents with concerns about a particular school tend to call on the support of other parents in the congregation or on officials from the Kingdom Hall. Given that the movement has only six million members worldwide, one is highly unlikely to find more than a handful of Witness pupils in a British school, and perhaps only one or two in the same class. Unlike the Kingdom Hall, the school is an environment in which young Witnesses find themselves in a small minority.

Few would doubt that the training involved in Witness ministry along with the amount of respect which children are expected to show their teachers complements the general principles on which school life operates. As I explained in Chapter 4, Witnessing requires the serious study of textual material and an inordinate amount of rote learning, mainly by preparing answers to hundreds of never-ending questions from tracts and magazines – a mechanistic system of stimulus-response that resembles traditional classroom teaching. It would be a mistake, however, to think that, because Witness children are disciplined readers and listeners, they are high academic achievers. There are two main reasons why this is not generally the case. First, the passive 'learning' that takes place in the Kingdom Hall and at Book Study meetings fails to procure the critical thinking, less still the analytical skills, required for high-level academic performance; and, second, the Society's message is unequivocally spiritual, which means that, whatever the academic potential of its younger members, evangelistic activities take priority over educational success. Young Witnesses who intend to undergo baptism rarely progress to college or university. This can be a source of regret in subsequent years among those who are reared in the organisation but who later defect. One former Witness told me:

> Witnesses don't push you with school work. If you're a Witness, education just doesn't seem to be an issue. Although my mum and dad always wanted me to do well, they didn't show a great deal of interest in my school work because, as far as the Witnesses are concerned, you're going to become a pioneer when you leave school and work part-time. You can't have a career because your 'career' is going to be in the Witness organisation. I started off at school with the best of intentions and I'd have liked to have done a lot better, but my parents never pushed me so I stopped trying. My sister who never questioned anything the Witnesses did went on to become a pioneer, worked part-time on a fruit and veg stall, has no direction, doesn't own her own house and doesn't have a pension scheme! I've been back to college since and done NVQs in Business Management and Administration.

This young woman's comments suggest that the Witnesses pay lip-service to compulsory education and that they fail to use it as an avenue for upward social mobility.[6] Although the Governing Body wants its younger members to be able to read, write and express themselves well (if only to improve their ministry work), it continues to worry that education for the sake of career success and material wealth might lead to the pursuit of personal interests at the expense of one's spiritual well-being:

> you will likely agree that success in life involves more than just material prosperity. In recent times men and women whose whole lives had become absorbed in their careers lost everything upon losing their jobs. Some parents have sacrificed their family life and the time that they could have spent with their children, missing out on helping them to grow up, because they were consumed by secular work. Clearly, a balanced education should take into account that more than material prosperity is needed to make us truly happy. Jesus Christ stated: 'It is written: "Man does not live on bread alone, but on every word that comes from the mouth of God." '
>
> (Watch Tower Bible and Tract Society of Pennsylvania
> 1995: 6–7)

Witness pupils who express an interest in pioneering maintain that work is simply a means to an end; a necessary evil that will enable them to earn a modest living while they carry out their door-to-door evangelism.[7] In the meantime, the Society urges children to attend school regularly, complete their homework and contribute as much as they can in lessons, while forbidding them to take part in anything that violates the movement's principles. They are also sternly advised to avoid situations that may cause this to happen. The 1970s and 1980s Watch Tower publications listed a multitude of school rituals and activities from which Witness pupils had to refrain including all forms of non-Witness worship, school politics, nationalistic practices such as saluting flags and singing anthems, curricular and extracurricular activities for Christmas and Easter, school dances and a whole host of other activities that could lead to 'unwholesome associations'. Parents were requested to keep a close eye on certain aspects of the school curriculum, particularly performing arts and media programmes, in order to ensure that their children were not being exposed to hedonistic culture.[8] Although the Society has no objection to religious studies syllabuses that contain factual information about world faiths, participation in religious worship continues to be strictly forbidden. This means that, like the Muslim community, the Witnesses may choose to withdraw their children from school assemblies that include Christian prayers and/or hymn-singing. It is, however, becoming increasingly common for Witness children to attend school assemblies while abstaining from these rituals. Participation in after-school clubs is still discouraged, partly because it is feared that it will leave less time for Witnessing activities but mainly because of the movement's concern that voluntary peer association may lead to undesirable secular influences.

Watch Tower precepts have a significant impact on the lives of young devotees at school. Witness parents, perhaps more than any others, find themselves in constant dialogue with governors, teachers and other educational administrators who work within a system that does not always operate in accordance with Watch Tower doctrines. Although a child from any background might wish to refrain from certain school activities, the larger than average number of objections made by the Watch Tower Society makes it impossible for its young members to experience an education that is completely free from tension with school authorities. Although it is true to say that Witness pupils who attend non-denominational schools are usually spared from having to conscientiously object to religious worship, they must continue to jettison those aspects of school culture that contravene the Watch Tower code if they are to show the outside world that they are Jehovah's faithful servants.[9] The young Witnesses I met all claimed that their teachers showed understanding by excusing them from activities that went against the Society's principles and by exercising diplomacy during such times as Christmas and Easter. British schools now produce comprehensive policy documents that contain guidelines on how to deal with children who follow heterodox religious creeds.[10] This puts an onus on teachers to think of different ways of occupying Witness pupils at those times of the year when the rest of the class are making Mother's Day cards, preparing turnips for Hallowe'en, designing floats for St George's Day carnivals, electing school representatives, rehearsing nativity plays and painting Easter bunnies. These examples convey the dissonance between British culture (that is, a culture rooted in the Judaeo-Christian tradition) and non-Trinitarian religion. At the same time, the fact that the education system makes concessions to parents who request that their children opt out of certain activities is indicative of its acknowledgement that Britain is a pluralistic society in which people's citizenship rights should be protected.

As far as Witness pupils themselves are concerned, having to manage a sectarian identity in an environment alongside hundreds of other youngsters who do not share their beliefs poses a difficult challenge. Unlike their parents, second-generation Witnesses have not made a conscious decision to become members of the Watch Tower community (until, that is, they agree to undergo baptism); hence, their involvement with the movement is compulsory, at least until the time that they leave school. The quality of school life for a Witness child is dependent on a number of social and psychological factors, and variations in experience are enormous. In general terms, those who accept the Society's precepts throughout the whole of their childhood tend to remain within the Watch Tower community as adults. These pupils, because they have been trained from a very young age to show respect for authority, are usually held in high regard by their teachers. With the exception of their refusal to co-operate fully with the school system because of their religious convictions, Witness children are renowned for their compliance and usually leave school on favourable terms, even if they are not the highest achievers. But, as I will argue shortly, some young Witnesses wage war against the Watch Tower regime while they are still under their parents' jurisdiction, and when this happens there is no reason to think that their rebellion is confined merely to the family unit. Although I have never met a young devotee who has been in legal trouble (at least not to my knowledge), I have interviewed anxious parents who have received letters from school informing them of their son's or daughter's mis-demeanours such as truancy, failure to submit homework or disruption in class. Psychologists have long argued that personality traits are as much to do with a child's willingness to conform as with social (or in this case, religious) conditioning, and there is no guarantee that Witness children will have a more trouble-free school life than their non-Witness counterparts. Whether or not this triggers second-generation defection from the Watch Tower Society is another matter.

There can be little doubt that schools are not the most pleasant environ-ments for members of millenarian movements. State schools are, on the whole, secular institutions attended by children whose behaviour is not governed by world-renouncing tenets. Youngsters who are religiously indifferent are consumers of a kind of education different from that of their forebears. Not only have we seen the erosion of religious ideology in the hidden curriculum, but there has also been a huge change in the ways in which teaching and learning are conceptualised; most notably, the emergence of new philosophies of discipline and control that no longer contain a religious element. In an age in which moral authority is questioned as never before, it is not unusual for children who have been brought up in accordance with ascetic values to be teased by their classmates. This became evident in an interview with Joshua, a thirteen-year-old Witness of rather sensitive character who shared with me his memories of what school was like in the days when he and his parents were members of the Watch Tower community:

> My school friends used to find it really odd because I didn't use to attend assembly or celebrate Christmas. They used to try to make me make Christmas cards, but I wouldn't do it; and they used to say, 'You're missing Christmas!', and they used to look at me and gossip about me like I was different, like I was some kind of freak, and they used to shout, 'Jovey!' 'Jovey!' But I wanted to go to Bethel and become a pioneer, so I tried to ignore it.

Joshua went on to explain how his religious identity made him feel more and more isolated as he progressed through school. Like his adult brethren, however, Joshua accepted that persecution was an endemic part of Watch Tower membership. Paradoxically, his awareness of his difference, exacerbated by his refusal to attend morning assemblies or to take part in any activity that violated Watch Tower teachings, seemed to have an empowering effect on him. This suggests that, if the religious convictions of teenagers like Joshua are anything like as strong as their co-believers at the Kingdom Hall, the humiliation they endure at school is more likely to affirm to them their exclusivity than to make them renounce their faith. For these young devotees, the prospect of becoming pioneers compensates for the mockery with which they must contend in an education system that they claim is unable to provide them with an opportunity to fulfil their spiritual potential.

Witness pupils with more forthright personalities than Joshua are perhaps better equipped to confront religious prejudice at school, but even they do not find it easy to remain composed when they are being ridiculed. For as long as she could remember, Tammy had resented her parents taking her to Kingdom Hall meetings and, unlike Joshua, left the movement while her parents were still members. She told me:

> My parents had taken me to meetings for as far back as I can remember, so I'd never known anything else; but, because of my strength of personality, I didn't take any flak from anybody at school for being a Jehovah's Witness. People knew I'd give just as good as I got; but I did

get tremendous stick for knocking on doors. I'd go and knock on my friends' doors knowing that I was lining myself up for a barrage of abuse at school. They thought I went knocking on doors of my own accord and they'd be laughing and joking and making me feel uncomfortable. It was terrible; total humiliation! I had a sheet and you had to tick off which doors you'd been to. So in the end, I used to go with my friend and we'd take this sheet and go and sit down a back alley and have a fag and cross a few things off this sheet.

Tammy's testimony conveys the different ways in which Witness children are affected by teasing from their non-Witness peers. Tammy's rebellion against the Society meant not only that she was more able than Joshua to embrace secular school culture but that she was indeed part of it. Her confident personality allowed her to make many friends at school despite having to comply with her parents' request that she abstain from activities that contravened Watch Tower injunctions. Her regular association with those more streetwise than she led to occasional truancy and a willingness to engage in deviant habits such as smoking tobacco and drinking alcohol. From the Witnesses' point of view, Tammy's refusal to comply with Watch Tower tenets makes her a very poor role model for other children in the movement to follow. Second-generation members who are as comfortable with the world as she are considered worryingly brazen, while Joshua, for all the jeering he faced, remained loyal to the organisation throughout his school life. This suggests that familiarity with school peers can be the beginning of more serious rebellion against parents and against the movement itself in subsequent years – a sequel that did in fact occur in Tammy's final two years of education. As far as Tammy was concerned, the time spent at school with people in 'the world' was intermittent relief from studying Watch Tower literature and knocking on doors. These were activities from which her school friends, by virtue of their non-Witness status, were exempt, and this caused her to envy them greatly. Nevertheless, there was little chance of Tammy accepting their frivolous jibes with humility.

Although Joshua and Tammy are only two individuals, their stories convey some of the struggles that the secular world presents both to Witness parents and to their children. Those responsible for education (particularly those who implement policy) are clearly in a difficult position; for, although we are living in an age in which ascetic religion is becoming less fashionable, teachers and governors must find a way of administering a system that reflects Britain's pluralistic character. Like them or loathe them, heterodox religious beliefs are here to stay. Jehovah's Witnesses, Muslims, Sikhs and Hindus have always been entitled (at least in principle) to the citizenship rights on which Britain prides itself.[11] State schools have extensive equal-opportunities policies that allow pupils from religious backgrounds to opt out of certain curricular and extracurricular activities without discrimination. In this respect, the Witnesses are beneficiaries of modern liberal democracy. But, as I have shown in this section, Witness pupils, because they belong to a movement that discourages assertiveness, can never be guaranteed a trouble-free life at school. This may well be the acid test of their conviction.

The ones who say 'no'

Continued membership of a totalitarian organisation is never unconditional. When Russell founded the Watch Tower Society in the late nineteenth century, his intention was to offer an alternative belief system to mainstream Christianity, and one (the only one) that represented the word of God. From the time of its inception, the Society was indisputably sectarian – it was small, it was intense, it claimed monopoly over truth; and, consequently, its members felt exclusive. Communities like this are dependent on those born into them for long-term survival. The movement owes much of its success to horizontal and vertical recruitment. Mothers, fathers, brothers, sisters, sons, daughters, aunts, uncles, nephews, nieces, cousins, in-laws, grandparents and grandchildren are all prime candidates for baptism – a rite of passage that boosts the Society's membership. Were it not for the significance of kinship, the Witnesses would not have had nearly the amount of success they have either in recruitment or in sustaining high levels of commitment. But what about children who express disdain for a movement they have been brought up to believe is so sacrosanct? What do the parents do *then*?

In a world in which people are allegedly free to choose from a whole range of options, children's acquiescence matters to the Society as never before. Most of the available research suggests that the Witnesses are successful in retaining their children. For example, Beckford (1975a) discovered that around two-thirds of second-generation Witnesses over sixteen remained active members. This was also borne out in the General Social Survey of 1994 that showed a retention rate of around 70 per cent.[12] The Witnesses nurture their young in accordance with Watch Tower doctrines because they believe it is the right thing to do, and, as far as they are concerned, that is the end of the matter. At the macro level, the Governing Body has a responsibility to ensure that parents in every congregation are supported to the *nth* degree, not only because it shares the same spiritual objectives but also because it must consider long-term survival. So long as children toe the line, all will be well; but those who break away from the movement do damage to its membership statistics. Children are the movement's bread and butter. Only a parent lacking in foresight would allow a child to miss Kingdom Hall meetings or to question the principles on which the theology is based. Only a foolish one would encourage excessive contact with the outside world or turn a blind eye to influences that could have serious consequences. For the Witnesses, an expedient parent is a forbidding parent. It is a parent who recognises those seductive forces that will lead their child astray and who drives them away before they are able to strike. It is someone who is aware that even the nicest outsider who offers their child friendship may be a wolf in sheep's clothing; skilled at making something sinister appear glamorous. Witness parents, wherever they are, must always be on their guard.

Rebellion within the Watch Tower community can take a number of forms, all of which are interesting from a social scientific standpoint. The following selective account is not about feckless youngsters who go missing on a warm summer evening a few minutes before they are due to set off with their parents to the Kingdom Hall, or those who ignore the elder's request for silence when a meeting is about to commence. Nor is it about children who fail to take seriously the words of an angry parent when their preparation for a Book Study meeting has been found wanting. Minor misdemeanours such as these constitute little more than general naughtiness and present no real threat to the Watch Tower regime. Instead, I have decided to focus on children of around fifteen upwards who have decided, without reservation, that Watch Tower life is no longer for them. These dissidents are the Society's *bêtes noires*. Their behaviour poses a more serious challenge, and it has much graver implications. A child who is unwilling to partake in activities that relate to worship is not like a child who does not want to go to bed. Children who wish to terminate their membership are making a *spiritual* statement, and the effects are catastrophic. Congregational elders hope that, by the age of about sixteen, a young person who has received a Witness upbringing will make the decision to become an official publisher, for which baptism is a prerequisite. But this is also the age at which children have reached legal independence, and there is nothing to prevent those who feel spiritually suffocated from leaving home. As far as the Witnesses are concerned, this is not the issue. Those who abandon the Society, whatever their legal rights, are playing with fire; far more than those in the outside world who at least can be excused on the grounds that they do not know any better. In this respect, voluntary defection is like involuntary expulsion; the first step to mayhem, perhaps even to annihilation. How, then, does this defiance manifest itself?

Whatever else might happen, the kind of rebellion I am describing begins or ends with the refusal to attend Watch Tower meetings. Although this is never well received either by loved ones or by other devotees, it can happen for a number of reasons. Some individuals may feel anxious about having to stand on a platform and present an imaginary doorstep sermon in front of the whole congregation the following week; hardly an easy feat for a young person. Others may be aware of events that take place elsewhere on the evenings when meetings are held; it could be a game of football or an extracurricular activity at school. Or, less commonly, there could be an unbelieving relative at home (as in the case of mixed marriages) who has the luxury of staying in and watching television while the rest of the family is at the Kingdom Hall. Whatever the reason, the alternatives to studying religious texts and listening to what seem like endless monologues can be very attractive to someone for whom studying is an altogether too demanding way of life. This is not to say that second-generation members who turn away from the movement necessarily renounce its *principles*. For all their objections, it would be very surprising if these youngsters did not accept at least some of the values that they had had their whole lives to internalise. Lapsed Witnesses are thus no different from lapsed Catholics or lapsed Methodists in that their defection is usually a rejection of the organisation's rituals rather than its values of honesty, charity and integrity; and in some cases, even of its doctrines.[13] Consider, for example, the following testimony by Laura, a 25-year-old former member who, after several years of turbulence with her parents, left the community at the age of sixteen:

> My earliest memories of childhood are of being dragged to meetings so often; it was the absolute centre of my life for two hours at a time, three times a week. By the time I was about eight or nine, I started thinking 'This is a bind. I'm not enjoying this.' You see, the truth makes parents stricter than parents who aren't Witnesses; it keeps you in this little circle of people that you never go outside of, except when you're at school . . . But, leaving aside their religion, my parents are two very loving people who would give their best at all times. Most of what they say is true and I do believe it, I just can't follow it . . . but being brought up a Witness has given me a good steady base. I know I'm a responsible person; I think about things before I do them, I take other people's feelings into consideration . . . all sorts of things the Witnesses are, they've passed down to me.

Laura's disdain for Watch Tower meetings is tempered with what seems almost like an apology for her defection. While there is no knowing how much of the movement's theology former members like Laura accept, there was certainly a desire from those I interviewed to remain close to their parents, for whom they undoubtedly had a lot of affection. Whatever resentment these individuals might previously have had to contain, I found no evidence of permanent estrangement. For one thing, teenage defectors are likely to be living in their parents' home during the initial stages of their departure from the organisation – a situation that requires mutual tolerance if the lid is to be kept on a simmering pot – and, for another, the strong kinship ties for which the Witnesses are renowned cannot easily be severed between parents and children, however aggrieved the parties might feel. But these might be the only factors that prevent a family (certainly a Witness family) from falling apart in the short term; for teenage rebellion within the Watch Tower ranks often involves much more than an unwillingness to attend meetings at the Kingdom Hall. The 'rebels' I met all regaled me with stories of how, in what sounded like desperation for freedom, they would do such things as climb out of their bedroom windows in the evenings to be with their friends when their parents were downstairs, smuggle alcohol and cigarettes into the house, take public transport to forbidden venues and, in some cases, even form illicit relationships with the opposite sex. Tammy's story illustrates some of this:

> I had a large circle of Witness friends and we were *all* doing things we shouldn't have been doing . . . we were all smoking, we were all drinking, we were all going out with the opposite sex, we all used to go home late. I remember one night, we were supposed to be going ice-skating and Martin, my cousin, had sneaked some Special Brew under his coat and we drank it together in the park . . . on that occasion, we got the bus back to his house 'cos we weren't being picked up . . . but I'd say a good half of us have now left the truth.

Tammy's recollection of her deviant behaviour as a fifteen-year-old suggests that second-generation rebellion within the organisation is more widespread than parents realise. Regardless of whether they remain in membership, youngsters such as Tammy are no different from any other teenagers hungry for freedom. What *is* clear is that these youngsters see themselves as far less privileged than other people their own age who are lucky enough not to have parents whose lives are governed by sectarian precepts. Tammy's rebellion can thus be seen as a response not merely to authority but to her parents' *brand* of authority; that is, to a set of controls which she considered unreasonable. She firmly believed that the conflict with her parents could have been greatly reduced had they been more liberal:

> By the time I was at secondary school, I started thinking to myself, 'I could be going out with my friends tonight to the park, just messing about doing this and doing that, not to do anything wrong, but just to go out to the youth club and things like that; but instead I've got to go to a meeting for two hours, and by the time I get home it'll be too late'. When I was about thirteen, my parents wanted to mould me and limit my association with certain people. Even when I was older and I was allowed out, there was always a curfew of half past eight; everybody else was going home at ten . . . mind you, other Witness children weren't allowed *any* association with any non-Witnesses apart from at school, so I suppose I had a lot of freedom! By the time I was in my final year at school, I was spending most of my time fighting my parents and, at that point, I decided I wasn't going to any more meetings. They were trying to control me and I didn't want to be controlled; they weren't willing to bend at all. If I'd just been left to do my own thing for a while with guidance rather than strict guidelines, I might still be a Witness now.

The lengths to which Tammy's parents were prepared to go to ensure that she remained within the parameters of the Watch Tower Society – their insistence that she attend all meetings, the limited amount of time she was allowed to spend with her non-Witness friends and the curfews she had to meet – demonstrate their suspicion of the secular world and their perceptions of its danger. This is the consequence of no ordinary generation gap. A great many parents who live in the modern West make the claim that, when they were teenagers, things were different; that it was safe to walk the streets without fear of attack, that they could leave their homes unlocked and know that they would not be burgled and that there was never any sex before marriage. But unless, like the Witnesses, they hold fundamentalist religious beliefs, their nostalgic memories of a world in which crime rates were low and moral standards were high do not generally cause them to impose anything like the constraints on their children to which Tammy was subjected. Tammy and her Witness friends are not necessarily indifferent to religious matters. Rather, they see themselves as products of parents who view the world with far deeper suspicion than is justified – parents who believe that children who have too much contact with secular influences tumble interminably into some vortex of depravity. Witness children who show signs of adapting their lives in accordance with the mores of the present day fill the Watch Tower community with fear. The Witnesses know that the modern world is vacuous (this is, after all, something on which their theology thrives), but their own children must give it a wide berth if Satan is to be restrained.

The rebellious acts in which Tammy engaged in her younger years – smoking tobacco, drinking alcohol and arranging illicit meetings with her friends in the park – are, however, minor aberrations compared with those of Natasha. Like Tammy, Natasha had quarrelled endlessly with her parents throughout her school years because she hated being made to attend Watch Tower meetings; but Natasha's story is much more dramatic. She had refused to attend meetings from the age of sixteen following an undignified exit from the Kingdom Hall one evening when she was about to take part in a role-play session:

> If you know anything about the Witnesses, you'll know that we have what we call the Ministry School where we do little household talks on the platform. Anyway, this particular lady from the congregation, I was her 'householder' and I'd been round and practised it the previous week, and I wasn't happy about it because of my age; I was quite self-conscious and I didn't want to appear a fool. Anyway, it came to the actual night, and just before I was about to walk on to the platform, I had a massive outburst and I just ran off to the toilets and I said, 'I'm not doing it, I'm NOT doing it, and I'm not coming again!' and my mum came running after me and she said, 'Oh yes you are!' and all hell broke loose, but I'd got it into my head that I was sixteen and that if I didn't

want to go any more, I wouldn't. I never went to another meeting after that.

Although both Natasha's parents were devout members of the movement, it was, in fact, her mother who claimed responsibility for ensuring that Natasha and her older sister completed their weekly Bible studies and door-to-door service work. Surprisingly, Natasha's father was less forthright than her mother, given that the Society equips husbands with greater authority than their wives in matters domestic as well as religious. This may be nothing more than the sum total of different personalities. On the other hand, it could be that, like most other women, Natasha's mother spent far more time than her husband looking after the children – also a consequence of a religion that operates along patriarchal lines. Needless to say, it was with her mother rather than with her father that Natasha most frequently remonstrated:

> Mum and I were at each other's throats constantly and it was a real hassle for my dad . . . he didn't want to get involved really. I remember one night when we were having tea, my mum and I were at it hammer and tongs, and he just picked up his plate and smashed it on the floor and he yelled, 'I've had enough of this!' He'd got to the point where he didn't know what to do next. My mum was so intense about things and he wasn't. She just kept pushing and pushing and pushing.

For the next two years, Natasha formed a steady relationship with her boyfriend, Lee, a lapsed Catholic who was four years older than she, and who had little time for religion of any kind. Naturally, Natasha's parents disapproved of the relationship and insisted that, while Natasha remained living under their roof, she came home every night and invite Lee round to the house only when they were present. They also forbade Lee and Natasha from going away together on holiday. Natasha's relationship with her parents finally reached an impasse when, a few weeks before her nineteenth birthday, she fell pregnant – a moral violation for which Natasha knew she would be evicted. With much foreboding, Natasha broke the news to her parents and went to live with Lee's sister. By the time Natasha had given birth to their baby girl, the couple had moved into their own home and planned to marry the following year. Meanwhile, Natasha's mother, who was probably at her lowest point in the crisis, told me:

> The problems we have had recently have taken their toll. This situation with Natasha has absolutely floored me. It all began when she said she didn't believe Armageddon's coming. We arranged for the elders from the congregation to come and talk to her, and since then, things went from bad to worse. She's gone living with her boyfriend now which obviously we don't approve of. She's even said that she's prepared to get

married in a Catholic church and the thoughts of that just smashes my mind to bits! I mean, there's no way we'd be able to go to the wedding . . . I've felt at times like I've been going demented. I've even considered going and speaking to a psychologist. I got books from the library on how to deal with teenagers. I've gone wrong somewhere! I feel like I've bent over backwards to show her loving kindness and I've kept getting slapped down. I find it very hard to talk about. Our theory is that it's the devil turning people away from doing what's right.

This whole family scenario warrants consideration for a number of reasons. Here we have a youngster who not only breaks away from the Watch Tower community but falls pregnant by and cohabits with someone who does not uphold its moral edicts – a bitter pill indeed for her parents to swallow. Natasha's behaviour epitomises everything the Witnesses deplore. Her family life from start to finish reveals how, even compared with other world-renouncing sectarians, the Witnesses have great difficulty in dealing with children who break the Society's ascetic rules. Though there are many wilful teenagers in the world, those who have grown up in the movement offend their parents in a very different way than those who have not. The austerity of Watch Tower tenets allows little scope for young members to embrace teenage culture without being considered at risk (or, more precisely, possessed by the devil). To the unsympathetic outsider, this 'risk' has been crudely exaggerated by a group of religious fundamentalists whose beliefs make it impossible for their teenage children to experience normal adolescence. From this point of view, the issue of rebellion is more about unrealistic parental expectations than about serious defiance.

As far as the Society itself is concerned, second-generation defectors are not treated with anything like the same contempt as those who are disfellowshipped; nor are Witnesses who remain in membership necessarily forbidden to liaise with them. Rather, Watch Tower literature appeals to parents to accept their prodigal child's decision to leave the community and to wait in hope for his or her return. *The Watchtower* regularly contains stories of young people who have abandoned the movement and who return at some later stage. Defectors are presented as frivolous, impressionable people who have taken leave of their senses, while those who are reinstated are portrayed as having learned a hard lesson in discernment, but who none the less deserve Jehovah's forgiveness. These stories often include personal testimonies from former lapsed members who explain how their craving for excitement led them into lives of debauchery, but how, by virtue of their former knowledge of 'the truth', they saw the error of their ways and returned remorsefully to the fold:

Are there people today who resemble the prodigal? Yes. Sadly, a relatively small number have left the secure 'home' of our heavenly Father, Jehovah. (1 Timothy 3: 15) Some of these feel that the environment of God's household is too restrictive, that Jehovah's watchful eye is more of a hindrance than a protection. (Compare Psalm 32: 8) Consider one Christian woman who was brought up according to Bible principles but who later became involved with abuse of alcohol and drugs. Looking back on that dark period in her life, she says: 'I wanted to prove that I could make a better life for myself. I wanted to do what I wanted to do, and I did not want anyone to tell me differently.' Like the prodigal, this young woman sought independence . . . The prodigal's dilemma was compounded by the fact that 'no one would give him anything.' Where were his new found friends? Now that he was penniless, he was as if 'an object of hatred' to them. (Proverbs 14: 20) Likewise, many today who stray from the faith discover that the allure- ments and views of this world amount to 'empty deception.' (Colossians 2: 8) 'I suffered much pain and heartache without Jehovah's guidance,' says one young woman who for a time left God's organization. 'I tried to fit in with the world, but because I was not truly like others, they rejected me. I felt like a lost child who needed a father to guide me. That is when I realized that I needed Jehovah. I never wanted to live independent of him again.'

(Watch Tower Bible and Tract Society of Pennsylvania 1998c: 9–11)

Parents, on the other hand, are depicted as God-fearing people for whom their child's departure is a devastating blow – a crisis that is said to affect them in much the same way as a bereavement:

'My daughter told me that she no longer wanted to be part of the Christian congregation,' says one Christian father. 'For days, weeks, even months afterward, I felt a gnawing pain in my body. It was worse than death.' . . . It is truly heartbreaking when a fellow believer manifests a desire to live contrary to God's standards. (Philippians 3: 18) When this happens, elders and others with spiritual qualifications strive to readjust the erring one. (Galatians 6: 1)

(ibid.: 8–9)

The passage also gives an indication of how the Society attempts to rescue potential defectors from what it will always see as the dangerous forces that pervade modern secular society. It is not uncommon for anxious parents to adopt a kamikaze approach to their child's obstinacy by calling on the support of other members as well as congregational officials. Elders and relatives use Watch Tower aids, particularly tracts that contain biblical references, in an attempt to steer the offender back on course – a strategy that rarely produces success with those who feel they have had more than their fair share of indoctrination. Second-generation Witnesses who do break away from the community usually manage to establish sufficient relations with the outside world to compensate for the reduced amount of contact with 'the truth'. These defectors are likely to have formed close friendships with non-Witnesses at school or, like Natasha, they may be dating an unbelieving partner. Unlike many of their older relatives, and probably even their parents, these individuals have not entered the movement as enthusiastic converts with the same kind of susceptible profiles as the people I described in Chapter 3. Moreover, they are youngsters whose rebellious behaviour enables them to see that the outside world, for all its shortfalls, offers an alternative way of life.

The evidence suggests that children who violate Watch Tower principles are children who are struggling to express their frustration with authority. Whatever stand one might take either against the Witnesses' *Weltanschauung* or against former members, few would deny that rebels are courageous individuals. The testimonies presented above are of young people who dare to express their independence of thought; people who share with us their stories of what sympathetic onlookers would see as a recoil from an oppressive regime. But it is also clear that relationships are as volatile in Witness households as any other, especially where dissident children are at loggerheads with their parents. Although levels of discipline vary, the effective socialisation of second-generation members is crucial if the authenticity of the movement is to be maintained. For this reason, parents continue to use anachronistic language when bemoaning their child's defiance. It is a fundamental axiom of the Watch Tower Society that youngsters who transgress boundaries cavort with the devil and thus lose the impetus to bequeath its sacred legacy to their own children. Its greatest challenge is to prevent the enemy without from becoming the enemy within.

Summary

By offering a glimpse into the lives of Witness children, I have highlighted some of the general dilemmas that modernity poses for the movement at both macro and micro levels. The available evidence exposes all the difficulties of belonging to an organisation that espouses heterodox beliefs in a rapidly changing world. There is little reason to think that the Witnesses will become more liberal as the twenty-first century evolves. For all its conservatism, orthodox Christianity is better able than the Watch Tower community to respond to modern society, particularly where children are concerned. Catholic, Anglican and other church leaders are acutely aware of the present difficulties in recruiting and retaining young people; and most recognise that teenage culture has undergone some enormous changes over the past few decades. At a time when mainstream churches have begun to provide drop-in centres for young people, temporary accommodation for homeless teenagers, pastoral support for unmarried mothers, help lines for gays and lesbians, health advisory clinics for pregnant schoolgirls and a whole host of confidential counselling services for adolescents with emotional problems, the Witnesses hold fast to an exclusive theology that they insist holds good for all people and for all time. As the world becomes increasingly fragmented, the Governing Body of the Society is less willing than ever to demand anything other than complete loyalty. At the moment, the movement is flourishing, and it is probably its fundamentalist message that enables it to do so; but it must ensure that its children remain in membership if it is to sustain its successful worldwide mission.

8 The fear of freedom

No story of the Watch Tower Society would be complete without an examination of why some of its fully baptised members choose to withdraw their support. Any religious organisation with an optional membership the size of this one will inevitably have a percentage of people who decide, for one reason or another, to exit at some point in their lives. From the movement's own perspective, there is never any valid reason for leaving. Its monopoly over truth does not allow members to make the claim that their search for salvation is causing them to seek new pastures or that their spiritual hunger has not been satisfied. Abandoning the Society is thus the ultimate betrayal since the individual voluntarily enters the world of Satan. In this chapter, I discuss the major sources of dissent and describe how the Governing Body of the movement responds to those who question its authority. I offer a detailed examination of the process of defection from the time of initial dissatisfaction to the point of departure. Personal testimonies are presented in order to establish what happens to those who leave the movement of their own accord. I also consider the implications of defection in the longer term, and explain how lapsed members adjust to a new way of life. There is, as one might expect, a wide range of biographical and auto-biographical literature on defection.[1] Close examination of this literature reveals that defection comes in various forms. For example, there are those who undertake Bible studies with the Witnesses and attend their meetings for several months, but never reach the point of baptism. Others are baptised members who, for one reason or another, stop attending meetings and lapse for while, only to return at a later stage. Some of these may even have been disfellowshipped several years earlier. Then there is a third group comprising fully baptised Witnesses who have been active in the Society for a considerable period of time and leave never to return. It is to these defectors that most of this chapter applies.

Suppressing ambivalence

There is little doubt that the Witnesses have many defectors. This can be inferred from the Society's own annual statistics which indicate year on year that the 'peak' number of active devotees outweighs the 'average' number. Moreover, the aggregate number of baptisms over a given period soon surpasses the reported increase in the number of members. But a high drop-out rate does not mean that the Society is dwindling or that its beliefs are weakening. An annual growth rate of 5 per cent is impressive by anyone's standards and can be seen as evidence of a movement that is successful in replacing apathetic members with committed ones. None the less, the figures show also that people leave the Society of their own accord. Reasons for defection vary from individual to individual, but in all the cases I encountered in my fieldwork it was triggered more by doctrinal dissatisfaction than by religious activities or social relations, although these can act as catalysts. The Governing Body's strategies for dealing with those who question its teachings force some individuals to spend several years, even most of their lives, suppressing doubts about the legitimacy of certain doctrines before deciding to leave. Others who have lost faith completely might never be able to break free because of their affective bond with friends and relatives in the movement.

The Society's record of prophecy failure has undoubtedly played a part in voluntary defection. The Witnesses expected the invisible return of Christ in 1874 (which was later changed to 1914 – the original date for Armageddon), the 1918 destruction of Christendom and the 1925 return of the prophets Abraham, Isaac and Jacob (see Barnes 1984, Quick 1989 and Reed 1989a). But it was the failure of Armageddon in 1975 that had the most devastating effect on Watch Tower membership – an event that had featured in the Society's publications since the mid-1960s:

> This seventh day, God's rest day, has progressed nearly 6,000 years, and there is still the 1,000-year reign of Christ to go before its end (Rev. 20: 3, 7). This seventh 1,000-year period of human existence could well be likened to a great sabbath day ... In what year, then, would the first 6,000 years of man's existence and also the first 6,000 years of God's rest day come to an end? The year 1975.
>
> (*Awake!* 8 October 1966: 19)

Tom, who had been in the movement since the early 1970s, explained how the 1975 prophecy failure made it impossible for him to remain an active member.[2] In a detailed testimony of how the prophecy governed his life during his initial stages of membership, he told me:

> Our main teaching book was called *The Truth Book* and there was a little graph in there which ended in 1975. I said it from the platform! We told everyone the end was near. When I became a Witness I gave up my insurance policies, I cancelled all my insurance endowments, I never bought a house because I knew I wouldn't need one, we didn't even want to put the kids' names down for school.

Tom went on to explain how some of his closest friends who were also members during the critical years leading up to 1975 decided to stop having children. This corresponds with the preparations made by other devotees in anticipation of the New Kingdom. For example, former member David Reed explains:

> Having already served some years in pioneer work, I had no home or property to sell. But I did neglect having necessary dental work done, figuring it would be better to devote my time and funds to spiritual things, since the end was so near and my body would be restored to perfection shortly after 1975.
>
> (Reed 1989a: 60)

Tom proceeded to inform me that he was so certain that the thousand-year reign of Christ would begin in 1975 that its failure to happen marked the beginning of his doubts about the authority of the Governing Body. When the autumn of 1975 came and went, millions of Witnesses became disillusioned. The movement was clearly in crisis. What, then, enabled it to survive? More importantly, how has it since managed to recruit and expand at such an impressive rate?

The answers to these conundrums lie in the strategies employed by the Governing Body in Brooklyn to stamp out disaffection, as well as an unwillingness on the part of the members themselves to abandon the community. Prophecy failure has been played down so successfully by the Society's leaders that long-standing Witnesses who have remained in membership appear to be unperturbed by it. In 1976, the Governing Body began to reinterpret the Books of Daniel and Revelation in the belief that Jehovah's plans remained unaltered, and it was this reinterpretation that helped the movement to survive in the years that followed. Meanwhile, Raymond Franz, who was to become President on 7 June 1977, managed to save it from complete loss of spiritual legitimacy. Speaking to a huge audience of Witnesses in 1976, Franz attempted to explain why the prophecy had failed. He told them, 'It was because *you* expected something to happen' (Penton 1997: 100). Franz suggested that, because Jesus had indicated that *no one* knew the day or the hour of the beginning of the Messianic Age, devotees had been wrong to pin all their hopes on the establishment of the New Kingdom in 1975.[3] Meanwhile, the leaders revised the Society's chronology and suggested that the prediction of Armageddon should have been calculated from Eve's creation rather than Adam's.[4]

These attempts to explain away the failure of prophecy are remarkably similar to the strategies adopted by the Azande in maintaining their faith in chicken oracles (Evans-Pritchard 1937). By a process which Evans-Pritchard calls *secondary elaboration*, the Azande are able to explain contradictory indications from their oracles in various ways, including the belief that the wrong kind of poison has been procured, or that a taboo has been broken, or that witchcraft is being used by someone in the village to damage the oracle and so forth. Thus, just as Evans-Pritchard argues that belief is sustained because magicians have elaborate procedures at their disposal that enable them to explain mishaps, the movement's leaders managed to avert scepticism by blaming the failure of the Armageddon prophecy on the devotees themselves. Wilson also comments on the successful way in which the Witnesses changed their eschatology. I have explained how they regard world events such as environmental pollution, increases in crime, scientific developments, earthquakes and wars as signs of the end. In the late 1970s, such events seemed to persuade those who might otherwise have questioned Watch Tower teachings that the predictions set out in Matthew 24 were surely coming to pass, and that this was still Jehovah's theocratic organisation. The Witnesses now claim that we are at the end of what they describe as 'extra time'; hence, prophecy failure has not brought about the abandonment of belief in the way one might expect. Simple as it seems, what sceptics regard as failure, the Governing Body regards as a test of faith. This is one way in which it is able to remove doubting Thomases.

It is highly unlikely that those who have joined the Society within the last two decades are aware either of the expectation of Armageddon in 1975 or of the previous eschatological errors. In all the Watch Tower literature that has been published since 1975, there has been no mention of these prophecies, except for the invisible return of Christ in 1914. The information conveyed to present members is carefully vetted in a way that typifies a totalitarian movement. On current calculation, more than 60 per cent of Jehovah's Witnesses in the world today joined the movement after 1975; hence, the Governing Body has no reason to discuss with them the failure of its earlier prophecies. The suppression of the 1975 prophecy failure by those who were active at the time but who have nevertheless remained in membership suggests an unusual degree of complicity. More importantly, it challenges the notion that religious movements are unable to survive empirical disconfirmations. As Wilson contends, it could well be that for individuals like these, remaining in a community that offers strong moral edicts as well as hope for the future would be less traumatic than defection:

> For people whose lives have become dominated by one powerful expectation, and whose activities are dictated by what that belief requires, abandonment of faith because of disappointment about a date would usually be too traumatic an experience to contemplate.
>
> (Wilson 1978: 184)

This is echoed in Barnes's autobiography:

> In early 1979, I confronted a Witness of long standing, with fully documented evidence of all false prophecies and discussed with him

the Bible's definition of a false prophet (Deut 18: 20). His reply was illuminating. He said, 'Oh well, you've got me over a barrel. But let me tell you why I intend to stay with the Jehovah's Witnesses. They don't go killing each other in times of war, they live up to high moral principles, they are the only people to uphold God's name . . .' This man provides a clear example of one of the psychological defence mechanisms in use among the Witnesses – the preponderance of good points over bad.

(Barnes 1984: 81)

When disillusioned members began to defect in 1976, Watch Tower leaders sought to defend themselves as follows:

At times explanations given by Jehovah's visible organization have shown adjustments, seemingly to previous points of view. But this has not actually been the case. This might be compared to what is known in navigational circles as 'tacking'. By manoeuvring the sails, the sailors can cause a ship to go from right to left, back and forth, but all the time making progress toward their destination in spite of contrary winds.

(Watch Tower Bible and Tract Society of Pennsylvania 1981: 27)

Next to this denial of any adjustments to prophecy, the magazine featured an illustration of a boat tacking into the wind and travelling in zigzags. To thousands, even millions of devotees for whom defection would lead to existential crisis, any attempt by the Governing Body to preserve its divine authority is likely to be successful. These attempts have been well documented by one of the best-known Watch Tower critics, Edmund Gruss. Gruss, himself a former member, is an anti-Witness polemicist who has produced an excellent critique of the movement's date-setting eschatology. He argues that the Governing Body has distorted its own history and indeed the Bible itself in order to enhance its hierarchical authority. Gruss's work is concerned with both the presentation of historical evidence and a detailed critical analysis of the Witnesses' own methods of prophetic understanding. He also comments on how, since 1975, the Society has cajoled its members into accepting its pronouncements by intensifying the threat of eternal damnation (Gruss 1972: 94–103). My fieldwork supports most of Gruss's claims. Devotees are warned of the danger of apostasy in all the Watch Tower literature and by congregational elders. Other systems of belief are in the usual style depicted as Babylon the Great, the world empire of false religion. The Society's control over potential dissenters is described succinctly by Botting and Botting:

One thing is clear: the Organization of Jehovah's Witnesses will not lie down and die, no matter how much dissention might be generated from within, and no matter how much persecution is generated from without. As long as its members believe that Jehovah is with them, as long as they assume that anything the Governing Body does is in perfect accordance with His will, they will support the organization to the end of the century and beyond. Individuals may come and individuals may go, but the society will continue; like Orwell's Ingsoc Party, it is 'immortal.' It may be a classic example of Orwellian oligarchical collectivism, but as long as committed Jehovah's Witnesses are prepared to accept their organization as a theocracy, that is what it shall remain.

(Botting and Botting 1984: 186)

Even Witnesses who start to doubt that the organisation is a theocracy still find ways of suppressing their doubts. Claire, a lapsed member in her late twenties, gave me several examples of sceptics she knew, all of whom she was very fond, who were still in membership at the time of the research, but were unwilling to break free:

Some of them seemed to know it was wrong. There are people in there who *know* it's not right. There are people who read apostate literature, but their excuse is that they're just checking up, but you're not telling me they're not aware of all the discrepancies.

Similarly, Eric told me how, not long after he had decided to dissociate himself from his local congregation, some of those who remained in membership contacted him and explained to him how they had harboured misgivings for a very long time, but all were too afraid to leave the community for fear of losing their closest friends and having no one else to whom they could turn.

Although the Society has had *some* success in silencing potential defectors, it has not been able to prevent every disillusioned Witness from spreading dissent. One man told me how he was visited by two congregational elders at his home when he continued to question Watch Tower chronology. Having collated evidence of prophecy failure from the Society's own literature, he began presenting the evidence to the elders, who immediately reported him to the presiding overseer for apostasy – an offence that can result in disfellowship. As I have explained elsewhere, disfellowshipped individuals must be shunned by the other members of the congregation, even if these members are close relatives. Witnesses maintaining any contact with disfellowshipped individuals also risk disfellowship. The people I interviewed offered accounts of how they were rejected by other members who were equally disillusioned, but who were too afraid to voice their concerns for fear of estranging their families. Control of this kind makes empirical measurement of sectarian dissatisfaction impossible. When Watch Tower doctrines fail to hold good, totalitarian forces are able to compensate, if only because life beyond the Society is impossible to imagine. The following story by Peter exemplifies the emotional anxiety experienced by Witnesses who seriously contemplate defection:

> More and more I began to discover things which caused me to become disillusioned and to be upset and to realise that there was something seriously wrong but I didn't know what it was . . . and also, there was nowhere else to go because this was the truth! I knew a number of other people who were likewise disillusioned and upset but they couldn't speak about it. Occasionally in conversation they would let a little bit out but they would soon pull themselves in. It was as if they couldn't openly discuss it. I knew a couple who were long-term Jehovah's Witnesses in the 1930s and 1940s, they never had children in fact, and eventually he died and I used to go and visit his wife, she was a lovely old lady and she was drinking heavily at the time, and, when I went to visit her, her defences would come down and she suddenly started criticising the organisation and saying, 'This is nothing new, what's happening now has happened before', but then she would pull herself together and say, 'Oh but it is the truth though, where else can I go?', and she was a very sad, disillusioned person, but where else could she go?

It is not uncommon for Witnesses who experience doubts about Watch Tower teachings to talk of having nowhere to go. Peter's description of this woman's dilemma is worth comparing with an extract from Barnes's autobiography:

> No sooner had this process of enlightenment begun than the powerful effects of Watch Tower brainwashing began to assert themselves . . . We felt the need to leave the Watch Tower Society because we didn't think we could go along with it anymore, but where could we turn? There wasn't anywhere to go . . . so we thought . . . The only alternative is to become an apostate, by going to some other church which is a part of Babylon the Great.
>
> (Barnes 1984: 90–1)

These two accounts reveal as much about former members' attitudes towards the outside world as they do their doctrinal dissatisfaction.[5] While the Governing Body's revised eschatology has no doubt been successful in retaining large numbers of people who may previously have considered defection, most of whom, after all, remain certain of the imminence of Armageddon, it is the powerful combination of the individual's affective bond with other devotees and their fear of the outside world that secure loyalty. For many, defection would not only mean rejection from close friends and relatives, it would also mean abandoning a community that has hitherto offered them psychological and emotional certainty for the biggest part of their lives. Though the inside may be fallible, the outside is potentially much worse. In his famous work *The Fear of Freedom* (1960), Erich Fromm suggests that this kind of submission to an all-powerful closed system is one way of escaping the problems of so-called liberal democracies. Though Fromm writes from a psychoanalytical perspective, he argues that the root causes of anxiety in the modern world are, in fact, social. Fromm argues that the collapse of medieval tradition and the development of modern capitalism, both of which ostensibly produced freedom, created isolation, doubt and emotional dependency.[6] In this sense, escaping freedom is a form of psychological liberation. Liberation *from* choice can lead to far greater security than liberation *as* choice. Fromm suggests that the rise of fascism in Germany in the twentieth century can, at least in part, be explained by a longing for the return to the authoritarianism of pre-individualistic society. For Fromm, withdrawal from the world and the destruction of others are mechanisms of escape and symptomatic of the need for authority. Whatever doubts individuals might experience within the Watch Tower community, it is most unlikely that they would regard life outside as better. When Witnesses suppress their ambivalence, they suppress the ambiguity that stems from the modern secular world. The aversion of risk is well worth the sacrifice of what others in their folly call 'freedom'.[7] If this analysis is correct, it would appear that the forces that lure people into membership are the very forces that prevent them from leaving. This notion that freedom exists *within* the Society was strongly supported by Maureen, who shared with me her perceptions of life outside:

> Some people look at Jehovah's Witnesses and think that the boundaries are incredibly tight, but I don't think they are personally. I think it gives you more freedom than somebody out there. You're free from a morbid fear of what might happen to you by going against God's laws, you don't believe you're going to be tormented by a fiery hell, you're free to think that God is a God of love and he wouldn't do something like that. I think you're free from being enslaved to a lot of superstition, whereas people will let themselves be ruled by all sorts of silly things like walking under ladders, or if they see a black cat, or how many magpies; it's amazing . . . and people who feel that their lives are ruled by the stars and they won't do a certain thing because their horoscope tells them not to do. So you're free from that. You're free because today's morals are so liberal and anything goes, because you stick within Jehovah's moral guidelines, you're free from outside immorality.

What appears from the outside to be a highly restrictive way of life is, from the inside, one of security and liberation. The oppressive forces of totalitarian control can be subjectively experienced as gratifying. Though they may doubt, Witnesses who continue to pledge their allegiance to the

Watch Tower community are removing the uncertainty that disempowers them. Suppressing ambivalence may be the only way in which they are able to resist the problems presented by modern life. Multiple options and individual choice are fertile soil for the restoration of moral authority. In short, the paradox (indeed, one of the many paradoxes) of modernity is that the freedom it promises is the freedom that is feared.

Breaking away: a new beginning?

Difficult though it might be, there are individuals who *do* abandon the Society, whatever the cost. As I began to study the autobiographical accounts of ex-members and the data from in-depth interviews, it became apparent that one of the most important catalysts in the cause of defection involves something that the majority of devotees never succeed in doing (not least because it is forbidden by the Governing Body); namely, studying the Bible without Watch Tower guidance. Officially, the Watch Tower leadership claims that its doctrines are based solely on the Bible, while Kingdom Hall meetings prepare the Witnesses for ministry. In practice, however, independent reading of the Bible is never possible, since the material recommended for reading serves a different purpose. In addition to studying the monthly bulletin *Kingdom Ministry* for midweek meetings, Witnesses worldwide are compelled to read the Society's *Yearbook* on a regular basis and to study the contents of *Watchtower* magazines in preparation for Sunday services. This means that although most of the material is packed with scriptural references, the Bible is seldom used systematically and meditatively.[8] All biblical interpretation is presented to the Witnesses by 'the faithful and discreet slave' (that is, the Governing Body), and this prevents them from engaging in individual Bible study or what Quick (1989) and Bowman (1991) call Biblical Hermeneutics. The Governing Body strongly discourages personal study in favour of 'guidelines' which critics argue enable Watch Tower expositors to align scriptural texts with current Watch Tower thinking (Quick 1989: 17–18). Both Quick and Bowman argue that, although devotees are adept in quoting scriptures when they deliver their sermons on our doorsteps, these scriptures are invariably misinterpreted and miscontextualised. Academic theologians who are trained in biblical scholarship often express concern at what they claim are inaccuracies in all the organisation's materials, including its own version of the scriptures (see for example Sire 1980, Franz 1983, Hoekema 1984, Reed 1986, Bowman 1991 and Wijngaards 1998).

   Any Witness found reading literature that attacks Watch Tower theology risks disfellowship, while those who are successful in undertaking their own study of an orthodox Bible such as the King James version claim they become immediately aware of inconsistencies. This was Quick's experience when he decided to use an independent translation of the New Testament.[9] Quick tells us that, after compiling a list of two hundred verses which he then subdivided into fifty-eight separate theological issues including the deity of Christ, the personality of the Holy Spirit, the year 1914 and the gospel message of salvation, he concluded:

> the gravity of what I had just done hit me like a ton of bricks. I had now succeeded in destroying all my deepest convictions concerning God, His people, the outworking of His plan of salvation and my place in this whole affair. I was now undeniably, utterly lost!
>
> (Quick 1989: 55–6)

Confessions of bewilderment at the time of personal Bible study are common among those who break free from the movement. This is the point at which Watch Tower doctrines start to be questioned. The one motivating factor for studying the Bible without the aid of the Society's literature was, according to those I interviewed, the quest for truth. This suggests that people who undertake a personal study of their own must initially be experiencing feelings of confusion or dissatisfaction with Watch Tower theology prior to their own research; but it is only when they begin to doubt fundamental doctrines that they are likely to do this.[10] The root cause of disagreement between the Witnesses and orthodox Christians lies in the way in which scriptural texts, particularly those of the New Testament, are interpreted.

Most former Witnesses who have written autobiographies have transferred their allegiance to one or other form of evangelical Christianity. It is perhaps no coincidence that Witnesses who undertake their own study of the Bible should elect this option, since nonconformist Christianity also uses the Bible as its fundamental source of authority.[11] The Witnesses' engagement in *personal* research exposes some of the issues raised in the previous chapter concerning privacy within a totalitarian system. But privacy of *belief* poses a potential outcome different from private acts in public places. This struggle for privacy was something to which Alison alluded in her discussion of how her rejection of some of the teachings – particularly the prohibition of voting, the refusal of blood and the subordination of women – caused her to defect. Similarly, Claire told me how she resented the inflexibility of the beliefs and the mechanical fashion in which they were imparted. Realising that there were no opportunities for her to express her concerns, she was forced either to remain silent or to abandon the Watch Tower cause. But individuals like Alison and Claire who part company with the Society enter the world of risk. From a modernity perspective, the inflexible mind-set of the Witnesses and the closed boundaries within which they operate are strong mechanisms for risk aversion. What the Witnesses regard as consistency, defectors regard as a violation of freedom and an obstacle to personal growth. Although this high degree of internal control may cause some dissatisfaction, it does not necessarily prevent those whom it affects from attending meetings or engaging in door-to-door evangelism. Those who show signs of inactivity, as indicated by their failure to attend meetings on a regular basis and/or to devote themselves to ministry, are encouraged by congregational officials to return to active fellowship.

Defectors who convert to orthodox Christianity refer frequently to their new-found belief in the deity of Christ, as exemplified in Quick's declaration:

> In earnest prayer I pleaded with God. 'Jehovah', I prayed, 'I've torn your book apart! Please, my God, help me to put it back together again . . .' I pulled out my New Testament again and read the next verse: 'The Spirit Himself bears witness with our spirit that we are children of God'. My eyes flooded with tears. That verse was talking to me! The Society had no part in this matter. God Himself was my Father, Jesus Christ, who had taken all my sins upon His own body and died for me was my only Lord and Saviour and the Holy Spirit had come to dwell with me and in me forever. I had been born again.
>
> (Quick 1989: 56 and 78)

Needless to say, it is important to exercise caution when examining testimonies such as this. The often pitiful stories of those who have at some point abandoned the Watch Tower movement in favour of something that they claim filled them with spiritual awe are likely to include the same kind of rhetoric as the embellished accounts of recent Witness converts. It would seem that the only time the Witnesses offer anything other than sanguine accounts of Watch Tower beliefs is when they decide to look elsewhere for their spiritual nourishment, at which point their stories become scathing. Former-Witness autobiographies invariably convey the emotional anxiety of people who have spent a considerable number of years in the organisation before discovering 'the real Christ'.[12] The following two accounts demonstrate this clearly:

> One Saturday morning, my wife and I got into our car to go to a nearby town to shop. My wife was driving and I sat next to her meditating on these things. I mentally reviewed all the texts that I had been studying, I weighed all the evidence. I suddenly said to myself, 'I know who Jesus is, He is God' . . . When we left the house that morning, I was *not* a person who believed that Jesus is God, when we returned home later that day, I did believe. *I believed totally, utterly and absolutely that Jesus Christ is God!*
>
> (Barnes 1984: 94)

Luke 4: 18, 19 opened up a whole new vision of Jesus' ministry for me. I had believed that His primary objective in coming to earth was to 'vindicate Jehovah's name'. But now I noticed the force of the word 'because' in that passage: 'The spirit of the Lord is upon me, *because* . . . he hath anointed me to preach the gospel to the poor . . .' Not a word about vindicating Jehovah's name! Gradually my eyes were opened . . . 'Lord!' I cried, 'Forgive me for making You a liar!'

(Trombley 1974: 30–1)[13]

The first account by Barnes is not dissimilar to that of Paul on the road to Damascus, while Trombley's testimony is particularly illuminating for those interested in how the mode of worship and expression of faith can change for former Witnesses who discover evangelical Christianity. Both auto-biographies are filled from beginning to end with references to spiritual gifts, miracles and speaking in tongues. Christian fundamentalist rhetoric contrasts sharply with the Witnesses' more rational concepts such as 'truth', 'studying', 'ministry' and 'Kingdom'. Defectors commonly claim that their new-found faith releases them from years of what they often describe as 'slavery'. Charismatic worship and healing services usually replace Kingdom Hall meetings and the serious study of Watch Tower literature.[14]

Once defectors claim to have discovered the deity of Christ, a new *Weltanschauung* replaces the old one. Many previously cherished beliefs are immediately called into question, none more seriously than the doctrine of how to earn salvation. For Christians more orthodox than the Witnesses, Christ's deity means that entry into heaven is available to the whole of humanity with faith as the only necessary requisite. This means that works such as delivering doorstep sermons, selling Watch Tower literature and attending weekly meetings are largely redundant. Alison shared with me her memories of the way in which she had devoted most of her life to serving the Society in the belief that works would eventually be rewarded in Jehovah's New Kingdom:

> There was a brownie points system for how many hours you'd been out on the doors. If you hadn't been out on the doors for three months consecutively and done enough hours, then one of the elders came round and gave you a pep talk and you get a little black mark on your file . . . they actually kept files on everybody which horrified me. There's a *lot* of work involved in being a Witness. There's a woman who lives near us, she's only got one eye and she's virtually crippled with arthritis, she has a walking stick and she's a full-time pioneer. She's out there forty-five hours a week. It's just dead work!

Misgivings about the movement's relentless control over the Witnesses are expressed in most autobiographies of former members. Here are three more examples:

> I used to love attending meetings. I never missed a single one. But when the Lord freed me of the hypnotic spell of the Watch Tower religion of

'buying and selling', He also freed me of all desire to go to the Kingdom Hall.

(Schnell 1956: 199)

I seemed continually to be thinking on lines different from the Witness teaching. My mind was in constant turmoil, with so many unanswered questions. By now, I had lost the vision of a caring, loving, merciful Heavenly Father, in whom I had put my trust in earlier years. He had been replaced for me by a wrathful Jehovah God, a hard task-master, never satisfied. Yet all the time I might have turned to my Bible and been liberated through the precious name of the Lord Jesus Christ and received the spirit of adoption.

(Tomsett 1971: 36–7)

I wanted to be eaten alive, devoured by Jehovah, to spend so much time in his service that my peevish spirit, humbled and exhausted, would no longer have time for querulous doubts . . . what I was doing by entering Bethel was making spiritual capital out of spiritual despair, quelling my restlessness by giving it a death in a new life.

(Harrison 1980: 202)

These accounts make constant reference to the feeling of never being able to *do* enough to achieve salvation.[15] When Witnesses decide to defect, they often regret the many hours they had previously spent studying, ministering and generally working for an organisation run by officials who they claim were never satisfied. The Witnesses' emphasis on works enables them to plan their own religious career with a view to enhancing their chances of entry into the New Kingdom. Tom told me about a brother he once knew who had aspired to become an elder. After many years of evangelism, the man's dream came true; but, as soon as it did, he lapsed. It later became apparent that he had doubted its authority for most of his life. This story not only illustrates the point that the most 'successful' Witnesses are those who devote the greatest number of hours over the longest number of years to Watch Tower activities, it also supports the point that ambivalence is often suppressed.[16]

The defectors' recognition of the superiority of faith over ministerial duties is part of their new belief that truth is a spiritual discovery.[17] Although the world is still regarded as sinister, the departing member is now in a position to enter new negotiations with the outside world. Nevertheless, the decision to defect is often hindered by emotional factors that add to the stress of the experience. Eric described the reactions of his friends when he announced his decision to bid the community farewell:

I visited most of my closest friends within the Watch Tower and I said, 'Look, I'm going to be resigning and I know that when I do you'll never speak to me again'. Some of the people shut the door. Some of the people I explained to why I was leaving cried. They said, 'Once you've gone, we'll never be able to speak to you again.' Others got so annoyed that they threw me out of the house!

Eric went on to explain how *all* the people with whom he used to go on holiday and out for dinner were Witnesses. He knew that, once he decided to leave, these friendships would be severed and he would be regarded as an apostate. All the former members with whom I spoke told me how they had been cut off by friends and family who refused to visit them, attend their weddings or even acknowledge them in the street.[18] This is why defectors who make the smoothest transition are those who have found an alternative belief system or have the support of outsiders who are able to distract them from the milieu of the Society (Holzer 1968). But finding alternatives is far from easy given the years of constraint placed on devotees to limit their contact with the outside world and to refrain from reading apostate literature. Those who do eventually break free are seldom allowed a dignified exit.[19] Not only is their disfellowshipping announced from the platform, they are also condemned as 'mentally diseased' or 'apostates'.

As far as the Governing Body is concerned, there is no difference between those who leave the Watch Tower community voluntarily and those who are disfellowshipped. Those known to be associating with apostates are shunned by the congregation. Shunning is a double-edged sword, since it rids the community of defilement and deters others from dissident behaviour. But, for the defector, shunning is evidence of an organisation that cannot be of God. Peter regaled me with a story of a widow in her eighties who had been disfellowshipped for making contact with a relative who had defected some years earlier. From the point at which the disfellowshipping became official, she duly took her place at the back of the Kingdom Hall. Several months later when she was still being shunned, she fell down the stairs at home and urgently needed assistance. Since she knew she would be refused help from members of her congregation, she rang Peter (who had now left the Society), with whom she had previously been close, and asked him for help. Fearful of jeopardising her chances of reinstatement, she pleaded with him not to tell the elders.

Strangely enough, allegiance to the movement may continue to exist even among those who renounce it. Once the process of breaking away has begun, defectors find themselves torn between the need to develop a new identity on the one hand, and the fear of relinquishing Watch Tower doctrines on the other. These two positions may for a long time be irreconcilable as Malcolm explained:

> I went and looked up a few of my old school friends to see what they'd done with their lives. We had a drink and a chat and they would say things to me like, 'We heard you'd gone a bit weird and become a

Jehovah's Witness', and even then I found myself defending the Watch Tower and when I came away I'd think, 'Why did you do that?' It still had a grip on me!

Malcolm's story confirms how, paradoxically, clinging to the theology can be symptomatic of a person's struggle to break free. It seems that, unless this hold over the individual can be broken, defection will simply be a case of Witnesses abandoning the Watch Tower community rather than the Watch Tower community abandoning Witnesses. Reed provides what is probably the most extreme example of this by quoting a woman who said, 'Even if someone could prove to me beyond doubt that the organization was false, I would still stick with it' (Reed 1989a: 17).

The refusal of disillusioned Witnesses to renounce the theology is part and parcel of the dilemma in which they are caught. Though they may feel certain that the Society's version of reality is distorted, they cannot imagine life without it. Those who do reach the point of departure often experience a crisis of identity, particularly if they have failed to find an alternative system of belief.[20] Claire explained, 'It's like a rug being whipped out from under your feet and you're just standing on air. There's nothing there. Everything you've been living for has just gone. You're just lost.'

In a much more sinister account, Tom told me:

> I started drinking to deaden the pain. Most Witnesses I knew drank *very* heavily. I began to doubt God. I became angry but I had no one to lash out at because whenever I spoke to the Witnesses they made me feel as though I was wrong. I felt like a worm. I'd built my whole life on the Watch Tower and I had nothing left. I broke down in the car and I drove to this couple's home – they'd been going through a similar thing and they said to me, 'We think we've found the answer', but I said, 'There is no answer'. I was utterly condemned. I was so busy going from door to door I just wasn't thinking, and it just stunned me because it meant that soon, we still believed that Armageddon was round the corner, soon Jehovah would kill my wife. I loved my wife and I was suddenly faced with this incredible situation that, when Armageddon comes, God would kill Carol! I also had three children at that point and the two eldest children knew that she wasn't going to the Kingdom Hall and they began to ask questions. I found out later that that caused one of them incredible distress. It was only years later that when my son became a Christian he was asked in a church to give his experiences of growing up as a Witness and he wrote some notes out, and I took a peek at the notes to see what he was going to say. It was a youth group he was speaking to; and one of the things he wrote in the notes was that he remembered when I told him that his mum wasn't going to the Kingdom Hall, he'd gone away and wept because he knew that very soon Jehovah would kill his mum![21]

The threat of annihilation at Armageddon is the Society's most powerful weapon for averting risk. Those contemplating defection are afraid of renouncing what they have always regarded as truth because of their fear of spiritual damnation. Peter provided a poignant example of how former Witnesses continue to regard the outside world as contaminated in his account of a visit to a Baptist church some weeks after his defection:

> I drove to this church and I couldn't go in. I just couldn't go in the building because it was still in my mind that it was Satan's Temple. I walked around outside. It was pure turmoil. When I finally went in, the service had almost ended. I sneaked through the door and I did meet one girl who said to me, 'Are you a Christian?', which didn't impress me at all; but they presented a very simple Christian gospel.

So ingrained was the belief that orthodox Christianity was riddled with paganism that, for Peter, the balance between reverting to Watch Tower evangelism and deconstructing the process which persuaded him to believe this in the first place was so fine that the scales could be tipped either way.[22] Those who start to lose faith in the Witnesses' message are often rescued from the seduction of the world by means of more Kingdom Hall meetings and the stepping up of door-to-door ministry (as was the case when the Armageddon prophecy failed in 1975). For those who no longer accept Watch Tower teachings, deindoctrination can be a lengthy and difficult process. Autobiographies that extol 'a new freedom in Christ' can be misleading, since not all of them indicate the time it took to adjust to a new way of life or how this was achieved. It is also impossible to know whether the Witnesses' worldview is completely removed from the psyche of the defector, or if it remains dormant. All the former Witnesses I met told me of their feelings of deep mistrust on leaving the organisation. Most of their resentment was directed towards the Watch Tower leadership and congregational officials who by now were regarded as tyrannical. However, all expressed feelings of genuine affection for their former brothers and sisters who were forbidden to speak to them. According to the Reachout Trust,[23] those who are able to rid themselves of cynicism on leaving religious movements tend to adjust more easily than those who are not. Though it is difficult for a social scientist like myself to verify this, two of the defectors did claim to be experiencing some difficulty in establishing a new way of life, despite their departure two years previously. These two people expressed paranoia about reading any material of a religious nature other than the Bible. Although they had started to attend Christian churches, they remained circumspect in their attitude towards other religious organisations. Like nomads, they drifted from church to church in search of an alternative, wary of anyone who claimed to monopolise truth.

The struggle to adjust to the outside world is common to all former Witnesses who have written autobiographies or who have spent a reasonable length of time in Watch Tower membership. Defectors claim that they have never been encouraged to think independently and are unable to abandon the movement without feeling disoriented.[24] Not only does breaking away involve acquiring a new *Weltanschauung*, it also means changing one's lifestyle and forming new relationships. This is far from easy for anyone who has lived by the principles of a closed religious community (see Skonovd 1983). However, one thing that did puzzle me at the time of the research was whether those who defect are able to renounce *all* Watch Tower doctrines. Though it was clear that my sample of defectors had rejected the Governing Body's message of salvation, I was interested to know how they felt about ethical and cultural practices such as annual celebrations, blood transfusions and voting in elections, all of which they had opposed for so long. These doctrines would clearly need to be renegotiated in the context of their new lives. So, how easy is it for lapsed Witnesses to rebuild their lives in a world they have hitherto rejected? Which, if any, of the Watch Tower Society's tenets do defectors continue to uphold? And what is the defector's new relationship with modernity?

Responses to these issues vary from individual to individual. Voluntary defection implies that the individual is amenable to change, but abandoning totalitarian regimes also brings with it feelings of guilt and betrayal. To a greater or lesser extent, all the defectors I met continued to renounce the world. For two people, this meant imitating the Witnesses in abstaining from voting in general elections, while only one man relented in his previous opposition to joining the armed forces. This confirms that pacifism and anti-nationalism among defectors remain strong, though it could also be symptomatic of conversion to Trinitarian Christianity which, like the Watch Tower Society, upholds the sanctity of life. In his description of how he gradually replaced Watch Tower theology with Baptist beliefs, Peter informed me:

> I've known some people leave the Watch Tower and move over to Baptist churches and take on board everything immediately. I couldn't do that. It might not *all* be wrong; but the basis was wrong – the basis of salvation. Over the years, I went through each doctrine bit by bit. Even when I became a Christian I had some difficulty with Christmas and birthdays, so we used to compromise. I said to my wife, 'You have this room and put all your Christmas decorations up and I'll have that room'. I don't have any problem with Christmas whatsoever now. There was one occasion when two Witnesses came to visit me – they were making a final attempt – and I took them into the front room which was all full of decorations and it was quite a joy to see these two guys standing there with their mouths open!

Peter went on to explain how annual celebrations had become 'side issues' which he believed had little effect on a person's salvation, although he claimed it took him a few years to reach this point. It would appear both from Peter's comments and from the aforementioned testimonies that, once dissident Witnesses renounce the movement's prescription for salvation, annual celebrations become less problematic and Watch Tower totalitarianism loses its grip. Defectors who move towards mainstream Christianity seem to acquire Quick's hermeneutic method of biblical interpretation mentioned above. A new belief system is then adopted which embraces aspects of life that had previously been avoided. It is exactly this process that comes into play when former Witnesses start to renegotiate what must be one of the most emotive Watch Tower doctrines – that of refusing blood transfusions. Peter told me, 'The blood transfusion issue I soon settled in my mind. I realised that God doesn't want sacrifice – after all, Christ shed his blood that we might have life.'

So much for the issue which could at one time have cost Peter either his life or his salvation! Ironically, this doctrine elicited the most radical change in the defectors' responses. All were able to offer a new interpretation of biblical injunctions which challenged those most commonly cited by the Governing Body such as Acts 15: 28–9 and Leviticus 17: 10. The defectors claimed that, after some considerable discussion with members of Christian churches, they were finally persuaded that the prohibition was one of many Jewish purity laws in the first century. Nevertheless, the more orthodox versions of Christianity adopted by former Witnesses have a certain resemblance to Watch Tower theology. When individuals decide to renounce Watch Tower doctrines, they are taking a stand against the Governing Body's interpretation of biblical references rather than its general worldview. Those who come to replace the Watch Tower reality with a Christian *Weltanschauung* are often unshaken in their belief that the world comprises good and evil forces, and that sin is the result of Satan's power to wreak havoc. For the people I interviewed, puritanical behaviour was still important. Sexual relationships outside Christian marriage, homosexuality, abortion and euthanasia continued to be condemned, but, unlike their former brethren, all agreed that clean living and respect for the sanctity of life without faith in Christ's deity were not enough to earn a person entry into heaven. What they *did* share with the Witnesses was the belief that they had a mission to accomplish – namely, to save as many sinners as possible before the Day of Judgement. These similarities show not only that there are parallels between evangelical Christianity and Watch Tower tenets, but that millenarianism and risk continue to play a central role in the lives of lapsed members. The defectors' persistent disdain for sexual impurity demonstrates their continued awareness of moral danger, despite their belief that absolution from sin could be achieved only by repentance and spiritual healing, rather than disfellowship and subsequent reinstatement. Although Armageddon was no longer part of their vocabulary, they retained their zeal for the repentance of sinners in anticipation of a Messianic Age. Their support for millenarian doctrines had far from disappeared.

To offer a complete examination of how former Witnesses replace Watch Tower doctrines with a new way of thinking would require extensive research over a very long period of time. However, both the primary and secondary data presented here reveal that lapsed Witnesses often tend to pursue their search for security. If, as Berger suggests, modernity is about the weakening of tradition and the erosion of collective life, the defectors with whom I chatted were no more products of it than the people they left behind. Abandoning the Watch Tower Society did not seem to stop them from wanting the support of a close-knit community. But, like Fromm, Berger also argues that modernity is characterised by a liberation that some people openly renounce in their endless yearning for certainty (Berger 1977: 109–10). The defectors' firm adherence to moral boundaries and belief in competing supernatural forces continue to lure them away from liberal society and cause them to condemn the world with as much vigour as they did in their previous religious lives. Whether or not the lapsed Witnesses I interviewed were typical of those who voluntarily defect is difficult to say, but what is clear is that they showed no more desire to embrace the modern world than when they were in regular attendance at the Kingdom Hall. Their withdrawal from the movement signifies a rejection of one system that renounces the world and the adoption of another. Their need to defer to an authority far greater than themselves in a world they still regard as morally reprehensible is indicative of their disdain for personal autonomy and individual liberty.

Like their former brethren, the defectors never once stated that their present religious convictions prevented them from *feeling* free. Predictably, they claimed that this freedom had never been possible in the Watch Tower Society, whatever they might have said before they decided to leave.[25] Claire explained:

> You can be a Pentecostalist, you can be a Baptist, you can be a Roman Catholic, you can be an Anglican, but we all come under the same umbrella of one God. There's a church for every one of us to celebrate differently and we can all worship in the way we feel comfortable, which is wonderful, because with the Witnesses there just wasn't. I now have the freedom to disagree and come away and still be friends.

Similarly, Tom told me:

> I have a view of God that is a bit bigger than I had as a Witness. I see God as more magnanimous than this 'Jehovah' who will strike you dead if you go inside a Catholic church or a Jewish synagogue or a Hindu temple. I believe that ex-Witnesses have got something really special about them because of where they've been. They've suffered, they've been through the same thing, and they can relate to each other and it's wonderful. I have friends who are Jewish, most of my family are Roman

Catholics . . . I have to acknowledge in my mind there's a wider picture
that I don't fully understand, and I'm quite willing to leave it with God.
God's bigger than all our churches. He can deal with all that.

Though these testimonies still contain a concept of freedom that would
appear highly restrictive to modern liberal thinkers, both Claire and Tom's
references to the virtues of choice and diversity bring them closer to the
modern world than would previously have been the case. More significant,
perhaps, is their apparent willingness to jettison their former exclusive
tenets for a universal message of religious tolerance that cannot allow any
one system of belief to monopolise truth. Their adoption of orthodox
Christianity can, however, be interpreted from a number of perspectives.
From the Witnesses' point of view, it signifies turning away from Jehovah
and mixing with apostates – an appalling act of defilement that jeopardises
salvation. For the defectors themselves, it marks the beginning of a new life
and an opportunity to discover the *real* truth. Such people are not merely
narrating a story of how they came to leave a religious movement; they are
setting the record straight. From a risk perspective, I have already shown
how the defectors continued to attack the forces of moral danger as defined
by the Judaeo-Christian tradition. Though these people claimed they had
found greater freedom, their departure did not allow them to abandon their
concept of sin or eschew divine authority. What defectors regard as a major
change in religious status, outsiders would see as minor differences.

From a modernity perspective, there is little reason to think that lapsed
Witnesses who embrace mainstream Christianity enter into a significantly
different relationship with secular society. Though they had become actively
involved in Baptist, Congregationalist and other nonconformist denominations, the defectors remained adamant in their belief that the Bible was
the inerrant word of God. Their relentless moral condemnation of sinful
practices, especially sexual promiscuity, adultery and hedonistic behaviour
such as drug use and the excessive consumption of alcohol, means that their
status in the world remains peripheral. Nevertheless, it would be wrong to
suggest that the defectors' transfer of allegiance would not be of interest
to modernity theorists. Their initial struggle for independence of thought
provided them with the means to break free from a totalitarian system
and to acquire a greater acceptance of religious diversity. Among other
things, this allowed them greater social interaction with outsiders, political
franchisement, freedom of speech and the freedom to read literature
other than that published by a world-renouncing community. Whatever
restrictions the defectors may have imposed on themselves, these changes
demonstrate their willingness to embrace aspects of modern life, particularly
those pertaining to individual liberty, which they had previously renounced.
The continuous yearning for certainty can be seen as an attempt, consciously
or unconsciously, to escape the dilemmas of modernity discussed in Chapter
2. The uncertainties of the twenty-first century cause some people more

anxiety than others, and there are clearly those who are unwilling to wrestle with ambiguity. The need for some people to seek the safety of a religious community is one way of circumventing powerlessness and maintaining a sense of belonging.[26] The endless search for absolute truth says as much about the modern world as it does about the individual's retreat from it. In the end, the comfort that can be obtained from a millenarian dream is often far greater than the desire to enter a world that can make no promises.

9 Conclusion

Throughout this book, I have argued that the relationship between the Witnesses and the modern world is ambivalent and contradictory. Until recently, sociological literature has tended to propound the view that world-renouncing sectarian religion cannot survive the onslaught of modernity which is, among other things, rational, secular and materialistic. But these theories offer scant empirical analysis of millenarian movements. The rise of the modern state, modern capitalism and modern science have no doubt been the cause of great tension between faith and reason, but they can in no way be shown to have brought about the death of God. The Watch Tower Bible and Tract Society is an example of a religious movement that has freed itself from traditional churches, and yet it has still managed to maintain a piety that is as ascetic and puritanical as any version of orthodox Christianity. Curiously enough, its tirade against the modern world is one of the factors that has contributed to its success.

Modernity theory has been useful for the analysis of the empirical data since it contains a number of themes that lend themselves to the narrative I have presented. I have drawn on these themes to examine the current status of the Witnesses at this point of time. This has not been an easy task. As I explained in Chapter 2, modernity has no real beginning or ultimate goal, and social scientists approach it from a number of perspectives. Rightly or wrongly, I am committed to the view that modernity is articulated by processes that have shaped Western societies and are amenable to socio-logical investigation. These processes involve social, political and economic dimensions, all of which impact on each other and out of which individuals construct their identities. The nation state, the expansionist capitalist economy, industrialism, large-scale administrative bureaucracies, individu-alism, the dominance of secular, cultural values and the formal separation of public and private life provide the backdrop for some of the issues on which I have focused my analysis. The issues I have discussed help to illuminate what is as yet unexplored territory in the sociology of religion – namely, a comprehensive examination of the relationship between the Watch Tower Society and the modern world. I have selected themes from the modernity literature which describe the development of Western societies from the beginning of the Enlightenment period. Since modernity comprises a range of contrasting principles, it should come as no surprise that the Witnesses' relationship both with other people and with modern social institutions is paradoxical. Modernity comprises certainties and uncertainties, liberty and discipline, rationalism and relativism and the combination of individual and collective authority.

One of the most serious attacks on Enlightenment thinking is that it failed to deliver its promise of liberation and progress to all people. Although the concepts of equality and freedom provoked a strong sense of excitement throughout the eighteenth and nineteenth centuries, particularly among those who sought emancipation from their social, economic and political positions, in reality, such rights did not extend beyond the privileged few. The modernity project excluded women, enslaved Africans (on whose forced labour the economic prosperity of the period depended), minority groups and the peasantry. In his discussion of the limitations of modernity to freedom, Bauman writes:

> There is . . . an intrinsic ambiguity in freedom in its modern edition, wed to capitalism. The effectiveness of freedom demands that some people stay unfree. To be free means to be allowed and to be able to keep others unfree. Thus freedom in its modern, economically defined form does not differ from its pre-modern applications in respect of its social-relations content. It is, as before, selective. It may be truly achieved (as distinct from philosophically postulated) only by a part of the society. It constitutes one pole in a relationship which has normative regulation, constraint and coercion as its other pole. . . . This crucial feature of modern freedom is more often than not concealed in philosophical generalization of an experience limited in fact to the privileged category of people. Self-awareness of mastery over one's conditions (mastery inevitably attained at the expense of somebody else's subordination) is articulated as the collective achievement of mankind; purposeful, efficiency-conscious, reason-guided conduct is identified with rational-ization of society as such. In the end, mystifying rather than clarifying statements about the achievements of an unspecified 'man' are made – of which the following is a good example: 'World-mastery, or at least the potential for it, has come to man through rationalisation. Humans have replaced God as the masters of their destiny'. What is left undefined, is whether the 'humans' whose destiny is mastered, are the same humans.
> (Bauman 1988: 45–6)

It would be crude, if not misleading, to suggest that the Witnesses are oppressed individuals whom modernity has excluded, but their limited life-chances and insular social horizons *prior* to conversion call into question the modern notion of freedom of which Bauman is also critical. Although freedom is, in principle, available to all people, in practice it is restrictive since not everyone has the same access to resources. The individual's relationship with secular society is influenced to a greater or lesser extent by income, occupation, ethnic membership, gender, family attachments, status in the community and a whole range of other factors which represent social reality. The Witnesses construct their identity around rational, romantic and authoritarian principles that are negotiated between public and private spheres. This means that their relationship with the outside world is in a constant state of ambivalence. Though the Witnesses have a deeply pessimistic view of life, they are also idealistic and romantic. Their woeful narrative of things becoming progressively worse contrasts sharply with their concept of utopian bliss and optimistic vision of the future. From the analysis I have presented, I would suggest that the Witnesses' social status at the beginning of the twenty-first century centres on the interplay between their *resistance to* and *alliance with* modern secular culture, both of which need separate consideration. This book has exposed some of this ambivalence.

The Witnesses' resistance to the tenets of modernity has a number of dimensions. Their refusal to become involved in political affairs *per se* means that they can in no way subscribe to civil liberties. The Governing Body's moral condemnation of homosexuality, abortion, freedom of sexual relations between consenting adults and the struggle of women to achieve equality with men in the labour market as well as within the family and marriage means that the Witnesses deny themselves a whole series of rights which aim to liberate individuals and protect them from social injustice. Despite their international expansion, they are likely to remain peripheral in the foreseeable future with little hope of advancing beyond sectarian status. The rapid evolution of the so-called pluralistic society in which people are free to select from a number of life options has failed to undermine the Watch Tower Society, which still manages to recruit those who are searching for a monosemic truth. The organisation's relentless adherence to biblical literalism poses a serious challenge to Shiner's claim that, as societies move towards secularisation, religious movements may adopt a 'this-worldly' orientation. There is little or no evidence that Watch Tower doctrines are compatible with a world in which the sacred is in decline.[1] The Witnesses' condemnation of all forms of ecumenicalism and of what they see as the satanic corruption of every other religious institution is indicative of their determination to prevent secular influences from eroding their rituals and beliefs. The Society's claim to exclusivity is a powerful armoury for protecting its members from a pluralistic and atomised world.

The Witnesses' resistance to outside forces can be seen as a (subconscious) means of deflecting the problems of modernity. While the rest of humanity must find its own way of dealing with the uncertainties and ambiguities of the modern world and the various crises to which they give rise, the Witnesses are able to avert these problems through the provision of a protective community. The difficulties in constructing a meaningful identity in a world that imprisons, dislocates and dehumanises can be avoided by deferring to the external authority of a totalitarian system. This option denies all ambiguity and releases the individual from what Berger describes as 'the terror of chaos' (Berger 1977: 109). The data presented in this book suggest that one of the key means by which the Watch Tower Society is able to prevent the undesirable influences of the outside world from threatening its doctrines is to heighten the Witnesses' awareness of risk. I have shown how the primary purpose of this concept is to establish moral parameters for the demarcation of acceptable and unacceptable behaviour in order to ensure that the daily conduct of devotees is consistent with the movement's principles. In the end, exposing themselves to risk carries penalties that jeopardise salvation. The antithetical concept of *safety* (or in this case, 'truth') blames modernity's ills on the devil, to which only those who have refused to secure their place in the New Kingdom must find the solution. Witnesses who transgress the Society's prescriptive boundaries gamble with eternal life.

The Society's version of risk, sin and certainty along with its firm forecast of future events enable it to exercise a high degree of control over those who adhere to its tenets. These are strong theological weapons that the Witnesses have used to fend off undesirable forces and which have helped them to maintain their position on the periphery of secular society. It should be clear from my description of the conversion process that the world-renouncing option appeals to individuals who have a generally pessimistic outlook that they have acquired from their life experiences. But one of my main arguments is that, although the Witnesses are resistant to the modern world, they are also dependent on it for legal protection and for physical and cultural resources. Despite their apolitical stand, the Witnesses' freedom to practise their faith in Western societies and elsewhere without fear of intimidation is a consequence of the legal sanctioning of modern democratic rights. Though Watch Tower evangelism has persisted over the years in countries where the movement has been banned, the ensuing conflict between Witness evangelists and secular authorities has hindered recruitment. In Britain, however, public respect for religious creed has allowed the Witnesses to distribute their literature, hold regular meetings and recruit those who are sympathetic to their cause. The Society has thus benefited from the liberty brought about by the later stages of modernity.

The Witnesses' dependence on the outside world can be seen also in their never-ending search for new members. Their recruitment methodology requires them to make use of modern communication techniques as well as sophisticated technology such as multimedia software. The Society operates an international business enterprise for the production and dissemination of tracts and magazines and the expansion of its membership. Photographs of gigantic office blocks representing its headquarters and printing works appear in glossy reading materials. These photographs do not seem to depict an organisation that is anti-modern or anti-materialistic, but rather one that prides itself on its modern rational image. This is, to all intents and purposes, a global, multicultural corporation. Nevertheless, the Witnesses maintain that their international success is the result of their devotion to an ascetic creed to which millions of good-living people have been willing to adhere. Their usage of *cultural* resources demonstrates not only their alliance with the outside world but their acceptance of some of the most central principles of modernity. The Witnesses are able to entice people into the movement not with the aid of mysticism or affection, but through the exceptional character of the community they have constructed. I have argued that one of the most seductive features of their theology is their millenarian message that promises heaven to 144,000 Witnesses and eternal paradise on earth to the rest. But I have also suggested that it is not so much the promises contained in this message as the way they are imparted that strengthens the movement's appeal. The Witnesses have drawn on modernist romantic themes such as persecution, love, heroism, self-abnegation, temporality and Brotherhood; all of which were an essential part of literary and philosophical thought at the beginning of the nineteenth century. These mythical concepts are the constituents of an authentic community that presages the new order after Armageddon, and which modernity theorists suggest derive from a period which marked a cultural reaction against seventeenth- and eighteenth-century rationalism. Paradoxically, the Watch Tower community is as dependent on the rational principles that have their origins in the Enlightenment as it is on the romantic ideas that followed. When the Witnesses ask each other, 'How long have you been in the truth?', they assume absolute conviction based on a revealed message from Jehovah who does not allow multiple interpretations of scriptural texts. The predictive value of Bible-like science makes possible the precise calculation of the Last Days and an unambiguous explanation of the whole of human existence from the beginning to the end of time. These are the rational tools with which the Witnesses are able to make sense of the world in its present state.

Postmodernist scholars argue that, at the beginning of the twenty-first century, social and political movements are characterised by an aestheticism that signifies a break with earlier representations. The postmodern age of fluidity and pastiche has de-centred the self, leaving it in a state of flux and disarray. Unified conceptions of who we are and where we belong have, according to such writers, given way to media-inspired, self-contrived aspirations and identities; yet the Witnesses continue to eschew creativity and aestheticism in favour of a non-mystical, rational religious expression. By peering through the Watch Tower I have been able to narrate a story of disaffection, tension, tenacious evangelism and the immutable expectation of a Kingdom still to come. Could this dull calculation and preparation for an eagerly awaited apocalypse be one of the few remaining manifestations of modernist imagination?

Notes

1 The end is nigh

1 The annual membership statistics are published in the 1 January copy of *The Watchtower*.
2 This is based on a 4 per cent growth rate projection.
3 This provides the basis for Beckford's later work (1976) in which his theoretical contribution is made more explicit.
4 The Witnesses are renowned for keeping their distance from non-members.
5 For a detailed discussion of reflexivity in the sociology of religion see Flanagan (2001).
6 Greeley (1972) refers to this as *resacralisation*.
7 Wilson (1982) suggests that most sects (particularly those of a world-renouncing nature) will nearly always be in tension with wider society because of their exclusivity and their demands of total allegiance. Moreover, Wallis (1984) argues that the new religions involve only small numbers of people whose motives for joining are largely secular.
8 Other available literature suggests that millenarian beliefs are most common among those under colonial rule (see, for example, Smelser 1962, Lanternari 1963, Aberle 1965 and Worsley 1968).
9 This is particularly surprising given that the movement was founded in the United States.

2 The Jehovah's Witnesses in the modern world

1 During this period, the legal authority of the Society belonged to seven directors.
2 To this day, the Witnesses believe that these two books contain prophecies concerning the annihilation of Christian clergy and the destruction of the wicked. Several texts from Revelation are used to support their prediction of Armageddon.
3 Although Russell had previously criticised the activities of the clergy, he had, unlike Rutherford, acknowledged that some clergymen were sincere.
4 Armageddon is the final battle between good and evil where Jehovah will destroy Satan and all the wicked.
5 This represents the 'peak' figure. The 'average' figure for 2000 was 120,592.
6 Arminius was a late sixteenth-century Dutch theologian who maintained the doctrine of free will against Calvin.
7 *The Watchtower*, 15 June 1900 (cited by Beckford 1975a: 3).
8 *Pioneers* are those who devote many more hours to the missionary effort than *publishers* (that is, ordinary members). Pioneers currently spend approximately seventy hours per month knocking on doors.

9 One couple with whom I spoke told me that they had known several men who were homosexual but who had given up their practices on becoming Witnesses. This couple believed that, once a homosexual made a personal vow of celibacy and converted to the Society, his or her homosexual orientation would disappear. To date, this issue appears to be a source of confusion among Witnesses.

10 www.jw-media.org; www.jw-russia.org and www.jw-temoinsdejehova.org

11 For example, Beckford (1975a: 122–33) discusses three main theoretical approaches with regard to these issues. These are *frustration-compensation*, *world-view construction* and *social solidarity*. However, it is Wilson (1982, 1990) who probably offers the most comprehensive theoretical analysis of sects in general.

12 There is considerable disagreement about the periodisation of modernity. Some writers associate it with the spread of capitalism between the fourteenth and eighteenth centuries, some with religious changes which began in the fifteenth century, others with eighteenth- and nineteenth-century industrialisation and others still with cultural changes which coincide with modernism at the end of the nineteenth and beginning of the twentieth century (see Hall and Gieben 1992).

13 Some of these ideas form the basis of *postmodernity* (see for example Featherstone 1990, McLennan 1992, Rosenau 1992, Brown 1996).

14 This notion has its origin in the work of Daniel Bell (1979), who argued that the different principles imparted by politicians, economists and cultural experts send out different messages which have led to a confused, multifaceted self without a firm sense of identity.

15 Hence, modernity should not be regarded as a *recent* phenomenon.

16 Even within Christianity, Davie suggests that there have been important changes in symbolic expression from premodern to postmodern society. One example of this is the respective shift in emphasis from God the Son to God the Holy Spirit (1994: 192–9).

17 Hence Marx's phrase 'all that is solid melts into air'.

18 Some sociologists refer to this phenomenon as *supermarket* religion.

19 Indeed, Bruce argues that moral relativism is to be found as much *within* Christianity as outside it; hence the difficulty faced by supernatural religions in maintaining an official version of truth.

20 Drawing on the contrasting ideas of Habermas and Lyotard, McLennan (1992) offers a useful summary of the debate between the modernity and postmodernity theorists. He shows how relativism has been used by postmodernists to attack the idea of *the metanarrative* that stems from the Enlightenment project.

21 This term is used commonly by the mass media to describe a multiplicity of movements throughout the world.

22 Indeed, Harris (1994) argues that doctrinal certainty is an essentially modern phenomenon.

23 Habgood (1992) sees fundamentalism as part of the reassertion of local and national identities which he argues are indicative of the need for psychological security. He argues that this has its origins in the turn of the century when there were great demands for economic stability.

24 Harris (1994) offers an excellent account of the importance of the monosemic text in his discussion of Jewish fundamentalism.

3 Finding a home

1 Similarly, Barker identifies several reasons why people embrace *new* religious movements. These include *the desire for success in careers, improved health, self-development, community* and *kingdom building* – all of which she believes play

an important part in persuading prospective recruits that something positive will be gained from their involvement (1989: 25–9). More recently, John Saliba (1995: 183–92) quotes a Vatican report which reflects on the appeal of new religious movements to young adults.

2 Penton, however, argues that the organisation sometimes recruits those who *feel* socially underprivileged (Penton 1997).

3 Considering that the Society is renowned for its door-to-door proselytising, it is not surprising that prospective recruits are approached by the Witnesses rather than the other way round.

4 In his later work on the Witnesses' *talk about conversion*, Beckford outlines four characteristics which he argues are central to the convert's experience. The first is that it involves what he calls *the progression of mental states*; second, it is *predominantly cognitive*; third, conversion is *achieved*; and fourth, it is followed by *practical work in organisational activities* (Beckford 1978: 249–62).

5 Over a quarter of the devotees in my sample became self-employed in window-cleaning, gardening, catering and textiles.

6 This confirms Stark and Iannaccone's research in the mid-1990s in which it was found that the Witnesses recruited better in nations where there were more Christians and worse in nations where there were more Muslims (Stark and Iannaccone 1997: 139–42).

7 This corresponds with the general decline in church membership over the last three decades (see Brierley and Longley 1993).

8 This concept was first introduced into sociology by Durkheim, who suggested that 'abnormalities' occurred in societies which failed to move from *mechanical* to *organic* solidarity. More specifically, he argued that anomic societies are characterised by increases in suicide (Durkheim 1897). The concept was later used by Merton to explain organised crime in the USA during the depression (Merton 1949).

9 However, Martin also argues that the recent move towards service industries may halt or even reverse the trend to secularisation.

10 Lash and Urry (1987) equate the conventional account of community and its dissolution with the shift from *organized* to *disorganized* capitalism. They argue that the loosening of spatial and class affiliations in the late twentieth century has eroded mutual trust and reciprocity.

11 Barker (1984) uses this notion of push and pull in her description of conversion to the Unification Church.

12 This term is often used to describe an overwhelming degree of affection bestowed on prospective recruits during their initial visits to a religious organisation.

13 Cohen (1986) uses the concept of *symbolic boundaries* to describe how those who belong to closed communities decide who is and who is not a member. In the case of Witnesses, such boundaries form the basis for acceptable and unacceptable behaviour.

14 Weeks cites the 1957 Wolfenden report on prostitution and male homosexuality which articulated this distinction. He argues that this report laid the basis for subsequent reforms.

15 I am not suggesting here that millenarian religion is the *only* way in which such individuals can secure their identity, but it is certainly *one* way.

4   Rational means to rational ends

1 Wilson offers some excellent examples of 'therapeutic' sects that adopt rational patterns of organisation. His two most interesting examples are Christian Science and the Church of Scientology (1982: 108–10).

2 Suitability for baptism is usually determined by the individual's own personal qualities and his or her ability to pass a short oral test. The test comprises a series of questions about Watch Tower doctrines.

3 Beckford argues that the probability of a person ever reaching the point of baptism is determined by the intensity and frequency of interaction with those already in the movement (1975a: 161).

4 Lofland and Skonovd (1983) identify six types of conversion. These are *intellectual, mystical, experimental, affectional, revivalist* and *coercive*.

5 Psychoanalyst Carl Christensen (1963) provides a fascinating description of the psychological effects of mystical conversion among born-again Christians.

6 This exemplifies the theological debate about whether *faith, works* or a combination of the two provide the route to salvation.

7 Fully baptised members always refer to their theology as 'the truth' and, in all the interviews I conducted, no one admitted to doubting *any* Watch Tower doctrines. It seems that those who do have doubts show only peripheral interest in the organisation and never reach the point of baptism.

8 Hamilton (1992) traces the origin of reason back to the seventeenth-century philosophers – particularly Descartes and Pascal – who used the concept to support their work on empiricism.

9 The Witnesses' belief in free will rather than predestination suggests that this pessimism derives from their knowledge that Jehovah has prepared a place for them as part of a much greater plan.

10 One interesting feature of Watch Tower theology is that expressions such as 'Good luck' are banned by the Society because they imply superstition. This exemplifies the reason for ethnographers to exercise caution when working in closed communities. Thankfully, I was aware of this particular injunction.

11 Witnesses quote biblical texts such as Exodus 20: 4 and Deuteronomy 27: 15 to support this injunction. In addition to idolatry, the organisation teaches that fortune-telling constitutes superstition as indicated in Acts 16: 16.

12 Interestingly, one of the most commonly used Watch Tower tracts is called *Reasoning from the Scriptures*.

13 It would, however, be misleading to suggest that the Witnesses do not hold a concept of sacredness. Rather, their rejection of mystical accoutrements is a rejection of what they see as idolatrous worship. Their 'sacredness' is thus expressed in a Protestant form.

14 Despite this rigidity, I was always allowed to sit where I wanted at the meetings and no one ever interfered with what I was trying to do.

15 Paradoxically, women are equally responsible for proselytising on doorsteps and are given the opportunity to pioneer. It would appear therefore that the organisation encourages women to be active mainly for the purpose of recruitment.

16 Though this tract was published over twenty years ago, it is still widely consulted by young people who have not reached the point of baptism.

17 Despite this, I did not meet anyone who said they found the meetings oppressive.

18 According to the Society, Satan is 'The spirit creature who is the chief adversary of Jehovah God and of all who worship the true God' (Watch Tower Bible and Tract Society of Pennsylvania 1989b: 361).

19 In this respect, the Watch Tower organisation could be regarded as an agent of late twentieth-century moral panics.

20 In her work on New Religious Movements, Eileen Barker refers to this as *kingdom building* (Barker 1982).

21 This work has been criticised by historians such as Tawney (1926) and Eisenstadt (1967), both of whom argue that Weber's account is chronologically incorrect. Notwithstanding this, it is Weber's description of the *work ethic* that is important here.

22 The movement is successful in recruiting from a wide range of ethnic groups. In the United States alone, African, Hispanic and Asian-Americans form the majority of self-identified Witnesses. This may enhance the success of the movement in Latin America, Africa and Asia (see Stark and Iannaccone 1997: 150).

23 This kind of feedback is not dissimilar to that offered to student teachers when they are learning to impart knowledge to their prospective pupils.

24 Newly baptised Witnesses usually learn to minister by accompanying established members, but it may be a long time before they acquire the necessary skill and confidence to present their own sermons. In some cases, this can be several months after baptism.

25 Similarly, Bruce (1990) discusses the ways in which Christian fundamentalists in the USA have made use of the electronic media as in the case of *televangelism*.

26 As scriptural literalists, the Witnesses do, of course, acknowledge the miracles of Jesus in the synoptic gospels. However, they maintain that these miracles were performed only for the purpose of spreading the *kerygma*. The Witnesses believe that, once Jesus had died and the ministry had expanded, miracles were no longer necessary.

27 It could be argued from this that the organisation represents a 'totally administered' system. According to the Frankfurt School of the 1930s, total administration damaged the promise of the Enlightenment – namely, to bring about progress and human emancipation.

28 Weber suggested that legal-rational authority gives rise to modern bureaucracies. He also identified two other types of authority: *traditional* and *charismatic*.

5   Returning to Eden

1 Such beliefs are prominent also among Christian Pentecostalists, Satanists, the Jesus People and members of the Unification Church (McGuire 1987).

2 This is one of the very few academic studies of the Watch Tower organisation that the Witnesses seem to applaud. This is undoubtedly because King's documentary material, though 'factual', reminds them of their exclusivity.

3 Witnesses often use images of lions or wolves to depict orthodox Christianity as false religion.

4 Beckford notes that some Kingdom Schools were established for those children in the United States who had been excluded from state schools (Beckford 1975a: 37).

5 There have been several cases of tension between the Watch Tower organisation and the state (particularly in the United States) in instances concerning children of Witnesses in need of such surgery (see Tierney *et al.* 1984).

6 Hall borrows this notion of the *imagined community* from Benedict Anderson (1983).

7 All pictorial images are of the New Kingdom *on earth* rather than in heaven. Since the organisation teaches that heaven is reserved for only 144,000 Witnesses (of which only a small number remain), these images would appear to depict future life for those *other than* the chosen few.

8 Theme parks, museums and The National Trust are examples of how people attempt to compensate for the loss of the past. The heritage industry revolves around the artificial reconstruction of history and shared memories.

9 Hence the Witnesses' slogan *Millions Now Living Will Never Die*.

6   Inside, outside

1 This would suggest that Durkheim was correct in his view that 'the cult of the individual' was a social product. However, if religion in the modern world

has indeed become privatised, Durkheim's work on 'positive' integration or collective effervescence has become, to a certain extent, irrelevant.

2 Luckmann calls this 'the invisibility of religion'. Incidentally, secularisation theorists have hitherto ignored the extent to which 'private' religion has enabled the individual to construct his/her own identity. However, this view is contested by Foucault (1976), who suggests that notions of individuality are moulded to suit the interests of the dominant powers.

3 Indeed, when Catholics accept Papal authority, differences in the interpretation of Canon law still remain.

4 In contrast with this, Casanova (1994) has recently examined the ways in which traditional religions, particularly throughout the 1980s, have undergone a process of *deprivatisation* throughout the world and inspired large-scale political revolt.

5 This is a state which anthropologist Victor Turner calls *liminality*.

6 This is not to suggest that all Witnesses within a congregation are compatible as friends by virtue of the fact that they share the same worldview.

7 I gleaned this information from casual conversation after a *Watchtower* study meeting. I then interviewed two of these women later on in the study.

8 Despite the generally optimistic nature of these accounts, I would question their validity. Although the marriages had clearly survived, there was no way of knowing how the husbands really felt about their wives' conversion. However, it did transpire in a subsequent interview that one of these marriages had resulted in a brief separation because of the husband's disapproval.

9 The organisation has also expressed concern in recent years about the increasing numbers of young Witnesses who are dating non-members and failing to attend Kingdom Hall meetings. Those who do this often fail to reach the point of baptism. But, since the organisation does not collect official data on young people who break away from 'the truth', it is difficult to assess the extent to which this is occurring.

10 There is, after all, no knowing what state some of these marriages are in *prior to* the husband or wife's conversion. Indeed, this argument applies to all religious organisations (see Barker 1989: 87–91).

11 This is consistent with the Witnesses' attitude towards aspiring to attain academic qualifications.

12 Legislation in the 1980s made closed shops illegal.

13 This is why Douglas rejects binary distinctions as a useful tool of analysis (see Douglas 1978).

7 Honour thy father and thy mother

1 At the time of writing, there is also a section for children entitled *Young People Ask . . .* in the Society's magazine *Awake!*

2 Sixteen is the legal age at which children can leave home.

3 This is, after all, a well-documented issue that concerns most parents. It is also one that has been frequently subjected to the rigours of empirical social science.

4 Concern for the socialisation of subsequent generations is one of the reasons devotees are discouraged from marrying someone outside the community.

5 Attitudes towards school sex education programmes vary among Witness parents. Although few object to the teaching of human reproduction and pregnancy in biology classes, most regard sex education as a matter for the family and may, therefore, exercise their legal right to withdraw their children from classes that include discussions of birth control (which the Witnesses do not object to within marriage) and sexually transmitted diseases. Schools that

emphasise the value of family life in their sex education programmes, however, tend to win the support of Witness parents.

6 Since so few adult Witnesses are employed in professional occupations, their failure to encourage their children to remain in education beyond the statutory leaving age is consistent with working-class groups in general.

7 This is clearly one of the reasons why so few Witnesses are employed in professional occupations.

8 One young Witness explained how her parents disapproved of her studying sociology at school because it addressed issues that they considered immoral.

9 The Society's objection to religious worship in schools means that most Witness parents select non-denominational state education for their children.

10 This is now a generally recognised equal-opportunities issue that most state schools incorporate into their mission statements.

11 At the time of writing, citizenship is becoming an integral part of the modern school curriculum.

12 Moreover, the American National Survey of Religious Identification found in the early 1990s that American Witnesses are more likely than other members of the general population to be married and to have large families (about one-third of Witness parents have four or more children).

13 I am referring here to second and subsequent generation Witnesses rather than those who convert later and subsequently leave the movement to join another religious denomination.

8   The fear of freedom

1 Among the most compelling of these are Schnell (1956), Dencher (1966), Stevenson (1967), Tomsett (1971), Harrison (1980), Franz (1983), Botting and Botting (1984) and Penton (1997).

2 Singelenberg (1988) describes the period between 1967 and 1975 as 'the prophecy phase', during which there was a huge growth in membership in nearly every country in the world. In contrast, the period between 1976 and 1979 is what he calls 'the disconfirmation phase', which saw a sharp decline in both evangelism and recruitment. It has been estimated that around a million members defected between 1976 and 1981 (Reed 1989a).

3 Beckford (1975a: 220) argues that one of the tactics adopted by the organisation was the suggestion that a full understanding of Jehovah's plan would become clear to the Witnesses only in much later years.

4 This was despite the organisation's previous teaching that Adam and Eve had been created in the same year.

5 The cynicism of former members needs to be treated with as much caution as the optimism of those still in membership. Both parties clearly have their own stories to tell.

6 This echoes Weber's concern that capitalist, bureaucratic society produces an 'iron cage' in which human freedom, creativity and ingenuity become trapped (see Bradley 1992b: 198).

7 According to Hamilton the freedom promised by the *philosophes* of the Enlightenment included 'an opposition to feudal and traditional constraints on beliefs, trade, communication, social interaction, sexuality and ownership of property' (1992: 22).

8 For a detailed description of the Witnesses' usage of study aids alongside their own translation of the Bible see Sire (1980) and Reed (1986).

9 Quick and other former Witnesses like him claim that, on checking Watch Tower translations of scriptures with the orthodox New International Bible, deliberate errors in the former text become apparent. With the help of Greek lexicons,

Quick cites examples of discrepancies between the two versions with regard to references such as John 1: 1, John 17: 3, Romans 10: 9–10 and Hebrews 13: 15, all of which, he claims, confirm Christ's equality with God and the necessary steps for salvation. Other discrepancies include references from the Book of Corinthians which, according to the critics, stress the need for a personal relationship with Christ if translated accurately from the original Greek and Hebrew.

10 It is difficult to know whether those who experience doubts but remain in membership ever reach the point of undertaking independent biblical research. This is clearly a crucial factor in defection.

11 Conversely, it is impossible to know how many Watch Tower defectors slip into agnosticism or fail to adopt an alternative system of religious belief.

12 This suggests that the defectors adopted Trinitarian beliefs in which Christ is co-equal with God the Father and God the Holy Spirit.

13 This is an example of what Lofland and Skonovd (1983) call *mystical* conversion.

14 Although references to 'the living Jesus' were common among the defectors I interviewed, most had in fact entered Baptist churches in which worship was conducted by ordained ministers.

15 See for example Gruss (1974) for a collection of other similar testimonies.

16 All the defectors in my study claimed that they were too afraid to discuss their ambivalence with other members for fear of being reported to congregational officials. Some explained how bonds were weakened with those with whom they tried to share their anxieties. This means that disaffected Witnesses are usually left to overcome their concerns alone.

17 Tom referred to his new-found faith as 'the spirit of truth'.

18 More traumatic still, Witnesses in membership are not allowed to attend the funerals of those who have lapsed.

19 As I have stressed throughout this book, the organisation operates in such a way that to question its teachings is tantamount to questioning the divine authority of the leadership. The anonymity of the Governing Body enables it to stamp out dissidence by imposing sanctions such as prohibiting those in fellowship to visit their 'apostate' relatives who have defected.

20 In this scenario, the pressure to return to meetings can be overwhelming. It is not uncommon for Witnesses who are experiencing doubts to stop attending meetings for weeks at a time, only to return at a later stage.

21 Tom explained that it was a long time before he was able to read the Bible independently. This would suggest that the greater the emotional trauma experienced by the individual, the greater the chance of defection without the possibility of return.

22 Festinger (1957) defines this experience of conflicting or contradictory thoughts as *cognitive dissonance*. He argues that consonance can be achieved only by reducing or increasing the validity of either position. In the case of totalitarian organisations, loyalty can be nothing less than absolute.

23 The Reachout Trust is an organisation based in Surrey which shares the same objectives as its American counterpart Free Minds – namely, to offer support to lapsed members of religious movements. These counter-cults have large networks of people who crusade for defectors. Lapsed Witnesses are widely represented by both these organisations.

24 There are now several internet websites that have been set up by former Jehovah's Witnesses. These sites are also visited by disillusioned devotees still in membership.

25 Alison explained how it was only when she had burnt all her Watch Tower reading material that she felt really free to make a new start. She regarded this as a symbolic act in which she was attempting to rid herself of unhappy memories.

26 In his book *Culture of Fear* (1997), sociologist Frank Furedi argues that safety has become a fundamental value in a world that has become obsessed with risks such as abuse, stranger danger, environmental damage and disease.

9 Conclusion

1 On the other hand, the fact that the Witnesses have steadily gained recruits does not necessarily mean that religious thinking, practice and institutions are losing social significance (Wilson 1966: xiv). It could be that heterodox religious movements are able to resist secularising influences and prosper at a time when orthodox Christianity has weakened.

Glossary

Below is a selection of terms used by the Jehovah's Witnesses that may require general clarification. The list is far from exhaustive, and, where there are terms that are not defined, the reader is advised to consult the Watch Tower Bible and Tract Society's own published sources.

Anointed, The   The 144,000 'chosen ones' of Revelation 14: 1–3 who are to reign with Christ for the duration of the millennium. The term is synonymous with 'Little Flock', 'Bride of Christ' and 'Faithful and Discreet Slave' classes.

Antichrist   All those who oppose what the Society teaches about Christ.

Apostasy   The rejection of the published doctrines of the Watch Tower Bible and Tract Society for some alternative doctrine. Also, the sin of attending an alternative religious institution.

Armageddon   The imminent battle between Christ and Satan. At Armageddon (or Har-Magedon) the world will be destroyed and Jehovah's New Kingdom be inaugurated.

Assembly   A gathering of Jehovah's Witnesses from several congregations or circuits. Circuit assemblies are held twice a year and district assemblies are held annually.

Babylon the Great   'The world empire of false religion' which the Society regards as all non-Witness teachings.

Baptism   Water immersion symbolising conversion to the Watch Tower Society.

Bethel   The residence and factory of the major branch office of the Witnesses.

Bethel family   Residents of Bethel; that is, those who live and work at the branch.

Bible   The sacred texts which the Witnesses regard as Jehovah's written word.

Bible Study   A study of the Society's doctrines under the guidance of a devotee.

Book Study   A weekly meeting where the Witnesses read and discuss Watch Tower publications.

Branch Committee   A group of three Witness officials who oversee the movement in a given country.

Bride of Christ   See 'The Anointed' above.

Brooklyn   The official headquarters of the movement.

Brother   Title given to a male baptised Witness.

Christendom   The collectivised mainstream Christian churches.

Christians   Jehovah's Witnesses.

Circuit   A collection of congregations in close proximity. Several circuits comprise a 'district'.

Convention   A large assembly of Jehovah's Witnesses.

Dedication   The spiritual commitment to Jehovah and the Watch Tower Society preceding baptism.

Disassociation   The voluntary removal of oneself from the Watch Tower Society.

Disfellowshipping   The expulsion of a member by the Watch Tower authorities.

District   A geographical area comprising several 'circuits'.

Elder   A (male) person in a position of leadership. He is usually responsible for overseeing a congregation.

Emblems, The   The bread and wine circulated at the Witnesses' Memorial Service (14 Nisan of the Jewish calendar) symbolising Christ's body and blood.

Faithful and Discreet Slave   See 'The Anointed' above.

Field Service   The house-to-house evangelism carried out by devotees.

Gilead   The Society's missionary school.

Goat   Anyone who opposes the Witnesses' teachings.

God   Jehovah, the creator of the universe who is omniscient, omnipresent and omnipotent.

Governing Body   The ruling committee of the Watch Tower Society, all of whom claim to be members of the Anointed class.

Great Crowd   The vast majority of Witnesses who will enjoy everlasting life in the post-Armageddon Kingdom.

Har-Magedon   See 'Armageddon' above.

Hell   Hades or Sheol (that is, The Grave). The Witnesses do not believe in eternal torture, but, rather, eternal mortality for the wicked.

Holy Spirit   Jehovah's 'active force'; the spiritual energy used by Jehovah to inspire humankind.

Jehovah   See 'God' above.

Jehovah's Witnesses   Devotees of the Watch Tower Bible and Tract Society.

Jesus Christ   The only begotten Son of Jehovah, the firstborn of all creation. He will shortly establish Jehovah's heavenly kingdom after Armageddon.

Judgement Day   The time of testing up to the inauguration of Armageddon.

Judicial Committee   A tribunal of officials who hear complaints and handle accusations of wrongdoing within the Watch Tower community.

Kingdom, The   The awaited post-Armageddon world.

Kingdom Hall   The official name for the Witnesses' meeting place.

Last Days   The time period between Christ's return in 1914 and Armageddon.

Memorial   A commemoration marking the death of Jesus Christ. Only the Anointed Class may partake of the emblems of bread and wine.

Millennium   Christ's thousand-year reign which begins after Armageddon. During this time, paradise will be restored, those who died in faith will be resurrected and the earth will be restored to perfection.

Minister   A baptised member of the Society.

Ministry   Service work involving preaching.

New Order   The anticipated paradise on earth after Armageddon.

New World Society   The Watch Tower Bible and Tract Society.

New World Translation   The Witnesses' own version of the Bible.

Old System   The current world prior to Armageddon, the ruler of which is Satan.

Overseer   A person in a position of leadership in a congregation, circuit or district.

Paradise   Eden or Eden-like conditions after Armageddon.

Pioneer   A full-time Witness evangelist who must work at least ninety hours per month proselytising.

Public Talk   A weekly meeting which involves a lecture at the Kingdom Hall.

Publisher   A baptised member who evangelises for the Society on a voluntary basis.

Ransom Sacrifice   The death of Jesus Christ.

Remnant Class   The remaining members of the Anointed (that is, the 144,000 'chosen ones') still alive on earth.

Resurrection   The process of being brought back to life after death. This may be either in spirit (as in the case of the 144,000) or in flesh (after Armageddon).

Return of Christ   The Second Coming of Jesus Christ as the enthroned king. The Witnesses believe that this happened invisibly in 1914.

Satan   Jehovah's adversary, once the archangel Lucifer, who turned against Jehovah. In 1914, Satan was cast out of heaven and has corrupted the world ever since. He will be tortured in an abyss during the millennium, released briefly at the end of it (when he will make a final attempt to deceive the nations), and then annihilated.

Second Coming   See 'Return of Christ' above.

Service Meeting   A weekly meeting to assist devotees in their ministry and to keep them informed of developments in the congregation.

Sin   Behaviour which the Witnesses regard as offensive to Jehovah.

Sister   Title given to a female baptised Witness.

Society, The   Abbreviation of the Watch Tower Bible and Tract Society.

Soul   The living body of humans and animals. *Not* to be confused with 'spirit'.

Spirit   (1) An invisible being such as an angel, a demon or the holy spirit (sometimes known as 'Jehovah's active force'); (2) breath of life.

Spiritual Food   The Witnesses' theological message.

Theocratic   Literally, 'governed by God'. Devotees use the term to describe their Society.

Theocratic Ministry School   A weekly meeting where devotees learn to evangelise and to speak in public.

Truth, The   The Witnesses' collection of beliefs, or a term used by devotees when referring to the Society itself.

Watch Tower Bible and Tract Society   The corporation of the Witnesses on earth.

***Watchtower* Study**   The most important of the Witnesses' weekly meetings in which articles are studied from the Society's magazine *The Watchtower*.

Witnessing   The evangelistic work of the Watch Tower Society.

World, The   A term used (often disparagingly) by devotees when referring to secular society.

Bibliography

Aberle, D. (1965) 'A note on relative deprivation theory as applied to millenarian movements and other cult movements', in Lessa, W.A. and Vogt, E.Z. (eds) *Reader in Comparative Religion: An Anthropological Approach*, New York: Harper and Row.

Aldridge, A. (2000) *Religion in the Contemporary World: A Sociological Introduction*, Cambridge: Polity.

Anderson, B. (1983) *Imagined Communities: Reflections on the Origin and Spread of Nationalism*, London: Verso.

Bailey, J. (1988) *Pessimism*, London: Routledge.

Bainbridge, W. (1978) *Satan's Power: A Deviant Psychotherapy Group*, Berkeley, CA: University of California Press.

Barker, E. (ed.) (1982) *New Religious Movements: A Perspective for Understanding Society*, New York and Toronto: Edwin Mellen.

—— (ed.) (1983) *Of Gods and Men: New Religious Movements in the West*, Macon, GA: Mercer University Press.

—— (1984) *The Making of a Moonie: Choice or Brainwashing?*, Oxford: Basil Blackwell.

—— (1987) 'Brahmins don't eat mushrooms: participant observation and the new religions', *LSE Quarterly* 1, 2: 127–52.

—— (1989) *New Religious Movements: A Practical Introduction*, London: HMSO.

Barnes, P. (1984) *Out of Darkness into Light*, San Diego, CA: Counter Cult Ministries.

Barraclough, G. (ed.) (1980) *The Christian World: A Social and Cultural History of Christianity*, New York: Abrams.

Bauman, Z. (1988) *Freedom*, Milton Keynes: Open University Press.

—— (1991) *Modernity and Ambivalence*, Cambridge: Polity.

Beck, U. (1992) *Risk Society: Towards a New Modernity*, translated by Mark Ritter, London: Sage.

Becker, H.S. (1960) 'Notes on the concept of commitment', *American Journal of Sociology* 66: 32–40.

—— (1967) 'Whose side are we on?', *Social Problems* 14, 3: 239–47.

Beckford, J.A. (1972) 'The embryonic stage of a religious sect's development: the Jehovah's Witnesses', in Hill, M. (ed.) *A Sociological Yearbook of Religion in Britain*, London: SCM Press.

—— (1973) 'Religious organization', *Current Sociology* 21, 2: 7–170.

—— (1975a) *The Trumpet of Prophecy: A Sociological Study of Jehovah's Witnesses*, Oxford: Basil Blackwell.

—— (1975b) 'Organization, ideology and recruitment: the structure of the Watch Tower Movement', *Sociological Review* 23, 4: 893–909.

—— (1976) 'New wine in new bottles: a departure from church-sect conceptual tradition', *Social Compass* 23, 1: 71–85.

—— (1978) 'Accounting for conversion', *British Journal of Sociology* 29: 249–62.

—— (1985) *Cult Controversies: The Societal Response to the New Religious Movements*, London: Tavistock.

—— (1986) (ed.) *New Religious Movements and Rapid Social Change*, London: Sage.

—— (1989) *Religion and Advanced Industrial Society*, London: Unwin Hyman.

Beckford, J.A. and Luckmann, T. (eds) (1989) *The Changing Face of Religion*, London: Sage.

Bell, D. (1962) *The End of Ideology: On the Exhaustion of Political Ideas in the Fifties*, London: Macmillan.

—— (1979) *The Cultural Contradictions of Capitalism*, London: Heinemann.

Bellah, R.N., Madsen, R., Sullivan, W.M., Swidler, A. and Tipton, S.M. (1985) *Habits of the Heart: Individualism and Commitment in American Life*, Berkeley, CA: University of California Press.

Berger, P.L. (1967) *The Sacred Canopy: Elements of a Sociological Theory of Religion*, New York: Doubleday.

—— (1977) *Facing Up to Modernity*, New York: Basic Books.

Berger, P.L., Berger, B. and Kellner, P. (1974) *The Homeless Mind: Modernization and Consciousness*, New York: Vintage.

Berger, T.R. (1981) *Fragile Freedoms: Human Rights and Dissent in Canada*, Toronto: Clarke Irwin.

Bergman, J.R. (1984) *Jehovah's Witnesses and Kindred Groups: Historical Compendium and Bibliography*, New York: Garland.

—— (1987) 'Religious objections to the flag salute', *The Flag Bulletin* 26, 4: 178–93.

Berlin, I. (1990) *The Crooked Timber of Humanity: Chapters in the History of Ideas*, London: John Murray.

Berman, M. (1983) *All that Is Solid Melts into Air: The Experience of Modernity*, London: Verso.

Bocock, R. (1992) 'The cultural formations of modern society', in Hall, S. and Gieben, B. (eds) *Formations of Modernity*, Cambridge: Polity.

Botting, H. and Botting, G. (1984) *The Orwellian World of Jehovah's Witnesses*, Toronto: University of Toronto Press.

Bowman, R.M. (1991) *Understanding Jehovah's Witnesses: Why They Read the Bible the Way They Do*, Grand Rapids, MI: Baker Book House.

Bradley, H. (1992a) 'Changing social divisions: class, gender and race', in Bocock, R. and Thompson, K. (eds) *Social and Cultural Forms of Modernity*, Cambridge: Polity.

—— (1992b) 'Changing social structures: class and gender', in Hall, S. and Gieben, B. (eds) *Formations of Modernity*, Cambridge: Polity.

Bram, J. (1956) 'Jehovah's Witnesses and the values of American culture', *Transactions of the New York Academy of Sciences* 2, 19: 47–54.

Brierley, P. (1991) *'Christian' England: What the 1989 English Church Census Reveals*, London: MARC Europe.

—— (1993) *Reaching and Keeping Teenagers*, London: Christian Research Association.

Brierley, P. and Longley, D. (eds) (1993) *UK Christian Handbook 1992/93*, London: MARC Europe.

Bromley, D.G. and Richardson, J.T. (eds) (1983) *The Brainwashing/Deprogramming Controversy: Sociological, Psychological, Legal and Historical Perspectives*, New York and Toronto: Edwin Mellen.

Brown, D. (1975) *Bury My Heart at Wounded Knee: An Indian History of the American West*, London: Pan Books.

Brown, P. (1996) 'Modernism, post-modernism and sociological theory', *Sociology Review 5*, 3: 22–5.

Bruce, S. (1990) 'Modernity and fundamentalism: the new Christian right in America', *The British Journal of Sociology* 41, 4: 477–96.

——(1992) 'The twilight of the gods', *Sociology Review* 2, 2: 11–14.

——(1995) *Religion in Modern Britain*, Oxford: Oxford University Press.

——(1996) *Religion in the Modern World: From Cathedrals to Cults*, Oxford: Oxford University Press.

Bruner, E.M. (1986) 'Ethnography as narrative', in Turner, V. and Bruner, E.M. (eds) *The Anthropology of Experience*, Urbana, IL: University of Illinois Press.

Bryman, A. and Burgess, R.G. (eds) (1994) *Analyzing Qualitative Data*, London: Routledge.

Burkitt, I. and Tester, K. (1996) 'Identity', in Haralambos, M. (ed.) *Developments in Sociology: An Annual Review* 12: 1–17, Ormskirk, Lancashire: Causeway.

Callinicos, A. (1991) *The Revenge of History: Marxism and the East European Revolutions*, Cambridge: Polity.

Carrier, H.S.J. (1965) *The Sociology of Religious Belonging*, London: Darton, Longman and Todd.

Carter, P. (1980) 'Religion at the grass-roots', in Barraclough, G. (ed.) (1980) *The Christian World*, New York: Abrams.

Casanova, J. (1994) *Public Religions in the Modern World*, Chicago: University of Chicago Press.

Christensen, C.W. (1963) 'Religious conversion', *Archives of General Psychiatry* 9: 207–16.

Clark, E.T. (1965) *The Small Sects in America*, New York: Ablingdon.

Cohen, A.P. (1985) *The Symbolic Construction of Community*, London: Tavistock.

——(ed.) (1986) *Symbolising Boundaries: Identity and Diversity in British Cultures*, Manchester: Manchester University Press.

Cohn, N. (1957) *The Pursuit of the Millennium*, London: Secker and Warburg.

——(1975) *Europe's Inner Demons*, Falmer, Sussex: Sussex University Press.

Cohn, W. (1955) 'Jehovah's Witnesses as a proletarian movement', *American Scholar* 24: 281–98.

Cole, M. (1956) *Jehovah's Witnesses: The New World Society*, London: Allen and Unwin.

Conway, J.S. (1968) *The Nazi Persecution of the Churches: 1933–1945*, London: Weidenfeld and Nicolson.

Cox, H. (1996) *Fire From Heaven: The Rise of Pentecostal Spirituality and the Reshaping of Religion in the Twenty-first Century*, London: Cassell.

Craib, I. (1992) *Anthony Giddens*, London: Routledge.

Darnton, R. (1979) *The Business of Enlightenment: A Publishing History of the Encylopédie 1775–1800*, Cambridge, MA: Harvard University Press.

Davie, G. (1989) 'Religion', in Haralambos, M. (ed.) *Developments in Sociology: An Annual Review* 5: 73–100, Ormskirk, Lancashire: Causeway.

—— (1994) *Religion in Britain Since 1945: Believing Without Belonging*, Oxford: Blackwell.

—— (1995) 'Competing fundamentalisms', *Sociology Review* 4, 4: 2–7.

Day, A. (1996) *Romanticism*, London: Routledge.

Day, G. (1996) 'Community, locality and social identity', in Haralambos, M. (ed.) *Developments in Sociology: An Annual Review* 12: 131–54, Ormskirk, Lancashire: Causeway.

Dencher, T. (1966) *Why I Left Jehovah's Witnesses*, London: Oliphants.

Dixon, J.L. and Smalley, M.G. (1981) 'Jehovah's Witnesses – the surgical/ethical challenge', *Journal of the American Medical Association* 246, 21: 2471–2.

Dobbelaere, K. (1981) 'Secularization: a multi-dimensional concept', *Current Sociology* 29, 2: 3–216.

Dobbelaere, K. and Wilson, B.R. (1980) 'Jehovah's Witnesses in a Catholic country: a survey of nine Belgian congregations', *Archives de Sciences des Religions* 25: 89–110.

Douglas, M. (1966) *Purity and Danger: An Analysis of the Concepts of Pollution and Taboo*, London: Routledge and Kegan Paul.

—— (1973a) *Natural Symbols: Explorations in Cosmology*, London: Barrie and Jenkins.

—— (1973b) *Rules and Meaning: The Anthropology of Everyday Life*, Harmondsworth: Penguin.

—— (1975) *Implicit Meanings: Essays in Anthropology*, London: Routledge and Kegan Paul.

—— (1978) 'Judgements on James Frazer', *Daedalus* 107, 4: 151–64.

—— (1986a) *How Institutions Think*, Syracuse: Syracuse University Press.

—— (1986b) *Risk Acceptability According to the Social Sciences*, London: Routledge.

—— (1990) 'Risk as a forensic resource', *Daedalus* 119, 4: 1–16.

—— (1992) *Risk and Blame: Essays in Cultural Theory*, London: Routledge.

Downton, J.V. (1980) 'An evolutionary theory of spiritual conversion and commitment: the case of the Divine Light Mission', *Journal for the Scientific Study of Religion* 19: 381–96.

Drew, N.C. (1981) 'The pregnant Jehovah's Witness', *Journal of Medical Ethics* 7, 3: 137–9.

Dunthorne, H. (1991) *The Enlightenment*, London: The Historical Association.

Durkheim, E. (1897) *Suicide: A Study in Sociology*, translated by John A. Spaulding and George Simpson, London: Routledge and Kegan Paul (1952).

—— (1912) *The Elementary Forms of the Religious Life*, translated by Joseph Swain, London: Allen and Unwin (1954).

Eisenstadt, S.N. (1967) 'The Protestant ethic thesis in analytical and comparative context', *Diogenes* 59.

Encyclopaedia Britannica (1964) vol. 3, London: William Benton.

Epstein, A.L. (1986) 'The millennium and the self: Jehovah's Witnesses on the Copperbelt in the '50s', *Anthropos* 81: 529–54.

Erdman, D.V. and Bloom, H. (eds) (1970) *The Poetry and Prose of William Blake*, New York: Doubleday.

Evans-Pritchard, E.E. (1937) *Witchcraft, Oracles and Magic Among the Azande*, Oxford: Clarendon.

—— (1956) *Nuer Religion*, Oxford: Clarendon.

Featherstone, M. (ed.) (1990) *Global Culture: Nationalism, Globalization and Modernity*, London: Sage.

Festinger, L. (1957) *A Theory of Cognitive Dissonance*, Evanston: Row.

Festinger, L., Riecken, H.W. and Schachter, S. (1956) *When Prophecy Fails: A Social and Psychological Study of a Modern Group that Predicted the End of the World*, New York: Harper and Row.

Feyerabend, P. (1975) *Against Method*, London: New Left Books.

—— (1987) *Farewell to Reason*, London: Verso.

Finch, J. (1984) ' "It's great to have someone to talk to": the ethics and politics of interviewing women', in Bell, C. and Roberts, H. (eds) *Social Researching: Politics, Problems and Practice*, London: Routledge and Kegan Paul.

Flanagan, K. (2001) 'Reflexivity, ethics and the teaching of the sociology of religion', *Sociology* 35, 1: 1–19.

Foster, H. (ed.) (1985) *Postmodern Culture*, London: Pluto.

Foucault, M. (1961) *Madness and Civilization*, London: Tavistock (1971).

—— (1963) *The Birth of the Clinic: An Archaeology of Medical Perception*, London: Tavistock (1976).

—— (1966) *The Order of Things: An Archaeology of the Human Sciences*, London: Tavistock (1974).

—— (1975) *Discipline and Punish: The Birth of the Prison*, London: Tavistock (1977).

—— (1976) *History of Sexuality*, London: Tavistock (1979).

Franz, R. (1983) *Crisis of Conscience*, Atlanta, GA: Commentary.

Friedrich, C. (1954) *Totalitarianism*, Cambridge, MA: Harvard University Press.

—— (1969) *Totalitarianism in Perspective: Three Views – Carl J. Friedrich, Michael Curtis and Benjamin R. Barber*, London: Pall Mall.

Fromm, E. (1960) *The Fear of Freedom*, London: Routledge and Kegan Paul.

Fukuyama, F. (1989) 'The end of history?', *The National Interest* 16: 3–18.

—— (1992) *The End of History and the Last Man*, New York: Free Press.

Furedi, F. (1997) *Culture of Fear: Risk-taking and the Morality of Low Expectation*, London: Cassell.

Gadamer, H. (1960) *Truth and Method*, translated by William Glen-Doepel, London: Sheed and Ward.

Gay, P. (1973) *The Enlightenment: An Interpretation Vol. 1: The Rise of Modern Paganism*, London: Wildwood House.

Geertz, C. (1957) 'Ritual and social change: a Javanese example', *American Anthropologist* 59: 23–54.

—— (1973) *The Interpretation of Cultures: Selected Essays*, London: Hutchinson.

—— (1983) *Local Knowledge: Further Essays in Interpretative Anthropology*, New York: Basic Books.

Gehlen, A. (1980) *Man in the Age of Technology*, New York: Columbia University Press.

Gellner, E. (1992) *Postmodernism, Reason and Religion*, London: Routledge.

Giddens, A. (1976) *New Rules of Sociological Method: A Positive Critique of Interpretative Sociologies*, London: Hutchinson.

—— (1984) *The Constitution of Society: Outline of the Theory of Structuration*, Cambridge: Polity.

—— (1990) *The Consequences of Modernity*, Cambridge: Polity.

—— (1991) *Modernity and Self-identity: Self and Society in the Late Modern Age*, Cambridge: Polity.

Glock, C.Y. (1964) 'The rôle of deprivation in the origin and evolution of religious groups', in Lee, R. and Marty, M.E. (eds) *Religion and Social Conflict*, Oxford: Oxford University Press.

Goffman, E. (1959) *The Presentation of Self in Everyday Life*, Harmondsworth: Penguin.

—— (1963) *Behaviour in Public Places: Notes on the Social Organization of Gatherings*, New York: Free Press.

—— (1967) *Interaction Ritual: Essays in Face-to-face Behaviour*, New York: Anchor Books.

—— (1971) *Relations in Public: Microstudies of the Public Order*, New York: Basic Books.

Gouldner, A.W. (1973) *For Sociology: Renewal and Critique in Sociology Today*, London: Allen Lane.

Greeley, A. (1972) *Unsecular Man: The Persistence of Religion*, New York: Shocken Books.

Greil, A.L. and Rudy, D.R. (1984) 'What have we learned from process models of conversion? An examination of ten studies', *Sociological Focus* 17, 4: 306–23.

Gruss, E.C. (1972) *The Jehovah's Witnesses and Prophetic Speculation*, Grand Rapids, PA: Presbyterian Reformed Publishing Company.

—— (ed.) (1974) *We Left Jehovah's Witnesses*, Grand Rapids, MI: Baker Book House.

—— (1975) *Apostles of Denial: An Examination and Exposé of the History, Doctrines and Claims of Jehovah's Witnesses*, Grand Rapids, PA: Presbyterian Reformed Publishing Company.

Habermas, J. (1981) *The Theory of Communicative Action*, Boston: Beacon Press, 2 volumes (1984).

—— (1985) 'Modernity: an incomplete project', in Foster, H. (ed.) *Postmodern Culture*, London: Pluto.

Habgood, J. (1992) 'Viewpoint', *The Independent*, 12 March.

Hall, S. (1992) 'The question of cultural identity', in Hall, S., Held, D. and McGrew, A. (eds) *Modernity and its Futures*, Cambridge: Polity.

Hall, S. and Gieben, B. (eds) (1992) *Formations of Modernity*, Cambridge: Polity.

Hall, S., Held, D. and McGrew A. (eds) (1992) *Modernity and its Futures*, Cambridge: Polity.

Hamilton, P. (1992) 'The Enlightenment and the birth of social science', in Hall, S. and Gieben, B. (eds) *Formations of Modernity*, Cambridge: Polity.

Hammersley, M. and Atkinson, P. (1983) *Ethnography: Principles in Practice*, London: Tavistock.

Hampson, N. (1969) *The Enlightenment*, Harmondsworth: Penguin.

Harding, S.F. (1987) 'Convicted by the Holy Spirit: the rhetoric of fundamentalist Baptist conversion', *American Ethnologist* 14: 167–81.

Hargrove, B. (ed.) (1984) *Religion and the Sociology of Knowledge: Modernization and Pluralism in Christian Thought and Structure*, New York: Edwin Mellen.

Harris, J.M. (1994) ' "Fundamentalism": objections from a modern Jewish historian', in Hawley, J.S. (ed.) (1994) *Fundamentalism and Gender*, Oxford: Oxford University Press.

Harrison, B.G. (1980) *Visions of Glory: A History and a Memory of Jehovah's Witnesses*, London: Hale.

Harrison, J.F.C. (1979) *The Second Coming: Popular Millenarianism 1780–1850*, London: Routledge.

Harrison, S. (1990) *Cults: The Battle for God*, London: Christopher Helm.

Harvey, D. (1989) *The Condition of Postmodernity: An Enquiry into the Origins of Cultural Change*, Oxford: Blackwell.

Hawley, J.S. (ed.) (1994) *Fundamentalism and Gender*, Oxford: Oxford University Press.

Heelas, P. (1996) *The New Age Movement: The Celebration of the Self and the Sacralization of Modernity*, Oxford: Blackwell.

Held, D., Anderson, J., Gieben, B., Harris, L., Parker, N. and Turok, B. (eds) (1983) *States and Societies*, Oxford: Robertson (in association with the Open University).

Held, D. (1989) *Political Theory and the Modern State*, Cambridge: Polity.

Hewitt, J. (1979) *I was Raised a Jehovah's Witness: The True Story of a Former Jehovah's Witness*, Denver, CO: Accent Books.

Hill, M. (ed.) (1972) *A Sociological Yearbook of Religion in Britain*, London: SCM Press.

Hoekema, A.A. (1984) *Jehovah's Witnesses*, Devon: Paternoster.

Holden, A. (1999) *Millenarianism, Risk and Modernity: An Ethnography of the Jehovah's Witnesses*, University of Lancaster: unpublished PhD thesis.

Holzer, B. (1968) *Reality Construction in Society*, Cambridge, MA: Schenkman.

Hughes, J.A., Martin, P.J. and Sharrock, W.W. (1995) *Understanding Classical Sociology: Marx, Weber, Durkheim*, London: Sage.

Hunter, J. (1991) 'Fundamentalism and social science', *Religion and Social Order* 1: 149–63.

Jenkins, J. (1987) *Contemporary Moral Issues*, Oxford: Heinemann Educational.

Jones, M. (1996) 'The Protestant ethic revisited', *Sociology Review* 6, 1: 26–7.

Jones, P. (1993) *Studying Society: Sociological Theories and Research Practices*, London: Collins Educational.

Jubber, K. (1977) 'The persecution of Jehovah's Witnesses in southern Africa', *Social Compass* 24, 1: 121–34.

Kant, I. (1963) *On History*, translated by L. White Beck, R.E. Anchor and E.L. Fackenheim, New York: Bobbs-Merrill.

Kaplan, W. (1989) *State and Salvation: The Jehovah's Witnesses and Their Fight for Civil Rights*, Toronto: University of Toronto Press.

Kautsky, K. (1953) *Foundations of Christianity: A Study in Christian Origins*, New York: Russell.

Kennedy, D. (1989) *In God's Country: Travels in the Bible Belt, USA*, New York: Unwin Hyman.

Kepel, G. (1994) *The Revenge of God: The Resurgence of Islam, Christianity and Judaism in the Modern World*, Cambridge: Polity.

King, A. (ed.) (1990) *Urbanism, Colonialism and the World-economy: Cultural and Spatial Foundations of the World Urban System*, London: Routledge.

King, C. (1982) 'The case of the Third Reich', in Barker, E. (ed.) *New Religious Movements: A Perspective for Understanding Society*, New York and Toronto: Edwin Mellen.

Kuhn, T.S. (1962) *The Structure of Scientific Revolutions*, Chicago: University of Chicago Press.

Kumar, K. (1991) *Utopia and Anti-Utopia in Modern Times*, Oxford: Blackwell.

Laclau, E. (1990) *New Reflections on the Revolution of Our Time*, London: Verso.

Lakoff, G. and Johnson, M. (1980) *Metaphors We Live By*, Chicago: University of Chicago Press.

Lanternari, V. (1963) *The Religions of the Oppressed: A Study of Modern Messianic Cults*, London: MacGibbon and Kee.

Lasch, C. (1980) *The Culture of Narcissism*, London: Abacus.

—— (1991) *The True and Only Heaven: Progress and its Critics*, London: W.W. Norton.

Lash, S. and Urry, J. (1987) *The End of Organized Capitalism*, Cambridge: Polity.

—— (1994) *Economies of Signs and Space*, London: Sage.

Lautmann, R. (1990) 'Categorization in concentration camps as a collective fate: a comparison of homosexuals, Jehovah's Witnesses and political prisoners', *Journal of Homosexuality* 19, 1: 67–88.

Lee, R. and Marty, M.E. (eds) (1964) *Religion and Social Conflict*, Oxford: Oxford University Press.

Lessa, W.A. and Vogt, E.Z. (eds) *Reader in Comparative Religion: An Anthropological Approach*, New York: Harper and Row.

Levine, E.M. 'Rural communes and religious cults: refuges for middle-class youth', *Adolescent Psychiatry* 8: 138–53.

Lofland, J. and Skonovd, N. (1983) 'Patterns of conversion', in Barker, E. (ed.) *Of Gods and Men: New Religious Movements in the West*, Macon, GA: Mercer University Press.

Lofland, J. and Stark, R. (1965) 'Becoming a world-saver: a theory of conversion to a deviant perspective', *American Sociological Review* 30, 6: 862–75.

Luckmann, T. (1967) *The Invisible Religion: The Problem of Religion in Modern Society*, New York: Macmillan.

Lyon, D. (1994) *Postmodernity*, Milton Keynes: Open University Press.

Lyotard, J.F. (1984) *The Postmodern Condition: A Report on Knowledge*, Manchester: Manchester University Press.

McGuire, M. (1987) *Religion: The Social Context*, Belmont, CA: Wadsworth.

Macklin, R. (1988) 'The inner workings of an ethics committee: latest battle over Jehovah's Witnesses', *Hastings Center Report* 18, 1: 15–20.

McLennan, G. (1992) 'The Enlightenment project revisited', in Hall, S., Held, D. and McGrew A. (eds) *Modernity and its Futures*, Cambridge: Polity.

Maduro, O. (1982) *Religion and Social Conflicts*, translated by Robert R. Barr, New York: Orbis.

Main, J. (1987) 'Trying to bend managers' minds', *Fortune* 23, November.

Marcus, G.E. and Fischer, M.J. (1986) *Anthropology as Cultural Critique: An Experimental Moment in the Human Sciences*, Chicago: University of Chicago Press.

Marsh, C. (1982) *The Survey Method: The Contribution of Surveys to Sociological Explanation*, London: Allen and Unwin.

Martin, B. (1983) *A Sociology of Contemporary Cultural Change*, Oxford: Blackwell.

Martin, D. (1978) *A General Theory of Secularisation*, Oxford: Blackwell.

—— (1990) *Tongues of Fire: The Explosion of Protestantism in Latin America*, Oxford: Blackwell.

Marx, K. (1964) *Capital*, London: Penguin.

May, T. (1993) *Social Research: Issues, Methods and Process*, Milton Keynes: Open University Press.

Merton, R. (1949) *Social Theory and Social Structure*, Glencoe: Free Press (3rd edn 1968).

Montague, H. (1977) 'The pessimistic sect's influence on the mental health of its members: the case of Jehovah's Witnesses', *Social Compass* 24, 1: 135–48.

Neibuhr, H.R. (1929) *The Social Sources of Denominationalism*, New York: World Publishing.

Oppenheim, F.E. (1961) *Dimensions of Freedom: An Analysis*, London: Macmillan.

O'Toole, R. (1984) *Religion: Classic Sociological Approaches*, Toronto: McGraw-Hill.

Pearson, G. (1983) *Hooligan: A History of Respectable Fears*, London: Macmillan.

Pearson, M. (1990) *Millennial Dreams and Moral Dilemmas*, Cambridge: Cambridge University Press.

Penton, M.J. (1979) 'Jehovah's Witnesses and the secular state', *Journal of Church and State* 21, 1: 55–72.

——(1997) *Apocalypse Delayed: The Story of Jehovah's Witnesses*, Toronto: University of Toronto Press.

Pickering, W.S.F. (1975) *Durkheim on Religion*, London: Routledge and Kegan Paul.

Porter, R. (1990) *The Enlightenment*, London: Macmillan.

Quick, G. (1940) 'Some aspects of the African Watch Tower movement in northern Rhodesia', *International Review of Missions* 29: 216–26.

Quick, K.R. (1989) *Pilgrimage Through the Watchtower*, Grand Rapids, MI: Baker Book House.

Reed, D.A. (1986) *Jehovah's Witnesses Answered Verse by Verse*, Grand Rapids, MI: Baker Book House.

——(1989a) *How to Rescue Your Loved One from the Watchtower*, Grand Rapids, MI: Baker Book House.

——(1989b) *Behind the Watchtower Curtain: The Secret Society of Jehovah's Witnesses*, Southbridge, MA: Crowne.

Richardson, J. (ed.) (1978) *Conversion Careers: In and Out of the New Religions*, London: Sage.

Ripley, F. (1982) *Jehovah's Witnesses*, London: Catholic Truth Society.

Ritzer, G. (1996) *Modern Sociological Theory*, London: McGraw-Hill.

Robbins, T. (1988) *Cults, Converts and Charisma: The Sociology of New Religious Movements*, London: Sage.

Rogerson, A. (1969) *Millions Now Living Will Never Die: A Study of Jehovah's Witnesses*, London: Constable.

Rosen, H. (1974) *Language and Class: A Critical Look at the Theories of Basil Bernstein*, Bristol: Falling Wall.

Rosenau, P.M. (1992) *Post-modernism and the Social Sciences: Insights, Inroads and Intrusions*, Princeton University Press.

Rushkoff, D. (1997) 'Designer apocalypse', *The Guardian*, 3 April.

Sachs, J. (1990) 'The persistence of faith', the Reith Lectures, Lecture 1 'The environment of faith', *The Listener*, 15 November, pp. 4–6.

Sacks, D.A. and Koppes, R.H. (1986) 'Blood transfusion and Jehovah's Witnesses: medical and legal issues in obstetrics and gynaecology', *American Journal of Obstetrics and Gynaecology* 154, 3: 483–6.

Saliba, J.A. (1995) *Perspectives on New Religious Movements*, London: Geoffrey Chapman.

Schnell, W.J. (1956) *Thirty Years a Watchtower Slave*, Grand Rapids, MI: Baker Book House.

Seggar, J. and Kunz, P. (1972) 'Conversion: evaluation of a step-like process for problem solving', *Review of Religious Research* 13, 3: 178–84.

Shiner, L. (1967) 'The concept of secularization in empirical research', *Journal for the Scientific Study of Religion* 6, 2: 207–20.

Simmonds, R.B. (1978) 'Conversion or addiction: consequences of joining a Jesus movement group', in Richardson, J. (ed.) *Conversion Careers: In and Out of the New Religions*, London: Sage.

Singelenberg, R. (1988) ' "It separated the wheat from the chaff": the "1975" prophecy and its impact among Dutch Jehovah's Witnesses', *Sociological Analysis* 50, 1: 23–40.

—— (1990) 'The blood transfusion taboo of Jehovah's Witnesses: origin, development and function of a controversial doctrine', *Social Science Medical* 31, 4: 515–23.

Sire, J.W. (1980) *Scripture Twisting*, Downers Grove, IL: Inter Varsity Press.

Sked, A. (1987) *Britain's Decline: Problems and Perspectives*, London: Blackwell.

Skonovd, N. (1983) 'Leaving the cultic religious milieu', in Bromley, D.G. and Richardson, J.T. (eds) *The Brainwashing/Deprogramming Controversy: Sociological, Psychological, Legal and Historical Perspectives*, New York and Toronto: Edwin Mellen.

Smart, B. (1992) *Modern Conditions, Postmodern Controversies*, London: Routledge.

Smelser, N.J. (1962) *Theory of Collective Behaviour*, London: Routledge and Kegan Paul.

Snow, D. and Machalek, R. (1984) 'The sociology of conversion', *Annual Review of Sociology* 10: 167–90.

Somit, A. (1968) 'Brainwashing', *International Encyclopaedia of the Social Sciences* 2: 138–43.

Sontag, S. (1989) *AIDS and its Metaphors*, London: Allen Lane.

Spencer, J. (1975) 'The mental health of Jehovah's Witnesses', *British Journal of Psychiatry* 126: 556–9.

Sprague, T. (1946) 'The "world" concept among Jehovah's Witnesses', *Harvard Theological Review* 39: 109–40.

Stark, R. and Bainbridge, W.A. (1985) *The Future of Religion: Secularization, Revival and Cult Formation*, Berkeley, CA: University of California Press.

Stark, R. and Iannaccone, L.R. (1997) 'Why the Jehovah's Witnesses grow so rapidly: a theoretical application', *Journal of Contemporary Religion* 12, 2: 133–57.

Stevenson, W.C. (1967) *The Inside Story of Jehovah's Witnesses*, New York: Hart.

Strinati, D. (1992) 'Postmodernism and popular culture', *Sociology Review* 1, 4: 2–7.

Swift, R. (1990) 'Fundamentalism: reaching for certainty', *New Internationalist*, 210, August.

Tawney, R.H. (1926) *Religion and the Rise of Capitalism: A Historical Study*, Harmondsworth: Penguin.

Thomas, J.M. (1983) 'Meeting the surgical and ethical challenge presented by Jehovah's Witnesses', *Canadian Medical Association Journal* 128, 10: 1153–4.

Thompson, K. (1986) *Beliefs and Ideology*, London: Tavistock.

Tierney, W.M., Weinberger, M., Greene, J.Y. and Studdard, P.A. (1984) 'Jehovah's Witnesses and blood transfusion: physicians' attitudes and legal precedents', *Southern Medical Journal* 77, 4: 473–86.

Tomsett, V. (1971) *Released from the Watchtower*, London: Lakeland.

Troeltsch, E. (1956) *The Social Teachings of the Christian Churches*, translated by Olive Wyon, London: Allen and Unwin (originally published in 1912).

Trombley, C. (1974) *Kicked Out of the Kingdom*, Monroeville, PA: Whitaker House.

Turner, B. (1983) *Religion and Social Theory*, London: Heinemann.

Turner, V. and Bruner, E.M. (eds) (1986) *The Anthropology of Experience*, Urbana, IL: University of Illinois Press.

Utley, R.M. (1963) *The Last Days of the Sioux Nation*, New Haven: Yale University Press.

Van Maanen, J. (1988) *Tales of the Field: On Writing Ethnography*, Chicago: University of Chicago Press.

Wagner, P. (1994) *A Sociology of Modernity: Liberty and Discipline*, London: Routledge.

Wallis, R. (ed.) (1975) *Sectarianism: Analyses of Religious and Non-religious Sects*, New York: John Wiley.

—— (1984) *The Elementary Forms of the New Religious Life*, London: Routledge and Kegan Paul.

—— (1985) 'The sociology of the new religions', *Social Studies Review* 1, 1: 3–7.

Wallis, R. and Bruce, S. (1989) 'Religion: the British contribution', *British Journal of Sociology* 40, 3: 493–520.

Watch Tower Bible and Tract Society of Pennsylvania (1943) *The Truth Shall Make You Free*, New York: Watch Tower Bible and Tract Society of New York, Inc.

—— (1945) *Theocratic Aid to Kingdom Publishers*, New York: Watch Tower Bible and Tract Society of New York, Inc.

—— (1946a) *Equipped for Every Good Work*, New York: Watch Tower Bible and Tract Society of New York, Inc.

—— (1946b) *Let God Be True*, New York: Watch Tower Bible and Tract Society of New York, Inc. (revised in 1952).

—— (1953) *Make Sure of All Things*, New York: Watch Tower Bible and Tract Society of New York, Inc. (revised in 1957).

—— (1955a) *Qualified to Be Ministers*, New York: Watch Tower Bible and Tract Society of New York, Inc.

—— (1955b) *You May Survive Armageddon in God's New World*, New York: Watch Tower Bible and Tract Society of New York, Inc.

—— (1958) *From Paradise Lost to Paradise Regained*, New York: Watch Tower Bible and Tract Society of New York, Inc.

—— (1959) *Jehovah's Witnesses in the Divine Purpose*, New York: Watch Tower Bible and Tract Society of New York, Inc.

—— (1966) *Awake!*, 8 October, New York: Watch Tower Bible and Tract Society of New York, Inc.

—— (1971) *The Watchtower*, 1 January, New York: Watch Tower Bible and Tract Society of New York, Inc.

—— (1974) *Kingdom Ministry*, 3 May, New York: Watch Tower Bible and Tract Society of New York, Inc.

—— (1976) *Your Youth: Getting the Best Out of It*, New York: Watch Tower Bible and Tract Society of New York, Inc.

—— (1981) *The Watchtower*, 12 December, New York: Watch Tower Bible and Tract Society of New York, Inc.

—— (1982) *Enjoy Life on Earth Forever!*, New York: Watch Tower Bible and Tract Society of New York, Inc.

—— (1983a) *The Watchtower*, 15 March, New York: Watch Tower Bible and Tract Society of New York, Inc.

—— (1983b) *United in Worship of the Only True God*, New York: Watch Tower Bible and Tract Society of New York, Inc.

—— (1983c) *School and Jehovah's Witnesses*, New York: Watch Tower Bible and Tract Society of New York, Inc.

—— (1986) *Look! I Am Making All Things New*, New York: Watch Tower Bible and Tract Society of New York, Inc.

—— (1988) *Awake!*, 22 June, New York: Watch Tower Bible and Tract Society of New York, Inc.

—— (1989a) *Questions Young People Ask: Answers that Work*, New York: Watch Tower Bible and Tract Society of New York, Inc.

—— (1989b) *Reasoning from the Scriptures*, New York: Watch Tower Bible and Tract Society of New York, Inc.

—— (1992a) *Comfort for the Depressed*, New York: Watch Tower Bible and Tract Society of New York, Inc.

—— (1992b) *Will This World Survive?*, New York: Watch Tower Bible and Tract Society of New York, Inc.

—— (1993a) *Awake!*, 8 May, New York: Watch Tower Bible and Tract Society of New York, Inc.

—— (1993b) *What is the Purpose of Life: How Can You Find It?*, New York: Watch Tower Bible and Tract Society of New York, Inc.

—— (1994) *When Someone You Love Dies*, New York: Watch Tower Bible and Tract Society of New York, Inc.

—— (1995) *Jehovah's Witnesses and Education*, New York: Watch Tower Bible and Tract Society of New York, Inc.

—— (1997) *The Watchtower*, 1 January, New York: Watch Tower Bible and Tract Society of New York, Inc.

—— (1998a) *The Watchtower*, 1 January, New York: Watch Tower Bible and Tract Society of New York, Inc.

—— (1998b) *The Watchtower*, 1 June, New York: Watch Tower Bible and Tract Society of New York, Inc.

—— (1998c) *The Watchtower*, 1 October, New York: Watch Tower Bible and Tract Society of New York, Inc.

—— (1999) *The Watchtower*, 1 January, New York: Watch Tower Bible and Tract Society of New York, Inc.

—— (2000) *The Watchtower*, 1 January, New York: Watch Tower Bible and Tract Society of New York, Inc.

—— (2001) *The Watchtower*, 1 January, New York: Watch Tower Bible and Tract Society of New York, Inc.

Waters, M. (1994) *Modern Sociological Theory*, London: Sage.

Watters, R. (1987) *Refuting Jehovah's Witnesses*, Manhattan Beach, CA: Bethel Ministries.

Weber, M. (1922) *Wirtschaft und Gesellschaft*, translated as *Economy and Society: An Outline of Interpretative Sociology*, by G. Roth and G. Wittich, New York: Bedminister (1968).

—— (1930) *The Protestant Ethic and the Spirit of Capitalism*, translated by Talcott Parsons, London: Allen and Unwin.

—— (1965) *The Sociology of Religion*, translated by Ephraim Fischoff, London: Methuen.

—— (1970) *From Max Weber: Essays in Sociology*, translated and edited by H. Gerth and C.W. Mills, London: Routledge and Kegan Paul.

Weeks, J. (1992) 'The body and sexuality', in Bocock, R. and Thompson, K. (eds) *Social and Cultural Forms of Modernity*, Cambridge: Polity.

Wijngaards, J. (1998) *Jehovah's Witnesses*, London: Catholic Truth Society.

Williams, R. (1975) *The Country and the City*, London: Paladin.

Wilson, B.R. (1963) 'A typology of sects in a dynamic and comparative perspective', *Archives de Sciences des Religions* 16: 49–53.

—— (1966) *Religion in Secular Society*, London: Watts.

—— (1969) 'A typology of sects', in Robertson, R. (ed.) *Sociology of Religion*, Harmondsworth: Penguin.

—— (1970) *Religious Sects: A Sociological Study*, London: Weidenfeld and Nicolson.

—— (1974) 'Jehovah's Witnesses in Kenya', *Journal of Religion in Africa* 5: 128–49.

—— (1977a) 'How religious are we?', *New Society*, 27 October, pp. 176–7.

—— (1977b) 'Aspects of kinship and the rise of Jehovah's Witnesses in Japan', *Social Compass* 24, 1: 97–120.

—— (1978) 'When prophecy failed', *New Society*, 26 January, pp. 183–4.

—— (1982) *Religion in Sociological Perspective*, Oxford: Oxford University Press.

—— (1990) *The Social Dimensions of Sectarianism*, Oxford: Clarendon.

—— (1992) (ed.) *Religion: Contemporary Issues*, London: Bellow.

Woodhead, L. and Heelas, P. (2000) (eds) *Religion in Modern Times: An Interpretive Anthology*, Oxford: Blackwell.

Worsley, P. (1968) *The Trumpet Shall Sound* (revised edn), London: MacGibbon and Kee.

Wuthnow, R. (1997) 'The cultural turn: studies, logic and the quest for identity in American religion', in Becker, P.E. and Eisland, N.L. (eds) *Contemporary American Religion: An Ethnographic Reader*, Walnut Creek, London and New Delhi: AltaMira.

Zygmunt, J.F. (1970) 'Prophetic failure and chiliastic identity: the case of Jehovah's Witnesses', *American Journal of Sociology* 75: 926–48.

—— (1977) 'Jehovah's Witnesses in the USA: 1942–1976', *Social Compass* 24, 1: 44–57.

Index

)

ut